Shakespeare

The Merchant of Venice

A CASEBOOK

EDITED BY

JOHN WILDERS

MACMILLAN

Selection and editorial matter © John Wilders 1969

First published 1969 by
MACMILLAN AND CO LTD
Little Essex Street London WC2
and also at Bombay Calcutta and Madras
Macmillan South Africa (Publishers) Pty Ltd Johannesburg
The Macmillan Company of Australia Pty Ltd Melbourne
The Macmillan Company of Canada Ltd Toronto
Gill and Macmillan Ltd Dublin

Printed in Great Britain by
WESTERN PRINTING SERVICES LTD
Bristol

CONTENTS

ACKNOWLEDGEMENTS

Richard G. Moulton, *Shakespeare as a Dramatic Artist* (The Clarendon Press); E. E. Stoll, *Shakespeare Studies* (The Macmillan Company, New York); Sigmund Freud, 'The Theme of the Three Caskets', from *The Complete Psychological Works of Sigmund Freud*, Standard Edition, vol. XII (Sigmund Freud Copyrights Ltd, Mrs Alix Strachey, The Hogarth Press Ltd and Basic Books Inc.); Harley Granville-Barker, '*The Merchant of Venice*', from *Prefaces to Shakespeare*, Second Series (Field Roscoe & Co.); Max Plowman, 'Money and the Merchant', from *Adelphi* (1931) (Mr Piers Plowman); G. Wilson Knight, *The Shakespearean Tempest* (Methuen & Co. Ltd); Mark Van Doren, *Shakespeare* (Holt, Rinehart & Winston, Inc.; © 1939; © Mark Van Doren 1967); John Palmer, *Political and Comic Characters of Shakespeare* (The Estate of the late John Palmer); M. C. Bradbrook, *Shakespeare and Elizabethan Poetry* (Chatto & Windus Ltd); '*The Merchant of Venice*', from *The Meaning of Shakespeare* (The University of Chicago Press; © Harold C. Goddard 1951, 1960); John Russell Brown, *Shakespeare and his Comedies* (Methuen & Co. Ltd); *Shakespeare's Festive Comedy: A Study of Dramatic Form and its Relation to Social Custom* (Princeton University Press; © C. L. Barber 1959); Graham Midgley, '*The Merchant of Venice*: A Reconsideration', from *Essays in Criticism* (1960) (Mr F. W. Bateson); Sigurd Burckhardt, '*The Merchant of Venice*: The Gentle Bond', from *Journal of English Literary History*, XXIX (1962) (The Johns Hopkins Press); W. H. Auden, 'Brothers and Others', from *The Dyer's Hand* (Faber & Faber Ltd and Random House Inc.).

GENERAL EDITOR'S PREFACE

EACH of this series of Casebooks concerns either one well-known and influential work of literature or two or three closely linked works. The main section consists of critical readings, mostly modern, brought together from journals and books. A selection of reviews and comments by the author's contemporaries is also included, and sometimes comments from the author himself. The Editor's Introduction charts the reputation of the work from its first appearance until the present time.

What is the purpose of such a collection? Chiefly, to assist reading. Our first response to literature may be, or seem to be, 'personal'. Certain qualities of vigour, profundity, beauty or 'truth to experience' strike us, and the work gains a foothold in our mind. Later, an isolated phrase or passage may return to haunt or illuminate. Where did we hear that? we wonder – it could scarcely be better put.

In these and similar ways appreciation begins, but major literature prompts to very much more. There are certain facts we need to know if we are to understand properly. Who were the author's original readers, and what assumptions did he share with them? What was his theory of literature? Was he committed to a particular historical situation, or to a set of beliefs? We need historians as well as critics to help us with this. But there are also more purely literary factors to take account of: the work's structure and rhetoric; its symbols and archetypes; its tone, genre and texture; its use of language; the words on the page. In all these matters critics can inform and enrich our individual responses by offering imaginative re-creations of their own.

For the life of a book is not, after all, merely 'personal'; it is more like a tripartite dialogue, between a writer living 'then', a reader living 'now', and whatever forces of survival and honour link the two. Criticism is the public manifestation of this dialogue, a witness to the continuing power of literature to arouse and excite. It illuminates the possibilities and rewards of the dialogue, pushing 'interpretation' as far forward as it can go.

And here, indeed, is the rub: how far can it go? Where does 'interpretation' end and nonsense begin? Why is one interpretation superior to another, and why does each age need to interpret for itself? The critic knows that his insights have value only in so far as they serve the text, and that he must take account of views differing sharply from his own. He knows that his own writing will be judged as well as the work he writes about, so that he cannot simply assert inner illumination or a differing taste.

The critical forum is a place of vigorous conflict and disagreement, but there is nothing in this to cause dismay. What is attested is the complexity of human experience and the richness of literature, not any chaos or relativity of taste. A critic is better seen, no doubt, as an explorer than as an 'authority', but explorers ought to be, and usually are, well equipped. The effect of good criticism is to convince us of what C. S. Lewis called 'the enormous extension of our being which we owe to authors'. A Casebook will be justified only if it helps to promote the same end.

A single volume can represent no more than a small selection of critical opinions. Some critics have been excluded for reasons of space, and it is hoped that readers will follow up the further suggestions in the Select Bibliography. Other contributions have been severed from their original context, to which some readers may wish to return. Indeed, if they take a hint from the critics represented here, they certainly will.

A. E. DYSON

INTRODUCTION

ALTHOUGH the dating of his plays is a matter for dispute, it seems clear that Shakespeare wrote *The Merchant of Venice* some time between August 1596 and July 1598.* This places it after *Richard II* and *A Midsummer Night's Dream* and before the two parts of *Henry IV* and the mature comedies *Much Ado, As You Like It* and *Twelfth Night.* It was first printed in a quarto edition of 1600. One reason why Shakespeare decided to write a 'Jewish' play may have been that anti-Jewish feeling had been running high at about this time and that he hoped to write a topical success which would be profitable to the Lord Chamberlain's Servants, the theatrical company with whom he acted and in which he was a shareholder. A celebrated trial had been held in 1594 at which the Queen's physician, a Portuguese Jew named Lopez, was exposed as a conspirator and charged with attempting to poison the sovereign. During the period of his trial and execution the actors, quick to exploit popular feeling, revived Marlowe's *Jew of Malta* and performed it at least fifteen times within the year. It would be characteristic of Shakespeare to compose a work which expressed his own insights and was at the same time a source of revenue to himself and his fellow actors.

He may have adapted *The Merchant* from an earlier play, now lost, called *The Jew.* Only one piece of evidence remains of the existence of this earlier play – a remark by the Puritan Stephen Gosson who praises it for 'representing the greedinesse of worldly chusers and the bloody mindes of Usurers'. Some scholars have argued that 'the greedinesse of worldly chusers' refers to the story of the caskets and 'the bloody mindes of

* The play's date of composition and its connection with the Lopez trial are examined in the introduction to the New Arden edition of the play, ed. John Russell Brown (1955).

Usurers' to the flesh-bond and that *The Jew*, like *The Merchant*, brought together both plots in the same play. The evidence is, however, not explicit enough to be convincing and, even if Shakespeare did find the two plots already combined, we are left with the conclusion that he chose to retain them, apparently because he realised that they could be significantly related to each other.

Like many of the plots which he adapted for his comedies, both are extremely ancient and had appeared in many different forms before they arrived on the stage.* The tale of the pound of flesh was originally an eastern folk-tale which began to take literary form in the twelfth century. It was one of the stories included in the medieval *Gesta Romanorum* and made its first appearance in English in a late-thirteenth-century poem, the *Cursor Mundi*. Shakespeare's immediate source was probably *Il Pecorone* ('The Dunce'), a collection of prose tales written by Ser Giovanni Fiorentino and published in Italy in 1558. Ser Giovanni includes several circumstantial details which Shakespeare could not have found in any of the earlier versions. The setting for the story is Venice where a rich merchant borrows money from a Jew to enable his godson to woo a lady of Belmont. The hero wins the lady but his godfather, unable to repay the Jew, is arrested and is about to lose a pound of his flesh when the lady arrives disguised as a lawyer and saves him by means of a legal quibble. The lady is finally identified by means of her ring. *Il Pecorone* does not, however, include the legend of the caskets which, as Freud realised (see pp. 59–61), also originated in folklore. The first written version was the work of Joannes Damascenus, a Greek monk, and dates from the ninth century. This was subsequently translated into Latin and reappeared in Boccaccio's *Decameron* and in the English poet John Gower's *Confessio Amantis*. The closest account to Shakespeare's is the one in the *Gesta Romanorum*, a selection from which, including the casket story, had been translated into English and published in 1577. The elopement of Lorenzo with Jessica was derived from yet

* The sources of the play are discussed and reproduced in Geoffrey Bullough's *Narrative and Dramatic Sources of Shakespeare* 1 (1957) 445–514.

another source, a story in the fifteenth-century Italian *Novellino* by Masuccio of Salerno.

If Shakespeare did in fact devise *The Merchant* in order to appeal to popular taste, he appears to have succeeded. It was, according to the title-page of the first edition 'divers times acted by the Lord Chamberlaine his Servants', the dramatist's own company. The first performance on record was given in the presence of James I on Shrove Sunday 1605, a successful one apparently since the King commanded a second performance the following week. Of its stage-history during the rest of the seventeenth century we know practically nothing, but it was 'improved' after the Restoration and for the first half of the eighteenth century was known to theatregoers only in an adaptation by George Granville, later Lord Lansdowne.* Granville renamed the play *The Jew of Venice*, removed a great many minor characters, rewrote much of Shakespeare's verse and introduced a banqueting-scene into the second Act where Shylock, feasted by Antonio and Bassanio, is entertained with a masque of Peleus and Thetis. It was not until Charles Macklin appeared as Shylock in 1741 that Shakespeare's text, though still incomplete, was used again in the theatre.

A brief sketch of the various ways in which Shylock has been interpreted on the stage reveals, perhaps more strongly than its critical history, the ambiguities in the play. In Granville's version the part was played originally by Thomas Doggett, a celebrated clown whose greatest successes had been in the portrayal of low comedy roles. The tradition of playing Shylock as a buffoon remained until Macklin took over the part and deliberately set out to astonish the first-night audience. Doggett had made Shylock a fool but Macklin presented him as a villain, malevolent, brooding and with what an eye-witness described as a 'sententious gloominess of expression . . . a sullen solemnity of deportment . . . a forcible and terrifying ferocity' (see p. 26). Macklin's became the accepted way of playing the role until a new and more subtle interpretation came in 1814 from Edmund Kean. 'We expected to see, what we had been used to see', wrote

* The fullest account of the stage-history of the play is Toby Lelyveld's *Shylock on the Stage* (1961).

Hazlitt, 'a decrepid old man, bent with age and ugly with mental deformity, grinning with deadly malice, with the venom of his heart congealed in the expression of his countenance, sullen, morose, gloomy, inflexible, brooding over one idea, that of his hatred. . . . We were disappointed, because we had taken our idea from other actors, not from the play' (see p. 28). Kean's performance was remarkable for its range, his awareness of the variations in Shylock's temperament from malevolent fawning to impassioned dignity. He was apparently the first actor to arouse the audience's sympathy for Shylock. According to Hazlitt he was 'more than half a Christian. Certainly our sympathies are much oftener with him than with his enemies'. It was Shylock's dignity and pathos which were exploited by Victorian actors, notably Henry Irving, who first played the role in 1879. Irving himself explained that he regarded Shylock as 'the type of a persecuted race; almost the only gentleman in the play and the most ill-used'. He conceived him as 'a representative of a race which generation after generation has been cruelly used, insulted, execrated. It is an hereditary hate, but to this as the play progresses are added individual wrongs that make him inexorable and fiendish.'* In the past Shylock had been played either as a buffoon or a villain; to Irving he was a tragic hero.

These widely varying interpretations of Shylock are all to some extent supported by Shakespeare's text. He is at times ridiculous, as in the scene with Tubal, at times diabolical, as he confronts Antonio at the trial, and at times he voices, as no other fictional character has done, the abject suffering of his race. An ideal performance of the role would include all these characteristics and reveal them to be not inconsistent in the same personality. But the apparent contradictions in the central character are only the most striking ambiguities in a play which is itself ambiguous, as we shall see.

The first critical remarks on the play of any interest are Nicholas Rowe's in the account of Shakespeare which he included in his 1709 edition of the poet's works (see p. 25). It is interesting to notice that even this early critic is aware of its

* Henry Irving, *Impressions of America* (1884) p. 265; *Herald*, 7 Nov. 1883, quoted in Lelyveld, pp. 82–3.

ambiguities and that, in one passing comment, he anticipates volumes of later controversy. 'Tho' we have seen that Play Receiv'd and Acted as a Comedy, and the Part of the *Jew* perform'd by an Excellent Comedian,' he remarks, alluding to Doggett, 'yet I cannot but think it was design'd Tragically by the Author.' He is also dissatisfied by the improbability of the casket story and indeed several eighteenth-century critics, notably Samuel Johnson, were offended by the implausibility of the comedies generally. A variety of arguments have been put forward in answer to this criticism. One of them – Granville-Barker's – is that both plots are nothing more than fairy-tales and that they were not intended to have any relevance to real life. 'There is no more reality in Shylock's bond and the Lord of Belmont's will', declares Barker, 'than in Jack and the Bean-stalk.'* Another answer, implicit in Miss Bradbrook's interpretation, is that the 'truth' of the play is to be found not in its veri-similitude but in the moral insights relating to justice and mercy to which the action is subservient (see p. 133). The action thus functions in the manner of an allegory or myth and we do not demand that it should be realistic. Nevertheless, it is clear that Shakespeare recognised the improbability of the stories as he found them in his sources and that, as Palmer demonstrates (see p. 119), he took pains to make them more convincing psychologically by the careful manipulation of events. As in all the mature comedies and romances 'real' people are caught up in 'unreal' situations, the extreme unreality of the action contributing to the dramatic – and thematic – heightening of the play.

Discussion of Shakespeare's themes was practically unknown in the eighteenth century, most critics remaining content to draw attention to the 'beauties' of the verse and to describe the leading characters. Their attempts to discover moral instruction and their more frequent expressions of frustration at finding none were clumsy experiments in thematic interpretation. Less literal-minded consideration of Shakespeare's themes begins to appear with the two nineteenth-century German critics Ulrici and Ger-vinus. I have included an excerpt from Ulrici's treatment of the

* *Prefaces to Shakespeare*, Second Series (1930) p. 67.

play, not because he gives anything like a full account of its meaning, but because he was the first critic to regard it as an examination of human values and because his essay elicited from his contemporary Gervinus the realisation that *The Merchant of Venice* is a play about 'the relation of man to property'. 'To examine the relation of man to property, to money', affirms Gervinus, 'is to place their intrinsic value on the finest scale, and to separate that which belongs to the unessential, to outward things, from that which in its inward nature relates to a higher destiny' (see pp. 34–5).

The most pertinent discussions of the themes of this play are those which have developed with more subtlety the theory originally advanced by Gervinus. Max Plowman, for example, declares that this 'romantic comedy of heart's desire' is 'designed to throw the life-value and the money-value into the strongest possible contrast' (see p. 79). John Russell Brown reminds us that, throughout his early plays, Shakespeare wrote of love 'as of a kind of wealth in which men and women traffic' and that '*The Merchant of Venice* is the most completely informed by Shakespeare's ideal of love's wealth' (see p. 163). Muriel Bradbrook sees the plainest statement of its theme in the trial scene where Shylock stands for the principle of justice and human law in opposition to Portia who stands for mercy and divine law. But these principles, she agrees, are intimately related to 'the gold of Venice' used strictly as a medium of exchange and 'the gold of Belmont' used generously as an expression of love.* Sigurd Burckhardt, in a valuable development of this view, points out that in the play the values of Venice and those of Belmont are not actually presented in opposition but are shown to be interdependent. It is only with the help of Antonio's money that Bassanio can go in quest of his bride; it is by submitting to her father's will, unlike Jessica, that Portia wins her lover, and it is not by transcending the law but by rigidly enforcing it that she is able to save Antonio. The play shows that money can be a currency of love as well as of business and that justice, rightly understood, need not be inhuman (see p. 220).

* See p. 133 and Nevill Coghill, 'The Basis of Shakespearean Comedy', in *Essays and Studies* III (1950) 21–3.

Support for these interpretations has been found in recent historical research into the social and economic background. Early scholarship was too exclusively preoccupied with Shylock's Jewishness and a great deal of material was unearthed about the social position of the Jews and popular attitudes towards them as shown in Elizabethan and medieval literature. It was once thought that Shakespeare might never actually have seen one, since they were expelled from England by Edward I and were still not officially allowed to enter the country. Shakespeare was therefore applauded in the mistaken belief that he had created a character on the basis of hearsay. We now know, however, that there was a sizeable Jewish community living in England, many of whom had fled from the Spanish Inquisition, and that, though they satisfied the law by the outward profession of Christianity, many conducted their own religious worship in private.* Shylock's distinctive mannerisms, his language and rhythms of speech were no doubt copied from life. The assumption behind such research was that *The Merchant* was essentially a play about Shylock and his persecution by society. Once it was realised, however, that the play is more centrally concerned with 'the relationship of man to money', scholars turned their attention to the more relevant subject of usury as a serious moral and economic problem. W. H. Auden and E. C. Pettet have pointed out that a large number of the nobility and gentry in Shakespeare's time were heavily in debt to professional moneylenders and that the play was a contribution to a contemporary debate between the Christian virtue of charity and the widespread practice of lending money on interest (see pp. 101–4 and 229–34). Not that the issue is a dead one. When Shylock perverts the word 'good' from the normal moral sense, in which it is used by Bassanio, to the sense of 'a good financial investment', the quibble is not without relevance to our own capitalist society (I iii 11–15).

The interpretations outlined above assume that the structure of the play rests upon the opposition between the characters of Shylock and Portia, the public relationship of law and commerce,

* See C. J. Sisson, 'A Colony of Jews in Shakespeare's London', in *Essays and Studies* XXIII (1937) 38–51.

and the private relationship of love and friendship. This struc-
tural design is, however, complicated by the further balancing of
Shylock against Antonio. Both are aliens in society, Shylock by
virtue of his race and profession, Antonio, it has been suggested,
by virtue of his sexual inclinations. The cause of Antonio's
melancholy is never revealed. To some readers it is simply the
malady of the rich and to others a sense of impending disaster.
But we do know that he 'only loves the world' for Bassanio
and that his sadness coincides with his friend's proposal to leave
Venice and seek a wife. W. H. Auden sees a special significance
in the fact that 'Shylock the usurer has as his antagonist a man
whose emotional life, though his conduct may be chaste, is
concentrated upon a member of his own sex', and reminds us of
Dante's association of usury with sodomy in the *Inferno* (see
p. 236). Graham Midgley goes further, seeing in Shylock and
Antonio 'the two focal points of the play'. 'As Shylock is to
Venetian society, so is Antonio to the world of love and marriage. . . . One cannot escape the parallel between the lonely
Shylock creeping from the stage . . . and this lonely Antonio
. . . following without joy the triumphant pairs of lovers (see pp.
195 and 207). Whether or not we agree with him that this
relationship is at the centre of the play, we must recognise that
it is an essential part of the total design.

This design is, moreover, not made up simply of contrasting
characters, principles and dramatic action but also of poetic
images. These have been most fully explored by Wilson Knight
whose work is also represented in this collection and who
recognises in *The Merchant* Shakespeare's characteristic opposition of images of storm and music (see p. 82). He remarks particularly the allusions to voyages and shipwreck in the opening
scene and the comparison of Shylock's fury to the raging of the
sea. Shylock has apparently no ear for music but it is to the
strains of a song that Bassanio wins Portia, and the last Act,
coming after the violence of the trial scene, opens with the love
discourse of Lorenzo and Jessica and with Shakespeare's fullest
exposition of the heavenly power of harmony. The accumulation
and release of dramatic tension in the play is thus achieved in part by
its images and these also are an essential element in its structure.

While there is little radical disagreement about the play's structure, the debate about Shylock continues. It became animated after Heine reported his celebrated visit to Drury Lane where, at the conclusion of the trial scene, 'a pale British beauty . . . wept passionately, and many times cried out, "The poor man is wronged!" ' (see p. 29). Heine, himself a Jew, produced the most sentimental account of Shylock. Its most severe rebuttal appeared almost a century later when the American scholar E. E. Stoll assembled a formidable array of evidence, political, social and literary, to prove that, for the Elizabethans, Jews were traditionally regarded as comic villains and that Shakespeare's Jew was no exception (see p. 47). Shylock's tragic pathos was, however, a quality which Stoll refused to recognise. Subsequent critics have rightly objected to Stoll's largely one-sided interpretation and to his assumption that Shakespeare unquestioningly shared the racial prejudices of his contemporaries. There have been further attempts to make Shylock an essentially tragic and sympathetic character, notably by H. B. Charlton in his lectures on *Shakespearean Comedy*.* Charlton's theory is that Shakespeare set out initially to depict Shylock as 'an ogre of medieval story', 'a cur to be execrated by all honest men', but that his creative imagination got the better of him and made a character of great sensitivity and humanity, thus destroying the 'artistic unity' of the play while enlarging our understanding of human nature. This theory may perhaps be right but it can never be proved nor is it easy to believe that such a skilful artist as Shakespeare was not wholly aware of what he was doing. Harold Goddard is still more extreme in his views and interprets the Jew's proposal of the bond as 'a sincere wish to wipe out the past and be friends'. His subsequent barbarity then appears as the result of circumstances for which Antonio is at least partially responsible (see p. 155). To sentimentalise Shylock, however, and to see him as 'more sinned against than sinning' is not only to hold an excessively liberal attitude towards attempted murder but to ignore the Jew's consistent

* H. B. Charlton, *Shakespearean Comedy* (1938). Charlton's account of Shylock is one of many serious omissions from this collection. It was too diffuse to abridge satisfactorily and too long to print in full.

preoccupation with wealth and property at the expense of human feeling. On the other hand to make Shylock into a monster is to neglect Shakespeare's ability to project himself into Shylock's situation and to suggest the social injuries – inflicted by Antonio and his associates – which have made him what he is.

A critic's view of Shylock, moreover, must inevitably influence his interpretation of the other major characters and will probably determine his reading of the entire play. If we are more aware of the Jew's suffering than his vindictiveness, then Antonio's most striking quality is not his love for Bassanio but his contempt for Shylock, and his ultimate plight the consequence not of his generosity to his friend but his inhumanity towards his enemy. Bassanio, like Gratiano, then becomes guilty by association, a type of Venetian gilded youth who abuses Antonio's love by sponging on him and whose apparent quest for a bride is really a gamble for money. Such a Bassanio, as Quiller-Couch remarked,* would be temperamentally incapable of choosing the right casket. Portia can also be seen from two different points of view. In the early scenes she is poised and witty but reveals little or no profundity of feeling. Then, when Bassanio has made his choice, she develops in stature. Her instinctive feeling is one of inadequacy as she commits herself and her possessions wholly to the man she loves. Like many of Shakespeare's heroines she expresses her love in terms of self-sacrifice and it is to this same generosity that she appeals when she pleads with Shylock for mercy. But is it this speech, as Granville-Barker believes, which 'gives the true Portia'? (see p. 72). Once she has Shylock in her grasp she is deaf to her own eloquence. She shows no mercy to him but demands the full penalty of the law in a way which some critics have regarded as quite ruthless. Her capacity for mercy does not apparently extend beyond the Gentiles.

The play as a whole may therefore be seen primarily as a celebration of love and mercy or as an ironic criticism of the very people who profess these virtues. Our interpretation will depend largely on our judgement of the central character. This judgement is made more difficult by the fact that the play is im-

* Sir Arthur Quiller-Couch, *Shakespeare's Workmanship* (1918) pp. 101–2.

perfectly balanced. Shylock is sympathetic in spite of his villainy not only because he speaks for a persecuted race but because he is more alive than the rest of the characters. Antonio's speeches seem hollow and platitudinous in comparison with the tough, flexible language given to Shylock.* Hence we can share more readily in the Jew's predicament than in the merchant's because Shylock is more recognisably a person.

The most profitable outcome of this debate has been to make us more conscious of the complexity of Shakespeare's achievement. Either of the two extreme views I have sketched above can be supported by the text but only if we neglect the inescapable evidence for the contrary. Neither will do justice to the unresolved contradictions and ironies within the central character and the play as a whole. Indeed, one of its fascinations lies in the very ambiguity of the motives which inspire its characters. Is Shylock's hatred of Antonio basically that of a victim towards his persecutor or, as he says, that of a moneylender towards his rival in business? Is Antonio's melancholy caused by a sense of doom or by his fear of losing Bassanio? Is Bassanio drawn to Belmont by Portia's beauty or by her dowry? Is Portia the agent of divine mercy or of inflexible justice? Should we applaud Jessica for escaping from her father or condemn her for making off with his money? Are Gratiano's sentiments the healthiest or the most unfeeling reaction to the trial scene? Is the last Act 'completely without irony' as one critic claims, or does it have that 'air of heartless frivolity' which another sees in it? There is no simple answer to any of these questions and to some there is no answer at all. *The Merchant of Venice* defies any simple schematic interpretation and refuses to come to heel at the command of producer or literary critic. What we can say, however, is that the ambiguities of the play are of a kind that we encounter without surprise in real life, for human motivation is never as simple in reality as it often appears in fiction. We can sympathise deeply with a Shylock for the pain he has suffered while recognising that its effects on his personality have been disastrous. We are most of us, like Portia, perfectly capable of defending the principle of mercy but are not always capable of exercising it –

* This point is made by Burckhardt. See p. 210.

especially when dealing with a man like Shylock. As she says, 'It is a good divine that follows his own instructions'. There are many charming young men like Bassanio whose irresponsibility about money does not diminish their charm. Shakespeare's plays, as Dr Johnson remarked, exhibit 'the real state of sublunary nature' in which 'the loss of one is the gain of another' in which, at the same time, the lovers are hasting to Belmont as Shylock is mourning in Venice. Shakespeare, unlike Ben Jonson, refuses to accommodate the ambiguities of 'life' to the formal requirements of 'art'. While involving us in the crises of the action and the power of his verse, he draws our attention to certain moral ambiguities in human experience. Is it right to punish a Shylock for his crime when we know of the agonies which lie behind his motivation? Does the possession of wealth necessarily produce a certain moral complacency? Can we comfortably share in the joyful reunion of the lovers, knowing that Shylock – and Antonio – are excluded? These are vexing questions which we continue to ask long after we have seen or read the play. It gives no easy satisfaction but has the more lasting power to disturb.

PART ONE
Earlier Criticism

NICHOLAS ROWE

THO' we have seen that Play Receiv'd and Acted as a Comedy, and the Part of the *Jew* perform'd by an Excellent Comedian,* yet I cannot but think it was design'd Tragically by the Author. There appears in it such a deadly Spirit of Revenge, such a savage Fierceness and Fellness, and such a bloody designation of Cruelty and Mischief, as cannot agree either with the Stile or Characters of Comedy. The Play it self, take it all together, seems to me to be one of the most finish'd of any of *Shakespear*'s. The Tale indeed, in that Part relating to the Caskets, and the extravagant and unusual kind of Bond given by *Antonio*, is a little too much remov'd from the Rules of Probability: But taking the Fact for granted, we must allow it to be very beautifully written. There is something in the Friendship of *Antonio* to *Bassanio* very Great, Generous and Tender.

(from *Some Account of the Life &c. of Mr William Shakespeare*, in Shakespeare, *Works*, ed. Rowe (1709))

FRANCIS GENTLEMAN

SHYLOCK'S servile and rapturous adoration of the supposed lawyer, for sustaining the solidity of the bond, is inimitably expressed by exclamations; and the cause works up against Antonio to a very pathetic crisis; when a very natural and most agreeable turn of Portia's, defeats the Jew's blood-thirsty hopes, frees the merchant, and gives general joy: there is not any incident in any drama, which strikes so sudden and so powerful an effect; the retorts of Gratiano are admirably pleasant, and the wretched state to which Shylock is in his turn reduced, is so

* The 'Excellent Comedian' is presumably Thomas Doggett. See Introduction, p. 13. J. W.

agreeable a sacrifice to justice, that it conveys inexpressible satisfaction to every feeling mind; the lenity of Antonio is judiciously opposed to the malevolence of his inexorable persecutor. . . .

What follows . . . is only a stratagem of the ladies to get those rings from their husbands, which they had made them swear not to part with; hence arises some matter to eke forward a piece which should undoubtedly have ended with the trial, as no event of equal force could follow the merchant's acquittal. . . .

Though we cannot trace a general moral, yet from many passages, useful, instructive inferences may be drawn, particularly the choice of the caskets, which shews that humility and judgement obtain meritoriously, what ostentation and vanity lose; from the Jew's fate may be learned, that persevering cruelty is very capable of drawing ruin on itself – in those scenes where sentiments and expressions of dignity are requisite, we find them amply provided, in less material passages, both are trifling.

Shylock, whose peculiarity of character and language we have hinted, is a most disgraceful picture of human nature; he is drawn what we think man never was, all shade, not a gleam of light; subtle, selfish, fawning, irrascible and tyrannic; as he is like no dramatic personage but himself, the mode of representation should be particular; as to figure and features, any person and countenance, by dress and other assistance, may be made suitable; however, there is no doubt but MR MACKLIN looks the part as much better than any other person as he plays it; in the level scenes his voice is most happily suited to that sententious gloominess of expression the author intended; which, with a sullen solemnity of deportment, marks the character strongly; in his malevolence, there is a forcible and terrifying ferocity; in the third act scene, where alternate passions reign, he breaks the tones of utterance, and varies his countenance admirably; in the dumb action of the trial scene, he is amazingly descriptive; and through the whole displays such unequalled merit, as justly entitles him to that very comprehensive, though concise compliment, paid him many years ago, 'This is the Jew, that SHAKESPEARE drew.'

(from *The Dramatic Censor or Critical Companion*, 1770)

WILLIAM HAZLITT

IN proportion as Shylock has ceased to be a popular bugbear, 'baited with the rabble's curse', he becomes a half-favourite with the philosophical part of the audience, who are disposed to think that Jewish revenge is at least as good as Christian injuries. Shylock is *a good hater*; 'a man no less sinned against than sinning'. If he carries his revenge too far, yet he has strong grounds for 'the lodged hate he bears Anthonio', which he explains with equal force of eloquence and reason. He seems the depositary of the vengeance of his race; and though the long habit of brooding over daily insults and injuries has crusted over his temper with inveterate misanthropy, and hardened him against the contempt of mankind, this adds but little to the triumphant pretensions of his enemies. There is a strong, quick, and deep sense of justice mixed up with the gall and bitterness of his resentment. The constant apprehension of being burnt alive, plundered, banished, reviled, and trampled on, might be supposed to sour the most forbearing nature, and to take something from that 'milk of human kindness', with which his persecutors contemplated his indignities. The desire of revenge is almost inseparable from the sense of wrong; and we can hardly help sympathising with the proud spirit, hid beneath his 'Jewish gaberdine', stung to madness by repeated undeserved provocations, and labouring to throw off the load of obloquy and oppression heaped upon him and all his tribe by one desperate act of 'lawful' revenge, till the ferociousness of the means by which he is to execute his purpose, and the pertinacity with which he adheres to it, turn us against him; but even at last, when disappointed of the sanguinary revenge with which he had glutted his hopes, and exposed to beggary and contempt by the letter of the law on which he had insisted with so little remorse, we pity him, and think him hardly dealt with by his judges. In all his answers and retorts upon his adversaries, he has the best not only of the argument but of the question, reasoning on their own principles and practice. They are so far from allowing of any measure of equal dealing, of common justice or humanity between themselves and the Jew, that even when they come to ask a favour of him, and Shylock reminds them that 'on such a day they spit upon him, another spurned him, another called him dog, and for these curtesies request he'll lend them so much monies' – Anthonio, his old enemy, instead of any acknowledgement of the shrewdness and justice of his remonstrance, which would have been preposterous in a respectable Catholic merchant in those times, threatens him with a repetition of the same treatment –

> I am as like to call thee so again,
> To spit on thee again, to spurn thee too.

After this, the appeal to the Jew's mercy, as if there were any common principle of right and wrong between them, is the rankest hypocrisy, or the blindest prejudice. . . .

The whole of the trial-scene, both before and after the entrance of Portia, is a master-piece of dramatic skill. The legal acuteness, the passionate declamations, the sound maxims of jurisprudence, the wit and irony interspersed in it, the fluctuations of hope and fear in the different persons, and the completeness and suddenness of the catastrophe, cannot be surpassed. Shylock, who is his own counsel, defends himself well, and is triumphant on all the general topics that are urged against him, and only fails through a legal flaw. . . .

When we first went to see Mr Kean in Shylock, we expected to see, what we had been used to see, a decrepid old man, bent with age and ugly with mental deformity, grinning with deadly malice, with the venom of his heart congealed in the expression of his countenance, sullen, morose, gloomy, inflexible, brooding over one idea, that of his hatred, and fixed on one unalterable purpose, that of his revenge. We were disappointed, because we had taken our idea from other actors, not from the play. There is no proof there that Shylock is old, but a single line, 'Bassanio and *old* Shylock, both stand forth' – which does not imply that he is infirm with age – and the circumstance that he has a daughter marriageable, which does not imply that he is old at all. It would be too much to say that his body should be made crooked and deformed to answer to his mind, which is bowed down and warped with prejudices and passion. That he has but one idea, is not true; he has more ideas than any other person in the piece; and if he is intense and inveterate in the pursuit of his purpose, he shews the utmost elasticity, vigour, and presence of mind, in the means of attaining it. But so rooted was our habitual impression of the part from seeing it caricatured in the representation, that it was only from a careful perusal of the play itself that we saw our error. The stage is not in general the best place to study our author's characters in.

(from *Characters of Shakespeare's Plays*, 1817)

HEINRICH HEINE

When I saw this piece played in Drury Lane there stood behind me in the box a pale British beauty who, at the end of the fourth Act, wept passionately, and many times cried out, 'The poor man is wronged!' It was a countenance of noblest Grecian cut, and the eyes were large and black. I have never been able to forget them, those great black eyes which wept for Shylock!

When I think of those tears I must include the *Merchant of Venice* among the tragedies, although the frame of the work is a composition of laughing masks and sunny faces, satyr forms and amorets, as though the poet meant to make a comedy. Shakespeare perhaps intended originally to please the mob, to represent a thorough going wehr-wolf, a hated fabulous being who yearns for blood, and pays for it with daughter and with ducats, and is over and above laughed to scorn. But the genius of the poet, the spirit of the wide world which ruled in him, was ever stronger than his own will, and so it came to pass that he in Shylock, despite the glaring grotesqueness, expressed the justification of an unfortunate sect which was oppressed by providence, from inscrutable motives, with the hatred of the lower and higher class, and which did not always return this hate with love. . . .

Truly Shakespeare would have written a satire against Christianity if he had made it consist of those characters who are the enemies of Shylock, but who are hardly worthy to unlace his shoes. The bankrupt Antonio is a weak creature without energy, without strength of hatred, and as little of love, a melancholy worm-heart whose flesh is really worth nothing save 'to bait fish withal'. He does not repay the swindled Jew the three thousand ducats. Nor does Bassanio repay him – this man is, as an English critic calls him, a real fortune-hunter; he borrows money to make a display so as to win a rich wife and a fat bridal portion.

As for Lorenzo, he is the accomplice of a most infamous theft, and according to the laws of Prussia he would have been branded, set in the pillory, and condemned to fifteen years' imprisonment, nothwithstanding his susceptibility to the beauties of nature, landscapes by moonlight, and music. As for the other noble Venetians who appear as allies of Antonio, they do not seem to have any special antipathy to money, and when their poor friend is in difficulties they have nothing for him but words or minted air.

(from *Shakespeare's Mädchen und Frauen* (1839),
trans. C. G. Leland, 1891)

HERMANN ULRICI

WE have three knots, each complicated enough, tangled together in the present fable: the money affair between Shylock and Antonio; the weddings of Bassanio and Portia, and of Gratiano and Nerissa; and lastly, Jessica's love for, and elopement with Lorenzo. These several events and interests are disposed with remarkable clearness and precision; each proceeds so naturally of itself, and alongside the others, that we never lose the thread, but the several parts are kept perfectly distinct, while at the same time a living, free, and organic principle pervades them all, and rounds them off into a well-organized and perfect whole. . . . In the same way that the noble Antonio is placed in delightful contrast to the hateful Shylock, so the strange bargain between them – which, although not absolutely impossible, is to the highest degree extraordinary—has its counterpart in the no less singular story of the courtship of Portia and Bassanio. The one is rendered less improbable by the other. So, again, as Portia's free choice is restrained by an odd whim of her deceased father, her attendant Nerissa voluntarily makes her own happiness to depend on the fate of her mistress. To this constraint of will and inclination, the violation of all respect of law and custom by the free choice of Jessica forms again a decided contrast. Thus are the manifold interests and situations of the plot skilfully disposed, so as to shew forth in strong light that contrariety from which life and movement uniformly issue. The next question, however, is, where then are we to look for that intrinsic unity of idea which alone can justify before the tribunal of criticism the combination in a single drama of so many different elements? . . .

The idea which lies at the bottom of the transaction between Antonio and Shylock, is evidently the old juristic maxim, 'Summum jus summa injuria', which is again founded on that high dialectic principle, which the experience of life enforces, that every one-sided and exclusive right produces in this world of limitation its direct negative, and necessarily passes into its opposite. Shylock has evidently the material right on his side, but by taking it, and following it out in its mere letter and one-sidedness, he falls into the deepest and foulest wrong, which by intrinsic necessity, and agreeably to the essential nature of sin, recoils fatally on his own head. The dead letter of the law can but kill. But the same dialectic, and the same view which is here presented in its sharpest and unqualified extreme, shine through all the other parts in various shades and refractions. The whim of Portia's father, which fetters her free-will and robs her of all participation in the choice of her husband, rests, no doubt, ultimately on parental rights and authority; but this extreme right is even extreme wrong, and Portia has good ground for her complaint:

> O! these naughty times
> Put bars between the owners and their rights.

Even if she had broken her oath, and by signs and hints had guided her well-beloved, amiable, and worthy lover to a right choice, would any of us have been ready to cast the first stone at her? The wrong which was involved in this capricious exercise of parental rights, might have issued in tragic misery, had not chance – again a lucky thought of the moment – led to a happy result. The flight and marriage of Jessica against her father's will is itself also a decided wrong. And, yet, who will condemn her for withdrawing herself from the rule, and for despising the rights of *such* a *parent*, who, if she had remained obedient to him, would have brought both her temporal and eternal welfare into peril. Here again, therefore, all revolves around the point of right, as Shakespeare himself plainly enough indicates, Act ii, sc. iii; and still more distinctly (Act iii, sc. v) in the conversations between Lancelot and Jessica. The penalty which the court imposes upon the Jew, by which he is compelled to sanction the marriage of his daughter with Lorenzo, annuls these struggling contrarieties externally and accidentally, rather than furnishes a true intrinsic adjustment of them. Lastly, right and wrong are in the same manner again carried to their extreme points, and consequently to a nicely balanced ambiguity, in the quarrel, with which the piece closes between Gratiano and Nerissa, and, Bassanio and Portia, about the rings which they have parted with, in violation of their sworn promises. Here, again, the maxim 'Summum jus summa injuria' is clearly reflected: here, too, right and wrong are driven dialectically to a strait – to that extreme boundary where both become indistinguishable and pass into each other.

Thus, then, does the intrinsic meaning and signification of these several and seemingly heterogeneous elements, combine them together into unity; they are but so many variations of the same theme. Human life is considered as a transaction of business, with right or justice as its foundation and centre. But the greater the stress that is laid upon this foundation, and the more it is built upon, the more unstable and weak it appears; and the more deeply and definitely it is taken, the more superficial and eccentric does it seem, and the more fatally is it disturbed by its own gravity. No doubt, the end of law and justice is to maintain and support human society. Nevertheless, they are not the true basis and centre of existence, and neither do they constitute the full value of life, nor comprise its whole truth. . . .

Ultimately, therefore, human life rests not on any arrogated right, but on the grace of God; and the divine mercy, which calls him to union with God, is the true and substantial basis of his existence. The conformity of the human with the divine will is the true life-giving morality of man; and this alone gives to right and wrong their true import and significance. This truth is thus beautifully expressed by Shakspeare:

> But mercy is above this sceptred sway,
> It is enthroned in the hearts of kings,
> It is an attribute to God himself;
> And earthly power doth then shew likest God's
> When mercy seasons justice. . . .

Right and wrong become indistinguishable when carried to their utmost limits, and are finally merged in the source of all true life – the love and mercy of God. And this consideration serves to prove how erroneous and unfounded is the oft-repeated objection, that the last Act is an unnecessary adjunct, which, after all interest has been exhausted, hobbles on feeble and languishing. It is nothing less than indispensable to the right understanding and completeness of the whole. It effaces the tragic impression which still lingers on the mind from the fourth Act; the last vibrations of the harsh tones which were there struck, here die away; *in the gay and amusing trifling of love the sharp contrarieties of right and wrong are playfully reconciled.* In the same way that in all the preceding scenes the tragic gloom, which the misfortunes of Antonio diffuse, is painted with the softest touch and lightest shades, and their bitterness seems dissolved into sweet, soothing, and melancholy strains, amid which a happier note may be not indistinctly heard, so the concluding Act impresses on the whole its appropriate comic stamp, and puts a playful mask on the profound seriousness of the entire subject. We cannot, in short, sufficiently admire the artistic skill of our poet, who, at the risk of censure, and of failure of effect on the weak-sighted and superficial reader, dares to appear indeed to be violating the rules of his art, while he is constantly and steadily pursuing it, and was attaining it so surely and un-erringly.

(from *Shakespeare's Dramatic Art and his Relation to Calderon and Goethe* (1839), English trans. 1846)

G. G. GERVINUS

ULRICI perceived the fundamental idea of the *Merchant of Venice* in the sentence: summum jus summa injuria. With ability and ingenuity he has referred the separate parts to this one central point. But when we look only upon the external structure of the piece, the essentially acting characters do not all stand in relation to this idea, a requirement fulfilled in all the maturer works of our poet. Bassanio, who is really the link uniting the principal actors in the two separate adventures, Antonio and Portia, has nothing to do with this idea. Just as little have the friends and parasites of Antonio, the suitors of Portia. Moreover Portia's father is called a virtuous holy man, who has left behind him the order concerning the caskets out of kindness, in a sort of inspiration, but in no wise in a severe employment of paternal power. . . .

To Ulrici the story of the piece is a given subject; to us – who do not so separate the dramatic forms, since even Shakespeare has not so separated them, for to him far rather out of every material a particular form arose naturally, fashioned according to inner laws – to us, the story grows out of the peculiar nature of the characters. *This* Shylock first connects the plot of the action with *this* Antonio, through *this* Bassanio; these men, their characters, and motives exist for our poet before the plot, which results from their co-operation. Granted, that the subject was transmitted to the poet, and that here as in *All's Well that Ends Well*, he held himself conscientiously bound to the strangest of all materials: that which most distinguishes him and his poetry, that in which he maintains his freest motion, that from which he designs the structure of his pieces, and even creates the given subject anew, is ever the characters themselves and the motives of their actions. . . . We could after our own fashion say in a more abstract and pretentious form, that the intention of the poet in the *Merchant of Venice* was to depict the relation of man to property. . . . The god of the world, the image of show, the symbol of all external things, is money, and it is so called by Shakespeare and in all proverbs. To examine the relation of man to property, to money, is to place their intrinsic value on the finest scale, and to separate that which belongs to the un-essential, to outward things, from that which in its inward nature relates to a higher destiny. As attributes of show, gold and silver, misleading and testing, are taken as the material of Portia's caskets, and Bassanio's comments on the caskets mark the true meaning of the piece:

> So may the outward shows be least themselves;
> The world is still deceived with ornament. . . .

The chooser therefore turns away from the gold and silver, as from the current and received image of that precarious show, and turns to the lead, 'which rather threatenest, than doth promise aught'. And so, not his relation alone, but the relation of a number of beings to this perishable false good, gold, is depicted in our piece. An abundance of characters and circumstances displays how the possession produces in men barbarity and cruelty, hatred and obduracy, anxiety and indifference, spleen and fickleness, and again how it calls forth the highest virtues and qualities, and by testing, confirms them. But essentially the relation of the outward possession to an inclination entirely inward, to friendship, is placed prominently forward. And this is indeed inserted by the poet in the original story, yet not arbitrarily inter-woven with it, but developed according to its inmost nature from the materials given. For the question of man's relation to property is ever at the same time a question of his relation to man, as it cannot be imagined apart from man. The miser, who seeks to deprive others of possession and to seize upon it him-self, will hate and will be hated. The spend-thrift, who gives and bestows, loves and will be loved. The relation of both to posses-sion, their riches or their poverty, will, as it changes, also change their relation to their fellow men. For this reason the old story of Timon, handled by our poet in its profoundest sense, is at once a history of prodigality, and a history of false friendship. And thus has Shakespeare, in the poem before us, represented a genuine brotherhood between the pictures he sets forth of avarice and prodigality, of hard usury and inconsiderate extrava-gance, so that the piece may just as well be called a song of true friendship. The most unselfish spiritual affection is placed in contrast to the most selfish worldly one, the most essential truth to unessential show. For even sexual love in its purest and deepest form, through the addition of sensual enjoyment, is not in the same measure free from selfishness, as friendship, an inclination of the soul, which is wholly based upon the absence of all egotism and self-love, and whose purity and elevation is tested by nothing so truly, as by the exact opposite, the point of possession, which excites most powerfully the selfishness and self-interest of men.

(from *Shakespeare Commentaries* (1849),
trans. F. E. Bunnett, 1863)

RICHARD G. MOULTON

THE starting-point in the treatment of any work of literature is its position in literary history: the recognition of this gives the attitude of mind which is most favourable for extracting from the work its full effect. The division of the universal Drama to which Shakespeare belongs is known as the 'Romantic Drama', one of its chief distinctions being that it uses the stories of Romance, together with histories treated as story-books, as the sources from which the matter of the plays is taken; Romances are the *raw material* out of which the Shakespearean Drama is manufactured. This very fact serves to illustrate the elevation of the Elizabethan Drama in the scale of literary development: just as the weaver uses as his raw material that which is the finished product of the spinner, so Shakespeare and his contemporaries start in their art of dramatising from Story which is already a form of art. . . . For illustration of this no play could be more suitable than *The Merchant of Venice*, in which two tales, already familiar in the story form, have been woven together into a single plot: the Story of the Cruel Jew, who entered into a bond with his enemy of which the forfeit was to be a pound of this enemy's own flesh, and the Story of the Heiress and the Caskets. The present study will deal with the stories themselves, considering them as if with the eye of a dramatic artist to catch the points in which they lend themselves to dramatic effect. . . .

In the Story of the Jew the main point is its special capability for bringing out the idea of *Nemesis*, one of the simplest and most universal of dramatic motives. Described broadly, Nemesis is retribution as it appears in the world of art. In reality the term covers two distinct conceptions: in ancient thought Nemesis was an artistic bond between excess and reaction, in modern thought it is an artistic bond between sin and retribution. . . . Now for this dramatic effect of Nemesis it would be difficult to find a story promising more scope than the Story of the Cruel Jew. It will be seen at once to contain a double nemesis, attaching to the Jew himself and to his victim. The two moreover represent the different conceptions of Nemesis in the ancient and modern world; Antonio's excess of moral confidence suffers a nemesis of reaction in his humiliation, and Shylock's sin of judicial murder finds a nemesis of retribution in his ruin by process of law. The nemesis, it will be observed, is not merely two-fold, but double in the way that a double flower is distinct from two flowers: it is a nemesis *on* a nemesis; the nemesis which visits Antonio's fault is the crime for which Shylock suffers his nemesis. Again, in that which gives artistic character to the reaction and the retribution the two nemeses differ. Let St Paul put the difference for us: 'Some men's sins are evident, going before unto judgment; and some they follow after.' So in cases like that of Shylock the nemesis is interesting from its very obviousness and the impatience with which we look for it; in the case of Antonio the nemesis is striking for the very opposite reason, that he of all men seemed most secure against it.

Antonio must be understood as a perfect character: for we must read the play in the light of its age, and intolerance was a mediaeval virtue. But there is no single good quality that does not carry with it its special temptation, and the sum of them all, or perfection, has its shadow in self-sufficiency. It is so with Antonio. Of all national types of character the Roman is the most self-sufficient, alike incorruptible by temptation and independent of the softer influences of life: we find that 'Roman honour' is the idea which Antonio's friends are accustomed to associate with him. Further the dramatist contrives to exhibit Antonio to us in circumstances calculated to bring out this drawback to his perfection. In the opening scene we see the dignified merchant-prince suffering under the infliction of frivolous visitors, to which his friendship with the young noble-man exposes him: his tone throughout the interview is that of the barest toleration, and suggests that his courtesies are felt rather as what is due to himself than what is due to those on whom they are bestowed. When Salarino makes flattering excuses for taking his leave, Antonio replies, first with conventional compliment,

> Your worth is very dear in my regard,

and then with blunt plainness, as if Salarino were not worth the trouble of keeping up polite fiction:

> I take it, your own business calls on you
> And you embrace the occasion to depart.

The visitors, trying to find explanation for Antonio's serious-ness, suggest that he is thinking of his vast commercial specula-tions; Antonio draws himself up:

> Believe me, no: I thank my fortune for it,
> My ventures are not in one bottom trusted,
> Nor to one place; nor is my whole estate
> Upon the fortune of this present year:
> Therefore my merchandise makes me not sad.

Antonio is saying in his prosperity that *he* shall never be moved. But the great temptation to self-sufficiency lies in his contact, not with social inferiors, but with a moral outcast such as Shylock: confident that the moral gulf between the two can never be bridged over, Antonio has violated dignity as well as mercy in the gross insults he has heaped upon the Jew whenever they have met. In the Bond Scene we see him unable to restrain his insults at the very moment in which he is soliciting a favour from his enemy; the effect reaches a climax as Shylock gathers up the situation in a single speech, reviewing the insults and taunting his oppressor with the solicited obligation:

> Well then, it now appears you need my help:
> Go to, then; you come to me, and you say,
> 'Shylock, we would have moneys': you say so;
> You, that did void your rheum upon my beard

> And foot me as you spurn a stranger cur
> Over your threshold: moneys is your suit.

There is such a foundation of justice for these taunts that for a moment our sympathies are transferred to Shylock's side. But Antonio, so far from taking warning, is betrayed beyond all bounds in his defiance; and in the challenge to fate with which he replies we catch the tone of infatuated confidence, the *hybris* in which Greek superstition saw the signal for the descent of Nemesis.

> I am as like to call thee so again,
> To spit on thee again, to spurn thee too.
> If thou wilt lend this money, lend it not
> As to thy friends . . .
> *But lend it rather to thine enemy,*
> *Who, if he break, thou may'st with better face*
> *Exact the penalty.*

To this challenge of self-sufficiency the sequel of the story is the answering Nemesis: the merchant becomes a bankrupt, the first citizen of Venice a prisoner at the bar, the morally perfect man holds his life and his all at the mercy of the reprobate he thought he might safely insult.

So Nemesis has surprised Antonio in spite of his perfectness: but the malice of Shylock is such as is perpetually crying for retribution, and the retribution is delayed only that it may descend with accumulated force. In the case of this second nemesis the Story of the Jew exhibits dramatic capability in the opportunity it affords for the sin and the retribution to be included within the same scene. Portia's happy thought is a turning-point in the Trial Scene on the two sides of which we have the Jew's triumph and the Jew's retribution; the two sides are bound together by the principle of measure for measure, and for each detail of vindictiveness that is developed in the first half of the scene there is a corresponding item of nemesis in the sequel. To begin with, Shylock appeals to the charter of the city. It is one of the distinctions between written and unwritten law that no flagrant injustice can arise out of the latter. If the analogy of former precedents would seem to threaten such an injustice, it is easy in a new case to meet the special emergency by establishing a new precedent; where, however, the letter of the written law involves a wrong, however great, it must, nevertheless, be exactly enforced. Shylock takes his stand upon written law; indeed upon the strictest of all kinds of written law, for the charter of the city would seem to be the instrument regulating the relations between citizens and aliens – an absolute necessity for a free port – which could not be superseded without international negotiations. But what is the result? As plaintiff in the cause Shylock would, in the natural course of justice, leave the court, when judgment had been given against him, with no further mortification than the loss of his suit. He is about to do so when he is recalled:

It is enacted in the laws of Venice, &c.

Unwittingly, he has, by the action he has taken, entangled himself with an old statute law, forgotten by all except the learned Bellario, which, going far beyond natural law, made the mere attempt upon a citizen's life by an alien punishable to the same extent as murder. Shylock had chosen the letter of the law, and by the letter of the law he is to suffer. Again, every one must feel that the plea on which Portia upsets the bond is in reality the merest quibble. It is appropriate enough in the mouth of a bright girl playing the lawyer, but no court of justice could seriously entertain it for a moment: by every principle of interpretation a bond that could justify the cutting of human flesh must also justify the shedding of blood, which is necessarily implied in such cutting. But, to balance this, we have Shylock in the earlier part of the scene refusing to listen to arguments of justice, and taking his stand upon his 'humour': if he has a whim, he pleads, for giving ten thousand ducats to have a rat poisoned, who shall prevent him? The suitor who rests his cause on a whim cannot complain if it is upset by a quibble. Similarly, throughout the scene, every point in Shylock's justice of malice meets its answer in the justice of nemesis. He is offered double the amount of his loan:

> If every ducat in six thousand ducats
> Were in six parts, and every part a ducat,

he answers, he would not accept them in lieu of his bond. The wheel of Nemesis goes round, and Shylock would gladly accept not only this offer but even the bare principal; but he is denied, on the ground that he had refused it in open court. They try to bend him to thoughts of mercy:

How shalt thou hope for mercy, rendering none?

He dares to reply:

What judgement shall I dread, doing no wrong?

The wheel of Nemesis goes round, and Shylock's life and all lie at the mercy of the victim to whom he had refused mercy and the judge to whose appeal for mercy he would not listen. In the flow of his success, when every point is being given in his favour, he breaks out into unseemly exultation:

A Daniel come to judgement! yea, a Daniel!

The ebb comes, and his enemies catch up the cry and turn it against him:

A Daniel, still say I, a second Daniel!
I thank thee, Jew, for *teaching* me that word.

Such then is the Story of the Jew, and so it exhibits nemesis clashing with nemesis, the nemesis of surprise with the nemesis of equality and intense satisfaction.

In the Caskets Story, which Shakespeare has associated with the Story of the Jew, the dramatic capabilities are of a totally different kind. In the artist's armoury one of the most effective weapons is Idealisation: inexplicable touches throwing an attractiveness over the repulsive, uncovering the truth and beauty which lie hidden in the commonplace, and showing how much can be brought out of how little with how little change. A story will be excellent material, then, for dramatic handling which contains at once some experience of ordinary life, and also the surroundings which can be made to exhibit this experience in a glorified form: the more commonplace the experience the greater the triumph of art if it can be idealised. The point of the Caskets

Story to the eye of an artist in Drama is the opportunity it affords for such an idealisation of the commonest problem in everyday experience – what may be called the Problem of Judgment by Appearances. . . .

Judgment by Appearances so defined is the only method of judgment proper to practical life, and accordingly an exalted exhibition of it must furnish a keen dramatic interest. How is such a process to be glorified? Clearly Judgment by Appearances will reach the ideal stage when there is the maximum of importance in the issue to be decided and the minimum of evidence by which to decide it. These two conditions are satisfied in the Caskets Story. In questions touching the individual life, that of marriage has this unique importance, that it is bound up with wide consequences which extend beyond the individual himself to his posterity. With the suitors of Portia the question is of marriage with the woman who is presented as supreme of her age in beauty, in wealth and in character; moreover, the other alternative is a vow of perpetual celibacy. So the question at issue in the Caskets Story concerns the most important act of life in the most important form in which it can be imagined to present itself. When we turn to the evidence on which this question is to be decided we find that of rational evidence there is absolutely none. The choice is to be made between three caskets distinguished by their metals and by the accompanying inscriptions:

> Who chooseth me shall gain what many men desire.
> Who chooseth me shall get as much as he deserves.
> Who chooseth me must give and hazard all he hath.

However individual fancies may incline, it is manifestly impossible to set up any train of *reasoning* which should discover a ground of preference amongst the three. And it is worth noting, as an example of Shakespeare's nicety in detail, that the successful chooser reads in the scroll which announces his victory,

> You that choose not by the view,
> Chance *as* fair, and choose *as* true:

Shakespeare does not say '*more* fair', '*more* true'. This equal balancing of the alternatives will appear still clearer when we

recollect that it is an intentional puzzle with which we are dealing, and accordingly that even if ingenuity could discover a
preponderance of reason in favour of any one of the three, there
would be the chance that this preponderance had been anticipated
by the father who set the puzzle. The case becomes like that of
children bidden to guess in which hand a sweetmeat is concealed. They are inclined to say the right hand, but hesitate
whether that answer may not have been foreseen and the sweetmeat put in the left hand; and if on this ground they are tempted
to be sharp and guess the left hand, there is the possibility that
this sharpness may have been anticipated, and the sweetmeat kept
after all in the right hand. If then the Caskets Story places before
us three suitors, going through three trains of intricate reasoning
for guidance in a matter on which their whole future depends,
whereas we, the spectators, can see that from the nature of the
case no reasoning can possibly avail them, we have clearly the
Problem of Judgment by Appearances drawn out in its ideal
form; and our sympathies are attracted by the sight of a process,
belonging to our everyday experience, yet developed before us
in all the force artistic setting can bestow.

But is this all? Does Shakespeare display before us the problem, yet give no help towards its solution? The key to the
suitors' fates is not to be found in the trains of reasoning they go
through. As if to warn us against looking for it in this direction,
Shakespeare contrives that we never hear the reasonings of the
successful suitor. By a natural touch Portia, who has chosen
Bassanio in her heart, is represented as unable to bear the
suspense of hearing him deliberate, and calls for music to drown
his meditations; it is only the conclusion to which he has come
that we catch as the music closes. The particular song selected on
this occasion points dimly in the direction in which we are to
look for the true solution of the problem:

> Tell me where is fancy bred,
> Or in the heart or in the head?

'Fancy' in Shakespearean English means 'love'; and the discussion, whether love belongs to the head or the heart, is no
inappropriate accompaniment to a reality which consists in this

– that the success in love of the suitors, which they are seeking to compass by their reasonings, is in fact being decided by their characters.

(from Shakespeare as a Dramatic Artist, 1885)

PART TWO
Recent Studies

E. E. Stoll

SHYLOCK (1927)

By all the devices of Shakespeare's dramaturgy Shylock is pro-
claimed, as by the triple repetition of a crier, to be the villain,
though a comic villain or butt. Nor does the poet let pass any of
the prejudices of that day which might heighten this impression.
A miser, a money-lender, a Jew – all three had from time im-
memorial been objects of popular detestation and ridicule,
whether in life or on the stage. The union of them in one person
is in Shakespeare's time the rule, both in plays and in 'character'-
writing: to the popular imagination a money-lender was a sordid
miser with a hooked nose. So it is in the acknowledged prototype
of Shylock, Marlowe's 'bottle-nosed' monster, Barabas, the Jew
of Malta. Though far more of a villain, he has the same traits of
craft and cruelty, the same unctuous friendliness hiding a thirst
for a Christian's blood, the same thirst for blood outreaching his
greed for gold, and the same spirit of unrelieved egoism which
thrusts aside the claims of his family, his nation, or even his faith.
If Barabas fawns like a spaniel when he pleases, grins when he
bites, heaves up his shoulders when they call him dog, Shylock,
for his part, 'still bears it with a patient shrug', and 'grows kind',
seeking the Christian's 'love' in the hypocritical fashion of
Barabas with the suitors and the friars. If Barabas ignores the
interests of his brother Jews, poisons his daughter, 'counts religion but a childish toy', and, in various forms, avows the wish
that 'so I live perish may all the world', Shylock has no word for
the generous soul but 'fool' and 'simpleton',* and cries ('fervid
patriot' that he is, 'martyr and avenger'): 'A diamond gone, cost
me two thousand ducats in Frankfort! The curse never fell upon

---

* Cf III iii, where the word, as Cowden-Clarke remarks, is significant. 'This is the fool that lent out money gratis'; – 'In low simplicity
he lends out money gratis.'

our nation until now. I never felt it till now.' Such is his love of
his race, which, Professor Raleigh says, is 'deep as life'.[1] And in
the next breath he cries, as 'the affectionate father': 'Two
thousand ducats in that, and other precious, precious jewels. I
would my daughter were dead at my foot, and the jewels in her
ear . . . and the ducats in her coffin.'

This alternation of daughter and ducats itself comes from
Marlowe's play, as well as other ludicrous touches, such as your
Jew's stinginess with food and horror of swine-eating, and the
confounding of Jew and devil. This last is an old, widespread
superstition: on the strength of holy writ the Fathers (with the
suffrage in this century of Luther) held that the Jews were devils
and the synagogue the house of Satan.[2] In both plays it affords
the standing joke, in the *Merchant of Venice* nine times repeated.[3]
'Let me say Amen betimes,' exclaims Salanio in the midst of his
good wishes for Antonio; 'lest the devil cross my prayer, for here
he comes in the likeness of a Jew.' And in keeping with these
notions Shylock's synagogue is, as Luther piously calls it, *ein
Teuffels Nest*, the nest for hatching his plot once he and Tubal
and the others of his 'tribe' can get together. 'Go, go Tubal,' he
cries in the unction of his guile, 'and meet me at our synagogue;
go, good Tubal, at our synagogue, Tubal!'[4] In any one such
eagerness for the sanctuary is suspicious; but all the more in those
times, when the congregation was of Jews and the business of a
Christian's flesh. These sly and insinuating Oriental repetitions
would of themselves have given the Saxon audience a shudder.

It is highly probable, moreover, that Shylock wore the red
hair and beard from the beginning, as well as the bottle-nose of
Barabas. So Judas was made up from of old; and in their im-
memorial orange-tawny, high-crowned hats and 'Jewish gabar-
dines', the very looks of the two usurers provoked derision. In
both plays the word Jew, itself a badge of opprobrium, is constantly in use instead of the proper name of the character and as a
byword for cruelty and cunning.

Now a popular dramatist, even more than other artists, cannot
play a lone hand, but must regard the established traditions of his
art, the rooted sentiments and prejudices of his public. In other

Elizabethan plays the Jew fares still worse. Few instances have come down to us; but in Abyssus in the anonymous *Timon*, Mammon in *Jack Drum's Entertainment*, Pisaro in Haughton's *Englishmen for My Money*, and Zariph in Day's *Travels of Three English Gentlemen*, are to be found, in various combinations, usurer and miser, villain and butt, devourer of Christian blood and coin, and limb of the devil[5] – all big-nosed,[6] or (in accordance with the vulgar error)[7] foul of breath, in some fashion or other egregiously 'Jewy'. In Mammon and Zariph, who are manifestly done under the influence of Shylock, prominence is given to outcries of avarice and of gloating revenge; while in Pisaro and Abyssus it is the nose, enormous and fiery, that bears the brunt. All these figures, the monstrous births of feeble poets, which owe all the humanity they have to Barabas and Shylock, are nevertheless of the same class, and show the same traits, an exaggeration of the same comic spirit. If they are travesties, they are such unconsciously, inevitably.

In two other plays, which certainly antedate the *Merchant of Venice*, and probably the *Jew of Malta* – Wilson's *Three Ladies of London* (1583) and the anonymous *Selimus* (1588) – the Jew has not developed so far. In the former play there is the single instance in the Elizabethan drama of an honourable Jew, one who forgives Mercatore a debt rather than let him go the length of abjuring his faith and turning Turk to escape it. But this episode is one with a purpose, that of satirizing the foreign merchants who are ruining England; and the Jews are painted fair only to blacken these. Gerontus is not held up to admiration as a whole, for his lending at interest is a practice bitterly attacked in this very play;[8] but intent as he is on recovering only interest and principal, he serves admirably as a foil to a love of lucre that knows no bounds. That Wilson is no advocate of the race appears from his crediting to Usury, in his next play, *The Three Lords and Three Ladies of London*, a purely Jewish parentage.[9] In the character of the usurer in Butler's and Overbury's collections, however, and in Rowley's *Search for Money* (1607), the usual conception prevails – that of one who lends money at interest, hoards it, skimps both himself and his dependants, and is an egoist and an atheist without either virtue or conscience. Butler and Overbury do not call him a Jew, but Rowley is sufficiently explicit in giving him a nose like the 'Jew of Maltae's', a foul odour, and Satan for patron. And the collections of medieval *exempla*[10] abound in stories of usurers who are fonder of gold than of their own souls and have given them up for it to the devil.

In the English mysteries which have come down to us few traces are to be found of a ludicrous treatment of the Jew. Like much of the other comic matter, it may have been such as does not appear in the dialogue – improvisations, gestures, noses, orange-tawny hats. Judas, with his red hair, red beard, and beetling brows, was no doubt comical; for these features the later drama never forgot, and there is a farcical scene in the York Plays where he is by Pilate's Porter refused admittance at sight. From medieval mysteries elsewhere, however, the omission may be supplied. By the Germans, who, unlike the English after 1290, had the Jews always with them, they are made ridiculous like the devils. Their looks, dress, speech, and proverbial greed are not spared, and the Jews' Song in double dutch is the standing-dish at the feast of fun. This blunt and boisterous satire goes the length, still attested pictorially, of representing them as drinking wine or beer as it gushes out of a sow or a calf.[11] In the Carnival plays, the newly converted are in a state of eager expectancy of the forbidden sausage; and once Hans Sachs delighted the audience by letting the devil, driven out of his patient by a physician, enter into a pair of Jewish usurers.[12] The Italian *carri*, popular plays presented on wagons drawn by oxen at the Carnival through the streets of Rome, were also called *giudate*, because in them the Jews played the main part – were abused and mocked, and, in the end, hanged, choked, impaled, and burned.[13] And to similar derision they were exposed among the Spanish.[14]

The closest parallel to Shylock and Barabas that I have seen is the Giudeo in Aretino's *Marescalco* (1526). He too is sly, fawning, and spiteful; and he even seems to have something of Shylock's trick of thought and speech.[15]

In the Elizabethan drama and character-writing, then, the Jew is both money-lender and miser, a villain who hankers after the Christian's blood, a gross egoist, even an atheist (though charged with dealings with the devil), and at the same time a butt, a hook-nosed niggard. And a similar spirit of rude carica-ture and boisterous burlesque, with even less of characterization, prevails, we have seen, in the treatment of the Jew in early popular drama on the Continent. Such is the soil from which the figure of Shylock grew; for almost everything in Shakespeare is a growth, and strikes root deep in the present and in the past, in stage tradition and in the life about him.

The tradition having been examined, it now remains to examine the opinions, or antipathies, of the time – a sorry tale to tell. Critics have wondered at the knowledge of Jewish character displayed by Shakespeare; but Sir Sidney Lee some years since[16] showed that although banished from England in 1290, and not re-admitted until the latter days of Cromwell, Jews were then not unknown. 'Store of Jewes we have in England', to quote *The Wandering Jew Telling Fortunes to Englishmen* (1640); 'a few in Court, many in the Citty, more in the Countrey'. In 1594, shortly before the *Merchant of Venice* was written, one of these Jews at court made something of a stir. Lopez, the Queen's physician, was tried for conspiracy against her life. Sir Sidney Lee has shown the bitterness of feeling which it provoked, and the weight that was given to the fact that the offender was a Jew by prosecutor, judges, and people. 'The perjured and mur-derous Jewish doctor', cried Coke, 'is worse than Judas him-self'; and 'of a religious profession', he said again, 'fit for any execrable undertaking'. Even his judges spoke of him as 'that vile Jew'. Though no longer a Jew by faith, when he protested from the scaffold that 'he loved the Queen as he loved Jesus Christ', such words 'from a man of the Jewish profession', says Camden, were 'heard not without laughter'; and 'He is a Jew!' men cried aloud as the breath passed from his body.[17] 'And what's his reason?' asks Shylock in the play; 'I am a Jew!'

Of itself this incident is enough to show that although there was by no means a Jewish peril in Shakespeare's day, the race-hatred of Angevin times had not burned out. Race-hatred, in-deed, or the desire to profit by it, may have prompted the writing of this play, that Shakespeare's company might in the present excitement compete with Henslowe's in their *Jew of Malta*. Even the Reformation, in England as in Germany, had done little to quench it:[18] only the later Puritans felt any relentings towards the chosen race. Hebrews of the Hebrews themselves, it was small wonder. The visionaries, the Fifth Monarchy men, the Root-and-Branch men, often looked almost kindly upon the Jews as they made the Jewish Sabbath henceforth and for ever the British Sabbath, contemplated surrounding Cromwell with a Sanhedrim of seventy councillors, and urged on Parliament the establishing of the Torah as the law of the realm. But the nation as a whole was not so minded; with it race-hatred went deeper than religion. Cromwell admitted the Jews in 1655; but it had to be, as Graetz remarks, by the back door, for the Commission designated to sit upon the measure was under the necessity of being admonished and dissolved like Parliament itself. Prynne, who for his own faith had lost his ears, wrote what was, measured by his own professional Dissenter's standard, a *Short Demurrer*, in Two Parts, in which, like Luther a century before him, he raked up all the charges against the Jews that had ever been made, including usury, coining, cheating and oppression, crucifixion of children, blasphemy and sacrilege, malice towards man and God, the murder of Christ, obstinacy and hardness of heart. 'Do not I hate them, O Lord, that hate thee?' he cries, with none to contradict him, in his zeal; 'I hate them with a perfect hatred.' And others there were like him, as appears from the petition to Parliament of Robert Rich, surnamed Mordecai, in 1653, on behalf of the Jews of England, Scotland, and Ireland: 'Ever since 1648, it was hoped that persecution for conscience' sake would cease and truth and mercy take its place, but contrary thereto, these three last years hundreds in England have been cast into dungeons and prisons, some have perished, and others endured whippings, stonings, and spoilings of goods for matters concerning their law and conscience', etc. Even after these persecutions had, under Cromwell's iron hand, been allayed, and the Jews admitted to the rights of worship, it was upon a precarious basis. The doors of the first synagogue were threefold and double-locked. In 1660, a remonstrance upon their usurious and fraudulent practices was made by the Lord Mayor and Aldermen to the King, praying for the imposition on them of special taxes, seizure of their personal property, and banishment for residence without a license.[19] Even after the Revolution, in 1689, a bill specially to tax the Jews was introduced into Parliament. Such were the disabilities under which the Jews laboured for a century after Shakespeare's day.

But the speech that to-day moves us most is 'Hath not a Jew eyes?' etc. This is the speech not so much of a comic character as of a villain; and like other villains in Shakespeare he is given his due – a full chance to speak up and to make a fair showing for himself – while he holds the floor. But it seems quite impossible to take it as pathetic, so hedged about is it with prejudice, beginning on a note of thwarted avarice and of revengefulness, and ending on one of rivalry in revenge, of beating the Christians at what, however justly, he chooses to think their own game. Certainly it is not the plea for toleration that it has generally been taken to be – here in the third Act, after all this cloud of prejudice has been raised up against him, and after his avowals of ignoble hatred, on which he is harping still:

He was wont to lend money for a Christian courtesy; let him look to his bond. . . . He hath disgraced me and hindered me half a million, laughed at my losses, mocked at my gains, etc.

As Dr Furness and others have observed, Shakespeare managed in this play very strangely if he meant to stand up for the Jews; but even the human appeal is deliberately thwarted.

We are alienated, not by Shylock's avarice and revengefulness alone – he seems just before his defence fairly to be hungering for the pound of flesh that shall 'feed' his revenge,* to him

---

* It must be remembered that Shakespeare is skirting the fringes of a horrible superstitious prejudice – the notion that the Jews not only crucified Christian children, but, when they had a chance, ate of a Christian's flesh. In John Day's *Travels of Three English Brothers* (1607), the Jew Zariph says:

Now by my soule 'twould my sprits much refresh
To tast a banket all of Christian's flesh. (p. 54)

Sweet gold, sweete Iewell! but the sweetest part
Of a Iewes feast is a Christian's heart. (p. 60)

more profitable (for all that he says that it is not) than the flesh of
muttons, beefs, or goats – but also by the comic circumstances.
Here is a remarkable case of comic preparations and precautions,
of 'isolation'. This is the 'daughter–ducats' scene, in which Shylock first appears after the ludicrous report given, in Act II,
scene viii, by Salanio to Salarino, of his strange and variable
lamentations; and to whom is he talking but to these two merry
gentlemen at this moment? If in the theatre it is to be pathos, he
should be speaking to some one more responsive on the stage; at
every word he is expected to burst out in his 'daughter–ducats'
vein once more; and presently so he does. Though we do
not laugh at Shylock when he asks, 'Hath not a Jew senses,
affections, passions?' good care has been taken that we shall not
weep.

Indeed, I cannot but think that even this speech has for genera-
tions been misread, simply taken, like the other supposedly
pathetic passages, out of its context, and a meaning super-
imposed. Not only does every one forget how it begins and how
it ends, but every one fails to see the thread running through it,
the idea, not that Jews have been inhumanly treated but that from
a Jew mistreated you may expect the same as from a Christian –
revenge, but in a richer measure. 'And what's his reason?' he
begins, 'I am a Jew.' And then and there, we, with our humanitarian impulses, jump the track – at once we are, one and all, over
on Shylock's side. But Shylock's answer is not meant to have
such a disconcerting effect; we must remember the cry of the
London mob when Lopez paid the penalty, and Antonio's words,
'I am like to call thee so again'; we must remember Luther, Coke,
Bishop Hall, James Howell, Jeremy Taylor, Robert Smith,
William Prynne, the Elizabethan dramatists, Shakespeare himself throughout his play.

> A perfect Judge will read each work of Wit
> With the same spirit that its author writ.

For *Jew*, read *German*, time 1914–18, place, Belgium or France,
England or America, and we have, with greater provocation, that
spirit approximately. Shakespeare does not jump the track himself. Hath not a Jew eyes? Hath not a Jew hands? and he proceeds

to show that a Jew, having the wit to perceive an injury, the hand to avenge it, quite the same organs, senses, and passions, in fact, that a Christian has, he will when hurt do all that a Christian will do, and a good bit besides. 'Let him look to his bond.' There is no suggestion that Christians should no longer do any hurt to the Jews, and we make Shylock overstate his case. He is only defending himself in what he intends to do; we make him defend his race against all that has been done to it. He is putting in a plea for the right of revenge; we turn it into a plea for equal treatment at the outset.

Of itself, to be sure, provided we can forget both beginning and end and the far from mitigating circumstances, this cele-brated defence might touch us. Shakespeare's method is not the ordinary method of caricature. He does not distort or grossly exaggerate the Jew's features, but flings a villainous or comic light upon them – does not turn him into a gargoyle or hob-goblin like Barabas, but gives him, to an extraordinary degree, the proportions and lineaments of humanity and of his race, scoundrel though he be. Shylock's Hebrew pride supports him, even when he crouches and cringes. Living in humiliation, he has within him a great bitter well of scorn and sarcasm – for bankrupts and prodigals, for the lazy and frivolous, for the light and weak of wit, and the frailties and inconsistencies of Chris-tians. He takes a Puritanic, or Pharisaic, pride in his sober house. He has a regard for law and the letter of it, is stiff-necked and tenacious in insisting on his rights, and keen and dexterous, though specious and cynical, in his defence of them. And like all Jews, he fights, in argument or lawsuit at least, to the last ditch. By force of circumstances it is he, not Launcelot, that is of Hagar's offspring, and his hand is against every man save his daughter and those of his tribe; but for them and for the memory of Leah he has traces of a racial, a patriarchal affection – they are his flesh, his blood. He remembers the past – having no particular reason to remember the present – the great but remote names of Scripture; and there is something of the dignity of such memories clinging to him, both in his bearing and his speech. And there is to his speech that indefinable individuality and identity of tone – in general, Shakespeare's greatest achievement in characterization

– perceptible in the cast of phrase, the sound and rhythm of it, his repetitions, exclamations, and rhetorical questions – a tone hard and grating, sly and dogged, and yet not without stateliness. Harsh and repellent, he is real and individual; and there is poetry in him, as there is in almost all of the characters of Shakespeare, even the villains and the grotesques, and more than there is in many of these.

Now, though, as I conceive it, there is nothing in the figure rightly to be taken as pathetic, one can see how easily, in forgetfulness of the context, it may be so taken by the modern sympathetic mind. The very dignity and isolation – the picturesque aspect – of the figure makes it pathetic for us, such sentimentalists are we! But in so doing we ignore the rest of Shylock, the traits not noble or appealing at all. Though not an ogre or scarecrow like Barabas, he is villainous enough and comic enough, as it were, in his own right. He is a trickster, a whining and fawning hypocrite, and he sweareth to another's hurt and changeth to avoid his own. His oath and his horror of perjury are belied, not only by his clutching afterwards at thrice the principal although he had refused it – or if not that, at least the principal alone – but also in his prompt abandonment of his suit the moment he hears that a drop of blood means the confiscation of his goods. To keep them in his grasp is to him of more moment than to lay perjury on his soul; though that he had said he would not do, no not for Venice. He could have commanded our respect if he had reverenced his oath, or if without swearing at all he had followed his losing suit (of which he is so proud) to the bitter end; but he is not a hero, even in racial revenge and hatred. His sacred nation he has forgotten long since; the curse upon it he had never felt until he lost his ducats; and in his suit, once fortune has turned against him, Shylock, in all his pretenses, shrivels up. He stands on his oath no longer; of law he has for once had enough; and if nothing else showed that his last words were meant to be comic – 'I pray you give me leave to go from hence, I am not well' – It is his whimpering before that – 'Give me my principal and let me go', 'Shall I not have barely my principal?' – his tearing the bond with a curse rather than take the forfeiture and declaring he will stay no longer question, and his abject miserly cry to the

Christians to take his life if they will take the means whereby he lives.* A losing bargain or suit, after all, is not in his line; his dignity is external, and vanishes once his fraud is revealed. And for this upshot there has been ample preparation. His hypocrisy and trickery glitter through his ruminations and repetitions when first he appears before us, and are fully revealed in his brief soliloquy. But drolly it has been idealized. Jacob and Rebecca he remembers reverently – Jacob because of his crafty dealing with Laban, and Rebecca because, in palming him off upon Isaac, as a 'wise mother she wrought in his behalf'. Sharp practise he respects, and he dwells fondly upon it in Scripture.

SOURCE: Abridged from an essay in *Shakespeare Studies* (1927).

NOTES

1. *Shakespeare* (London and New York, 1907) p. 150: 'More sinned against than sinning', which Swinburne, in 1909, rightly contradicts.

2. See *Jewish Encyclopædia*, 12 vols (London and New York, 1901–6), article 'Church Fathers'. Prynne in his *Short Demurrer* (1656) pt I, p. 35, quotes Matthew Paris and Eadmerus, in passages where the Jew is identified with the Devil. In the cases cited here and below, *devil* is not used loosely as the equivalent of *villain*; Shylock is a devil because he is a Jew.

3. John Bartlett, *A New and Complete Concordance to Shakespeare* (London and New York, 1906), 'Jew', 'devil'.

4. There is a medieval picture of such a meeting to be found in Paul Lacroix, t. i, folio viii, *Conspiration des Juifs*, a miniature in *Le Pèlerinage de la vie humaine*. How they lay their heads together! For the unrealistic red hair and beard put upon Judas and the Jews in medieval literature and art, and lingering on in popular lore, English, French and German, to the present day, there is a deal of evidence, too bulky for me to reproduce. There are Jews, of course, with red hair, but they are rare.

5. *Jack Drum*, lines 53 ff, 91, etc.

* Certainly Mr Poel is right in saying that at line 345 Shylock should tear the bond, as he does in *Il Pecorone*. Cf line 234: 'Be merciful; take thrice thy money; bid me tear the bond.' Now, to get away, he does it himself.

6. Ibid. pp. 140, 142, 143, etc.; *Englishmen for my Money*, in Robert Dodsley, *A Select Collection of Old Plays*, ed. W. C. Hazlitt, 4th ed., 15 vols (1874–6) x 481, 522; *Timon*, in W. C. Hazlitt, *Shakespeare's Library* (1875) pt II, vol. II, pp. 396–7. In neither of the last-named plays is the usurer expressly stated to be a Jew. Cf Thomas Nashe, *Pierce Penilesse* (1592), in *Works*, ed. R. B. McKerrow, 5 vols (1910) I 163, for a usurer with an enormous nose; *Jack Wilton* (1594), in ibid. II 304 ff, for the Jews Zadock and Zacharia, big-nosed, covetous, stingy, treacherous, revengeful, bloody-minded, addicted to poisoning and (like Barabas and Shylock) to casting up to Christians the inconsistency of their lives; William Rowley, *Search for Money* (1609), Percy Soc. II 19.

7. Much is made of this in *Timon*.

8. Dodsley, VI 332 ff. Usury, robbing Love and Conscience of their house, sets them on the downward path; and he assassinates Hospitality.

9. Dodsley, VI 457. Cf Dr Fernow's *Programm* (Hamburg, 1885), to which I am here indebted.

10. Those of Jacques de Vitry, for instance, ed. T. F. Crane (Folk-Lore Society 26: 1890).

11. V. Flögel-Ebeling, *Geschichte des Grotesk-Komischen*, Tafel 20; W. M. A. Creizenach, *Geschichte des Neueren Dramas*, 5 vols (Halle, 1893–1913).

12. For the German plays, see Creizenach (1893) I 205, 406, 419.

13. J. L. Klein, *Geschichte des Dramas* (1865–76) IV 239–40.

14. Creizenach (1903) III 199–207, for the Portuguese.

15. 'Orsù, dieci scudi e quattro sesini vi costeranno le maniglie, vi dono la fattura, che sarà mai? guadagnerò con qualche miserone' (III ii). *Shylock*. 'What of that? Tubal, a wealthy Hebrew of my tribe, will furnish me' (I iii 57).

16. *Gentleman's Magazine* (1880) pp. 187 ff; *Academy*, 14 May 1887; *Transactions of New Shakespeare Society*, 1888. Commonly they followed the trade of old-clothes dealer, it appears from a passage quoted by Sir Sidney Lee from *Every Woman in her Humour* (1609), and from Rowley's *Search for Money*, p. 15 – as both now and in the days of St Jerome. Creizenach quotes Heywood's *Challenge for Beauty* (1635) on their character: 'Your English Jewes, they'le buy and sell their fathers, prostrate their wives, and make money of their own children, the male stewes can witness that' (Thomas Heywood, *Works*, ed. R. H. Shepherd, 6 vols (1874) V 26).

17. William Camden, *Annales* (1635 ed.) p. 431. All the evidence used in the paragraph is Sir Sidney's.

18. H. Graetz, *History of the Jews*, 5 vols (London and Philadelphia, 1891) IV 540–2.

19. For this and the above, see *Calendar of State Papers: Domestic*.

Sigmund Freud

THE THEME OF THE THREE CASKETS (1913)

Two scenes from Shakespeare, one from a comedy and the other from a tragedy, have lately given me occasion for setting and solving a little problem.

The former scene is the suitors' choice between the three caskets in *The Merchant of Venice*. The fair and wise Portia, at her father's bidding, is bound to take for her husband only that one among her suitors who chooses the right casket from among the three before him. The three caskets are of gold, silver and lead: the right one is that containing her portrait. Two suitors have already withdrawn, unsuccessful: they have chosen gold and silver. Bassanio, the third, elects for the lead; he thereby wins the bride, whose affection was already his before the trial of fortune. Each of the suitors had given reasons for his choice in a speech in which he praised the metal he preferred, while depreciating the other two. The most difficult task thus fell to the share of the third fortunate suitor; what he finds to say in glorification of lead as against gold and silver is but little and has a forced ring about it. If in psycho-analytic practice we were confronted with such a speech, we should suspect concealed motives behind the unsatisfying argument.

Shakespeare did not invent this oracle of choosing a casket; he took it from a tale in the *Gesta Romanorum*, in which a girl undertakes the same choice to win the son of the Emperor. Here too the third metal, the lead, is the bringer of fortune. It is not hard to guess that we have here an ancient theme, which requires to be interpreted and traced back to its origin. A preliminary conjecture about the meaning of this choice between gold, silver and lead is soon confirmed by a statement from E. Stucken,[1] who

has made a study of the same material in far-reaching connec-
tions. He says, 'The identity of the three suitors of Portia is clear
from their choice: the Prince of Morocco chooses the gold
casket: he is the sun; the Prince of Arragon chooses the silver
casket: he is the moon; Bassanio chooses the leaden casket: he is
the star youth.' In support of this explanation he cites an episode
from the Esthonian folk-epic *Kalewipoeg*, in which the three
suitors appear undisguisedly as the sun, moon and star youths
('the eldest son of the Pole star') and the bride again falls to the
lot of the third.

Thus our little problem leads to an astral myth. The only pity
is that with this explanation we have not got to the end of the
matter. The question goes further, for we do not share the belief
of many investigators that myths were read off, direct from the
heavens; we are more inclined to judge with Otto Rank[2] that
they were projected on to the heavens after having arisen quite
otherwise under purely human conditions. Now our interest is
in this human content.

Let us glance once more at our material. In the Esthonian epic,
as in the tale from the *Gesta Romanorum*, the subject is the choice
of a maiden among three suitors; in the scene from *The Merchant
of Venice* apparently the subject is the same, but at the same time
in this last something in the nature of an inversion of the idea
makes its appearance: a man chooses between three – caskets. If
we had to do with a dream, it would at once occur to us that
caskets are also women, symbols of the essential thing in woman,
and therefore of a woman herself, like boxes, large or small,
baskets, and so on. If we let ourselves assume the same symbolic
substitution in the story, then the casket scene in *The Merchant
of Venice* really becomes the inversion we suspected. With one
wave of the hand, such as usually only happens in fairy-tales, we
have stripped the astral garment from our theme; and now we
see that the subject is an idea from human life, a man's choice
between three women.

This same content, however, is to be found in another scene of
Shakespeare's, in one of his most powerfully moving dramas;
this time not the choice of a bride, yet linked by many mysterious resemblances to the casket-choice in *The Merchant of*

Venice. The old King Lear resolves to divide his kingdom while he yet lives among his three daughters, according to the love they each in turn express for him. The two elder ones, Goneril and Regan, exhaust themselves in asseverations and glorifications of their love for him, the third, Cordelia, refuses to join in these. He should have recognized the unassuming, speechless love of the third and rewarded it, but he misinterprets it, banishes Cordelia, and divides the kingdom between the other two, to his own and the general ruin. Is not this once more a scene of choosing between three women, of whom the youngest is the best, the supreme one?

There immediately occur to us other scenes from myth, folk-tale and literature, with the same situation as their content: the shepherd Paris has to choose between three goddesses, of whom he declares the third to be the fairest. Cinderella is another such youngest, and is preferred by the prince to the two elder sisters; Psyche in the tale of Apuleius is the youngest and fairest of three sisters; on the one hand, she becomes human and is revered as Aphrodite, on the other, she is treated by the goddess as Cinderella was treated by her stepmother and has to sort a heap of mixed seeds, which she accomplishes with the help of little creatures (doves for Cinderella, ants for Psyche).[3] Anyone who cared to look more closely into the material could undoubtedly discover other versions of the same idea in which the same essential features had been retained.

Let us content ourselves with Cordelia, Aphrodite, Cinderella and Psyche! The three women, of whom the third surpasses the other two, must surely be regarded as in some way alike if they are represented as sisters. It must not lead us astray if in *Lear* the three are the daughters of him who makes the choice; this means probably nothing more than that Lear has to be represented as an old man. An old man cannot very well choose between three women in any other way: thus they become his daughters.

But who are these three sisters and why must the choice fall on the third? If we could answer this question, we should be in possession of the solution we are seeking. We have once already availed ourselves of an application of psycho-analytic technique,

in explaining the three caskets as symbolic of three women. If we
have the courage to continue the process, we shall be setting
foot on a path which leads us first to something unexpected and
incomprehensible, but perhaps by a devious route to a goal.

It may strike us that this surpassing third one has in several
instances certain peculiar qualities besides her beauty. They are
qualities that seem to be tending towards some kind of unity; we
certainly may not expect to find them equally well marked in
every example. Cordelia masks her true self, becomes as unassuming as lead, she remains dumb, she 'loves and is silent'.
Cinderella hides herself, so that she is not to be found. We may
perhaps equate concealment and dumbness. These would of
course be only two instances out of the five we have picked out.
But there is an intimation of the same thing to be found, curiously enough, in two other cases. We have decided to compare
Cordelia, with her obstinate refusal, to lead. In Bassanio's short
speech during the choice of the caskets these are his words of the
lead – properly speaking, without any connection:

> Thy paleness moves me more than eloquence
> ['plainness', according to another reading].

Thus: Thy plainness moves me more than the blatant nature of
the other two. Gold and silver are 'loud'; lead is dumb, in effect
like Cordelia, who 'loves and is silent'.

In the ancient Greek tales of the Judgement of Paris, nothing
is said of such a withholding of herself on the part of Aphrodite.
Each of the three goddesses speaks to the youth and tries to win
him by promises. But, curiously enough, in a quite modern
handling of the same scene this characteristic of the third that has
struck us makes its appearance again. In the libretto of Offen-
bach's *La Belle Hélène*, Paris, after telling of the solicitations of
the other two goddesses, relates how Aphrodite bore herself in
this contest for the prize of beauty:

> La troisième, ah! la troisième!
> La troisième ne dit rien,
> Elle eut le prix tout de même. . . .

If we decide to regard the peculiarities of our 'third one' as concentrated in the 'dumbness', then psycho-analysis has to say that dumbness is in dreams a familiar representation of death.[4]

More than ten years ago a highly intelligent man told me a dream which he wanted to look upon as proof of the telepathic nature of dreams. He saw an absent friend from whom he had received no news for a very long time, and reproached him warmly for his silence. The friend made no reply. It then proved that he had met his death by suicide about the time of the dream. Let us leave the problem of telepathy on one side: there seems to be no doubt that here the dumbness in the dream represents death. Concealment, disappearance from view, too, which the prince in the fairy-tale of Cinderella has to experience three times, is in dreams an unmistakable symbol of death; and no less so is a striking pallor, of which the paleness of the lead in one reading of Shakespeare's text reminds us.[5] The difficulty of translating these significations from the language of dreams into the mode of expression in the myth now occupying our attention is much lightened if we can show with any probability that dumbness must be interpreted as a sign of death in other productions that are not dreams.

I will single out at this point the ninth of Grimm's *Fairy Tales*, the one with the title 'The Twelve Brothers'. A king and a queen have twelve children, all boys. Thereupon the king says, 'If the thirteenth child is a girl, the boys must die.' In expectation of this birth he has twelve coffins made. The twelve sons flee with their mother's help into a secret wood, and swear death to every maiden they shall meet.

A girl-child is born, grows up, and learns one day from her mother that she had twelve brothers. She decides to seek them out, and finds the youngest in the wood; he recognizes her but wants to hide her on account of the brothers' oath. The sister says: 'I will gladly die, if thereby I can save my twelve brothers.' The brothers welcome her gladly, however, and she stays with them and looks after their house for them.

In a little garden near the house grow twelve lilies: the maiden plucks these to give one to each brother. At that moment the brothers are changed into ravens, and disappear, together with the house and garden. Ravens are spirit-birds, the killing of the twelve brothers by their sister is thus again represented by the plucking of the flowers, as at the beginning of the story by the coffins and the disappearance of the brothers. The maiden, who is once more ready to save her brothers from death, is now told that as a condition she is to be dumb for seven years, and not speak one single word. She submits to this test, by which she herself goes into danger, i.e. she herself dies for her brothers, as she promised before meeting with them. By remaining dumb she succeeds at last in delivering the ravens.

In the story of 'The Six Swans' the brothers who are changed into birds are released in exactly the same way, i.e. restored to life by the dumbness of the sister. The maiden has taken the firm resolve to release her brothers, 'an if it cost her life'; as the king's wife she again risks her own life because she will not relinquish her dumbness to defend herself against evil accusations.

Further proofs could undoubtedly be gathered from fairy-tales that dumbness is to be understood as representing death. If we follow these indications, then the third one of the sisters between whom the choice lies would be a dead woman. She may, however, be something else, namely, Death itself, the Goddess of Death. By virtue of a displacement that is not infrequent, the qualities that a deity imparts to men are ascribed to the deity himself. Such a displacement will astonish us least of all in relation to the Goddess of Death, since in modern thought and artistic representation, which would thus be anticipated in these stories, death itself is nothing but a dead man.

But if the third of the sisters is the Goddess of Death, we know the sisters. They are the Fates, the Moerae, the Parcae or the Norns, the third of whom is called Atropos, the inexorable.

II

Let us leave on one side for a while the task of inserting this new-found meaning into our myth, and let us hear what the mythologists have to say about the origin of and the part played by the Fates.[6]

The earliest Greek mythology only knows one Μοῖρα, per-sonifying the inevitable doom (in Homer). The further development of this one Moera into a group of three sisters – goddesses – less often two, probably came about in connection with other divine figures to which the Moerae are clearly related: the Graces and the Horae, the Hours.

The Hours are originally goddesses of the waters of the sky, dispensing rain and dew, and of the clouds from which rain falls; and since these clouds are conceived of as a kind of web it comes about that these goddesses are looked on as spinners, a character that then became attached to the Moerae. In the sun-favoured Mediterranean lands it is the rain on which the fertility of the soil depends, and thus the Hours become the goddesses of vegetation. The beauty of flowers and the abundance of fruit is their doing, and man endows them plentifully with charming and graceful traits. They become the divine representatives of the Seasons, and possibly in this connection acquire their triple number, if the sacred nature of the number three is not sufficient explanation of this. For these ancient peoples at first distinguished only three seasons: winter, spring, summer. Autumn was only added in late Graeco-Roman times, after which four Hours were often represented in art.

The relation to time remained attached to the Hours: later they presided over the time of day, as at first over the periods of the year: at last their name came to be merely a designation for the period of sixty minutes (hour, *heure*, *ora*). The Norns of German mythology are akin to the Hours and the Moerae and exhibit this time-signification in their names. The nature of these deities could not fail, however, to be apprehended more profoundly in time, so that the essential thing about them was shifted until it came to consist of the abiding law at work in the passage of time: the Hours thus became guardians of the law of Nature, and of the divine order of things whereby the constant recurrence of the same things in unalterable succession in the natural world takes place.

This knowledge of nature reacted on the conception of human life. The nature-myth changed into a myth of human life: the weather-goddesses became goddesses of destiny. But this aspect of the Hours only found expression in the Moerae, who watch over the needful ordering of human life as inexorably as do the

Hours over the regular order of nature. The implacable severity of this law, the affinity of it with death and ruin, avoided in the winsome figures of the Hours, was now stamped upon the Moerae, as though mankind had only perceived the full solemnity of natural law when he had to submit his own personality to its working.

The names of the three spinners have been interpreted significantly by mythologists. Lachesis, the name of the second, seems to mean 'the accidental within the decrees of destiny'[7] – we might say 'that which is experienced' – while Atropos means 'the inevitable' – Death – and then for Clotho there remains 'the fateful tendencies each one of us brings into the world'.

And now it is time to return to the idea contained in the choice between the three sisters, which we are endeavouring to interpret. It is with deep dissatisfaction that we find how unintelligible insertion of the new interpretation makes the situations we are considering and what contradictions of the apparent content then result. The third of the sisters should be the Goddess of Death, nay, Death itself; in the Judgement of Paris she is the Goddess of Love, in the tale of Apuleius one comparable to the goddess for her beauty, in *The Merchant of Venice* the fairest and wisest of women, in *Lear* the one faithful daughter. Can a contradiction be more complete? Yet perhaps close at hand there lies even this, improbable as it is – the acme of contradiction. It is certainly forthcoming if every time in this theme of ours there occurs a free choice between the women, and if the choice is thereupon to fall on death – that which no man chooses, to which by destiny alone man falls a victim.

However, contradictions of a certain kind, replacements by the exact opposite, offer no serious difficulty to analytic interpretation. We shall not this time take our stand on the fact that contraries are constantly represented by one and the same element in the modes of expression used by the unconscious, such as dreams. But we shall remember that there are forces in mental life tending to bring about replacement by the opposite, such as the so-called reaction-formation, and it is just in the discovery of such hidden forces that we look for the reward of our labours. The Moerae were created as a result of a recognition which warns man that he too is a part of nature and therefore subject to the immutable law of death. Against this subjection something in man was bound to struggle, for it is only with extreme unwillingness that he gives up his claim to an exceptional position. We know that man makes use of his imaginative faculty (phantasy) to satisfy those wishes that reality does not satisfy. So his imagination rebelled against the recognition of the truth embodied in the myth of the Moerae, and constructed instead the myth derived from it, in which the Goddess of Death was replaced by the Goddess of Love and by that which most resembles her in human shape. The third of the sisters is no longer Death, she is the fairest, best, most desirable and the most lovable among women. Nor was this substitution in any way difficult: it was prepared for by an ancient ambivalence, it fulfilled itself along the lines of an ancient context which could at that time not long have been forgotten. The Goddess of Love herself, who now took the place of the Goddess of Death, had once been identical with her. Even the Greek Aphrodite had not wholly relinquished her connection with the underworld, although she had long surrendered her rôle of goddess of that region to other divine shapes, to Persephone, or to the tri-form Artemis-Hecate. The great Mother-goddesses of the oriental peoples, however, all seem to have been both founts of being and destroyers; goddesses of life and fertility, and death-goddesses. Thus the replacement by the wish-opposite of which we have spoken in our theme is built upon an ancient identity.

The same consideration answers the question how the episode of a choice came into the myth of the three sisters. A wished-for reversal is again found here. Choice stands in the place of necessity, of destiny. Thus man overcomes death, which in thought he has acknowledged. No greater triumph of wish-fulfilment is conceivable. Just where in reality he obeys compulsion, he exercises choice; and that which he chooses is not a thing of horror, but the fairest and most desirable thing in life.

On a closer inspection we observe, to be sure, that the original myth is not so much disguised that traces of it do not show through and betray its presence. The free choice between the three sisters is, properly speaking, no free choice, for it must necessarily fall on the third if every kind of evil is not to come about, as in *Lear*. The fairest and the best, she who has stepped into the place of the Death-goddess, has kept certain characteristics that border on the uncanny, so that from them we might guess at what lay beneath.[8]

SOURCE: *Collected Papers*, 5 vols (1924–50).

NOTES

1. Eduard Stucken, *Astralmythen der Hebraeer, Babylonier und Aegypter*, 5 vols (Leipzig, 1896–1907).

2. O. Rank, *Der Mythus von der Geburt des Helden* (Leipzig and Vienna, 1909) pp. 8 ff.

3. I have to thank Dr Otto Rank for calling my attention to these similarities.

4. In Wilhelm Stekel's *Sprache des Traumes* (Wiesbaden, 1911) dumbness is also mentioned among the 'death' symbols (p. 351).

5. Stekel, loc. cit.

6. What follows is taken from W. H. Roscher's *Lexikon der griechischen und römischen Mythologie* (Leipzig, 1884–1937), under the relevant headings.

7. Roscher, after Preller-Robert's *Griechische Mythologie*.

8. The Psyche of Apuleius's story has kept many traits that remind us of her kinship with death. Her wedding is celebrated like a funeral, she has to descend into the underworld, and afterwards sinks into a death-like sleep (Otto Rank).

On the significance of Psyche as goddess of the spring and as 'Bride of Death', cf A. Zinzow, *Psyche und Eros* (Halle, 1881).

In another of Grimm's Tales ('The Goose-girl at the Fountain') there is, as in 'Cinderella', an alternation between the ugly and the beautiful aspect of the third sister, in which may be seen an indication of her double nature – before and after the substitution. This third one is repudiated by her father, after a test which nearly corresponds with that in *King Lear*. Like the other sisters, she has to say how dear she holds their father, and finds no expression for her love except the comparison of it with salt. (Kindly communicated by Dr Hanns Sachs.)

Harley Granville-Barker

SHAKESPEARE'S VENICE (1930)

IF Lorenzo and Jessica and a little poetry and the consort of music, which no well-regulated great household of his time would be without, are Shakespeare's resources (he had no other; and what better should we ask?) for the painting of the star-lit garden of Belmont at the play's end, for its beginning he must show us Venice. He troubles with no verbal scene-painting here; throughout the first scene the very word is but spoken twice, and quite casually. We might be anywhere in the city, or out of it, even. Thereafter we hear of the Rialto, of a gondola, of the common ferry and such-like incidentals; but of the picturesque environment to which modern staging has accustomed us there is no suggestion at all. Yet he does present a Venice that lived in the Elizabethan mind, and it is the Venice of his dramatic needs; a city of royal merchants trading to the gorgeous East, of Jews, in their gaberdines (as rare a sight, remember, as to us a Chinese mandarin is, walking the London streets to-day), and of splendid gentlemen rustling in silks. To the lucky young Englishman who could hope to travel there Venice stood for culture and manners and the luxury of civilisation; and this – without one word of description – is how Shakespeare pictures it.

We are used nowadays to see the play begun by the entry of a depressed, sober-suited, middle-aged man and two skipping youths, who make their way with a sort of desperate merriment through such lines as the producer's blue pencil has left them, vanish shamefacedly, reappear at intervals to speak the remnant of another speech or two, and slip at last unregarded into oblivion. These are Solanio and Salarino, cursed by actors as the two worst bores in the whole Shakespearean canon; not except-ing, even, those other twin brethren in nonentity, Rosencrantz

and Guildenstern.* As characters, Shakespeare has certainly not
been at much pains with them; they could exchange speeches and
no one would be the wiser, and they move about at everybody's
convenience but their own. But they have their use, and it is an
important one; realise it, and there may be some credit in fulfilling
it. They are there to paint Venice for us, the Venice of the magnificent young man. Bassanio embodies it also; but there are
other calls on him, and he will be off to Belmont soon. So do
Gratiano and Lorenzo; but they will be gone too. Solanio and
Salarino will not fail us; they hoist this flag at the play's beginning and keep it bravely flying for as long as need be. When
Salarino, for a beginning, addresses Antonio with

> There, where your argosies with portly sail,
> Like signiors and rich burghers on the flood,
> Or, as it were, the pageants of the sea,
> Do overpeer the petty traffickers,
> That curt'sy to them, do them reverence
> As they fly by them with their woven wings. . . .

– there should be no skipping merriment in this.

They are argosies themselves, these magnificent young men,
of high-flowing speech; pageants to overpeer the callow English
ruffians, to whom they are here displayed. The talk passes from
spices and silks into fine classical phrases; and with what elaborate, dignified dandyism it ends!

> *Enter Bassanio, Lorenzo and Gratiano.*
> Solanio.   Here comes Bassanio, your most noble kinsman,
>   Gratiano, and Lorenzo; Fare ye well;
>   We leave you now with better company.
> Salarino. I would have staid till I had made you merry,
>   If worthier friends had not prevented me.
> Antonio.   Your worth is very dear in my regard,
>   I take it, your own business calls on you,
>   And you embrace the occasion to depart.
> Salarino. Good-morrow, my good lords.

* But Rosencrantz and Guildenstern, as Shakespeare wrote them,
are not the mere puppets that the usual mangling of the text leaves
them.

Bassanio. Good signiors both, when shall we laugh? Say,
    when?
    You grow exceeding strange: Must it be so?
Salarino. We'll make our leisures to attend on yours.

No apologetic gabbling here: but such a polish, polish as
might have satisfied Mr Turveydrop. Solanio – if one could distinguish between them – might cut the finer figure of the two.
When the Mask is in question:

> 'Tis vile [he says] unless it may be quaintly ordered,
> And better, in my mind, not undertook.

Salarino has a cultured young gentleman's turn for classical
allusion. He ranges happily from two-headed Janus and Nestor
to Venus' pigeons.

But it is, as we said, when Bassanio and Gratiano and Lorenzo
with his Jessica have departed, that the use these two are to the
play becomes plainest. They give us the first news of Antonio's
losses, and hearsay, filtering through them, keeps the disaster
conveniently vague. If we saw the blow fall on Antonio, the far
more dramatic scene in which Shylock is thrown from depth to
heights and from heights to depth as ill news and this good news
strike upon him would be left at a discount. In this scene they are
most useful (if they are not made mere targets for a star actor to
shoot at). For here again is Venice, in the contrast between sordid Shylock and Tubal and our magnificent young gentlemen,
superfine still of speech and manner, but not above a little Jew-
baiting. They sustain that theme – and it must be sustained – till
it can be fully and finally orchestrated in the trial scene. It is a
simple stagecraft which thus employs them, and their vacuity as
characters inclines us to forget this, their very real utility. For-
getting it, Shakespeare's histrionic Venice is too often forgotten
also.

PORTIA (1930)

Shakespeare can do little enough with Portia while she is still
the slave of the caskets; incidentally, the actress must resist the

temptation to try and do more. She has the picture of an enchanted princess to present, verse and prose to speak perfectly, and she had better be content with that. But we feel, nevertheless (and to this, very discreetly, she may encourage us), that here, pent up and primed for escape is one of that eminent succession of candid and fearless souls: Rosaline, Helena, Beatrice, Rosalind – they embodied an ideal lodged for long in Shakespeare's imagination; he gave it expression whenever he could. Once he can set his Portia free to be herself, he quickly makes up for lost time. He has need to; for from the moment of that revealing

You see me, Lord Bassanio, where I stand. . . .

not half the play's life is left her, and during a good part of this she must pose as the young doctor of Rome whose name is Balthasar. He does not very deliberately develop her character; he seems by now to know too much about her to need to do that. He reveals it to us mainly in little things, and lets us feel its whole happy virtue in the melody of her speech. This it is that casts its spell upon the strict court of Venice. The

Shed thou no blood. . . .

is an effective trick. But

The quality of mercy is not strained;
It droppeth as the gentle rain from heaven
Upon the place beneath. . . .

with its continuing beauty, gives the true Portia. To the very end she expands in her fine freedom, growing in authority and dignity, fresh touches of humour enlightening her, new traits of graciousness showing. She is a great lady in her perfect simplicity, in her ready tact (see how she keeps her guest Antonio free from the mock quarrel about the rings), and in her quite unconscious self-sufficiency (she jokes without embarrassment about taking the mythical Balthasar to her bed, but she snubs Gratiano the next minute for talking of cuckoldry, even as she snubbed Nerissa for a very mild indelicacy – she is fond of Nerissa, but no forward waiting-women for her!). Yet she is no more than a girl.

Here is an effect that we are always apt to miss in the acting of Shakespeare to-day. It is not the actress's fault that she cannot be what her predecessor, the boy-Portia, was; and she brings us compensation for losses which should leave us – if she will mitigate the losses as far as she can – gainers on the whole. But the constant play made in the Comedies upon the contrast between womanly passion or wisdom and its very virginal enshrining gives a delicacy and humour to these figures of romance which the limited resources of the boy left vivid, which the ampler endowment of the woman too often obscures. This is no paradox, but the obvious result of a practical artistry making the most of its materials. Portia does not abide in this dichotomy as fully as, for instance, Rosalind and Viola do; but Shakespeare turns it to account with her in half a hundred little ways, and to blur the effect of them is to rob her of much distinction.

The very first line she speaks, the

> By my troth, Nerissa, my little body is aweary of this great world

is likely to come from the mature actress robbed of half its point. This will not matter so much. But couple that 'little body' with her self-surrender to Bassanio as

> . . . an unlessoned girl, unschooled, unpractised;
> Happy in this, she is not yet so old
> But she may learn . . .

and with the mischief that hides behind the formal courtesies of the welcome to Aragon and Morocco, with the innocence of the amazed

> What no more!
> Pay him six thousand and deface the bond . . .

with the pretty sententiousness of her talk of herself, her

> I never did repent of doing good,
> Nor shall not now. . . .

followed by the artless

> This comes too near the praising of myself . . .

and the figure built up for us of the heiress and great lady of Belmont is seen to be a mere child too, who lives remote in her enchanted world. Set beside this the Portia of resource and command, who sends Bassanio post haste to his friend, and beside that the schoolgirl laughing with Nerissa over the trick they are to play their new lords and masters. Know them all for one Portia, a wise and gallant spirit so virginally enshrined; and we see to what profit Shakespeare turned his disabilities. There is, in this play, a twofold artistry in the achievement. Unlikelihood of plot is redeemed by veracity of character; while the artifice of the medium, the verse and its convention, and the stylised acting of boy as woman, re-reconciles us to the fantasy of the plot.

But a boy-Portia's advantage was chiefly manifest, of course, in the scene of the trial; and here in particular the actress of today must see that she lessens it no more than she need. The curious process of what we may call the 'double negative', by which an Elizabethan audience first admitted a boy as a girl and then enjoyed the pretence that the girl was a boy, is obsolete for us; make-believe being the game, there was probably some pleasure just in this complication of it. This beside, there was the direct dramatic effect, which the boy made supremely well in his own person, of the wise young judge, the Daniel come to judgment. Shylock (and Shakespeare) plucks the allusion from the popular story of Susanna; but there may be some happy confusion, perhaps, with that other Daniel who was among '. . . the children of Israel, of the king's seede and of the Prince's: Springaldes without any blemish, but well-favoured, studious in all wisdome, skillful for knowledge, able to utter knowledge, and such as have livelinesse in them, that they might stand in the king's palace . . .' For this is the very figure we should see. Here is the strict court of Venice, like enough to any law court, from East to West, from Shakespeare's time to now, in that it will seem to the stranger there very dry and discouraging, airless, lifeless. Age and incredulity preside; and if passion and life do enter, they must play upon muted strings. The fiercely passionate Shylock is anomaly enough in such surroundings. Then comes this youth, as brisk and businesslike as you please, and stands before the judges' bench, alert, athletic, modest, confident. He is life incarnate and destined to victory; and such a victory is the fitting climax to a fairy-tale. So the Portia that will – as most Portias do – lapse into feminine softness and pitch the whole scene in the key of the speech on mercy, and that in a key of sentiment, damns the scene and herself and the speech, all three. This amazing youth has the ear of the Court at once; but he'll only hold it by strict attention to business. Then, suddenly, out of this, comes the famous appeal, and catches us and the Court unaware, catches us by the throat, enkindles us. In this lies the effect. Prepare for it, or make the beauty of it over-beautiful (all the more now, because it is famous and hackneyed) and it becomes a dose of soothing syrup.

This, be it further remembered, is not the scene's top note; conflict and climax are to come. They are brought about simply and directly; the mechanical trick of the 'No jot of blood' that is to resolve them asks nothing else. Shakespeare keeps the medium of the verse as simple; it flows on with hardly a broken line. The conflict is between Portia and Shylock. Bassanio's agony, Antonio's stoic resignation cannot be given great play; the artifice of the story will not even now sustain cross-currents of human passion. But the constraint of the business of a court accounts well enough for their quiescence (the actors need do nothing to mitigate it) and the few notes that are struck from them suffice. The action must sweep ahead and no chance be given us to question its likelihood. Even when all is over the Duke departs with not much more comment upon this amazing case than an invitation to the learned young doctor to come to dinner, and Antonio and his friends are as casual about it and almost as calm. There is tactful skill in this. Shylock has gone, that fairy-tale is done with; the less we look back and the sooner we come to fresh comedy again the better.

Throughout the scene a Portia must, of course, by no smallest sign betray to us – as well betray it to Bassanio – that she is other than she now seems. No difficulty here, as we said, for Shakespeare's Portia, or his audience either. There was no wondering as he faced the judges why they never saw this was a woman (since very obviously he now wasn't) nor why Bassanio did not know his wife a yard off. The liquid sentences of the Mercy speech were no betrayal, nor did the brusque aside of a young lawyer, intent upon his brief –

> Your wife would give you little thanks for that,
> If she were by to hear you make the offer.

– lose its quite casual humour. All this straightforwardness the modern actress must, as far as she can, restore.

SOURCE: *Prefaces to Shakespeare*, Second series (1930).

Max Plowman

MONEY AND *THE MERCHANT* (1931)

MONEY is a dangerous subject. Polite conversation avoids it. You may talk about economics, but not raw money. While it is fashionable to belong to a school of economics, university lecturers have to be careful how they talk to undergraduates about the vulgarity of money. For money is a great mystery. I will lend you my books, my house, even my car; but my money has a rate of interest. You will freely offer me a drink, food and cigarettes; but I must not ask you for sixpence, and if you offer it me, I am offended. Yes, money is a great mystery. Only one race understands it.

There is something sinister about money. It flows around us like water in an English August; yet it is sacrosanct. It is so unstable that the bright sun of credit will melt it into thin air; but the guns of war will bring it out of the sky like rain. Yet it is as hard as rock; the irreducible minimum of social necessity; to-day a collection of figures on paper from which a puff of opinion will blow off the noughts, to-morrow a handful of hard coins wherewith to build the only barrier that will stand between us and ignominy.

Money is so commonly the measure we unconsciously apply to men that he who speaks of it critically will be quickly 'sized up'. The shrewd never tell of their own. 'Put money in thy purse,' says Iago; and we take his advice, as secretly as possible. Income tax communications are strictly private, and what a man is 'worth' is divulged only at his death. Rate money higher than wisdom, and in the world of men you will pass unreproved; for money is the token of civilised self-preservation, and fear insists upon the first law of nature. So money has a permanent place in all our thoughts. Our social roots are in money; no one can be allowed to live without it. We are tied to money. It is the shore to which every human craft is anchored, and will remain anchored until mankind has learnt the greatest lesson history can teach it – how to live by a more spiritual means of exchange.

A large measure of disregard for money is one of the few things fools and wise men have in common; but they have it between them with this difference, that whereas wise men have a higher sense of value, fools have none at all. The task of the wise is to make the object of their higher esteem apparent, so that in the eyes of all men the regard for money will go by default. And this is difficult, because the object of their higher esteem is life itself, which is indefinable. The value of life we can only appreciate obliquely: the value of money is immediate and direct. So the money-bird in the hand is esteemed above the living-bird in the bush. The task of wisdom is to teach men to love and enjoy what they cannot grasp.

The arts provide us with the wise man's talisman. They proclaim consistently the higher value, and they constitute the only activity of man that does this consistently. Science does not proclaim the value of life any more than it proclaims the value of money, though pure science may be almost an art. But pure science would soon die were it not for the human sustenance constantly given to it by applied science; for knowledge is in itself, strictly speaking, valueless: to be humanly appreciable it must be made serviceable. Art, on the other hand, is directly appreciable. Its worth lies in its assertion of the value of life above all other values. Art cannot be bought, for its value is beyond money in the sense that it is beyond the valuation money is capable of making. Therefore to appreciate art is to take the first step towards a world in which men will live by a more spiritual means of exchange than money. The farmer who loves to grow corn for its own sake has taken this step. Anything appreciated for its own sake destroys the money-value. This explains the truth of Blake's aphorism: 'Where any view of money exists art cannot be carried on.'

Of course the idea of living by a more spiritual means of exchange than money is highly romantic: it has never been done – at least, not successfully for any length of time. But the idea persists in spite of experience, and its persistence is prophetic. Sooner or later we shall have to translate it from the region of romance to the world of fact, or the idea will poison us. The perpetual rule of life by money life will not endure.

That is really what Shakespeare was saying in *The Merchant of Venice* – his most often misinterpreted play. It is undoubtedly a romantic comedy of heart's desire, designed to throw the life-value and the money-value into the strongest possible contrast.

A play that ends where it begins, in a world in which good-fellowship is the ruling principle. The only currency these Venetians understand is the currency of friendship where he who has is debtor to him who has not, where the only enemy is the man who will not accept such currency but exalts a lower meed of worth and sanctifies it in the name of justice. He is the enemy because the gratification of his desires would drag life back from a civilised to a comparatively barbaric state. He is the enemy because he would check the free flow of money, which should move as healthfully as blood in the human body, and by the incision of usury play the vampire. Shylock is a symbol of the Mammon that can only be served by the negation of God; to sentimentalise him, after the modern fashion, is not merely to damage but to destroy the action of the play. Shakespeare made him human and so pointed the way to his redemption; but he left him inhuman as well, and thereby showed a subtlety and a truth to life which he emphasised again in the character of Iago.

Money is to-day what Shylock was to the world of Venice – the forbidding aspect, the dark principle, the shadow in the sun, the grim necessity. Its logic is inhuman. It has principle, but its principle is insufficient for the flexibility of human life. The problem is how to circumvent it without destroying the foundations of justice. And the answer is, by compelling it to the strictest interpretation of its own logic.

That was how Portia solved the problem. She took the Jew at his word and kept him to it. 'A verbal quibble?' Not at all; on the contrary, the turning upon itself of the weapon of logic basely misused in its attack upon life. And Shylock was convinced by the only means that would carry conviction.

By such a piece of strict rationalisation would money be convinced to-day. 'Realise your wealth,' said Portia. 'Liquidate it in the open court. If you cannot do this, your inability disproves your claim. There is no entity in money. Even as flesh is mingled with blood, so inseparably and inextricably is this, for which you claim a sovran right, woven in the fibres of life.' Compel money to be strictly honest, and it will lose its power to terrorise. Confine it to the work of exchange, and it will lose its power to beget. For money that breeds is the anomaly: in the act it has assumed an attribute of the creature, and when its life is threatened what can it do but seek compensation in flesh?

The theme of *The Merchant* is the interdependence of human beings in civilised society – an inviolable interdependence. This is the idea that Shylock outrages. It appears most obviously in the Trial Scene where a man stands wholly dependent upon a woman. It is shown in Portia's dependence upon her father's will, her maid's cheerfulness, and Bassanio's love. It runs like a thread through the play showing itself in the dependence of Bassanio upon Antonio, of Gratiano upon his friends, of Old Gobbo upon Launcelot, of Lorenzo upon Jessica, even of Shylock upon his daughter and his friend, and in the dependence of all of them upon favour and circumstance. All the sympathetic characters are shown as living in happy human interdependence. On them the sun of fortune shines in the end: they come to weal. All who arrogate to themselves wealth or merit (not only Shylock, but the braggart Princes of Morocco and Aragon) come to woe.

There is a harmony in *The Merchant of Venice* too fine for us to hear while the muddy vesture of economic security doth grossly close us in. . . . Can we hear it? Perhaps not. But Shakespeare trusted to an audience so romantic at heart and so adventurous in spirit that it could readily imagine a world in which the principle of avarice might, without pity, be given leave to hang itself, and another world, foreshadowed in the closing scene, wherein the principle of friendship inspires such exquisite concord heaven and earth are constrained to join in the marriage-making.

SOURCE: Abridged from an essay in the *Adelphi*, II (1931) 508.

G. Wilson Knight

TEMPEST AND MUSIC (1932)

IN no play of this period is there so clear and significant a contrast between the tempests of tragedy and the music of romance. The play opens with a fine description of Antonio's argosies:

> *Salarino.* Your mind is tossing on the ocean,
>   There, where your argosies with portly sail,
>   Like signiors and rich burghers on the flood,
>   Or, as it were, the pageants of the sea,
>   Do overpeer the petty traffickers,
>   That curtsy to them, do them reverence,
>   As they fly by them with their woven wings.
> *Salanio.* Believe me, sir, had I such venture forth,
>   The better part of my affections would
>   Be with my hopes abroad. I should be still
>   Plucking the grass, to know where sits the wind,
>   Peering in maps for ports, and piers, and roads;
>   And every object that might make me fear
>   Misfortune to my ventures, out of doubt
>   Would make me sad.
> *Salarino.*   My wind cooling my broth
>   Would blow me to an ague, when I thought
>   What harm a wind too great might do at sea.
>   I should not see the sandy hour-glass run,
>   But I should think of shallows and of flats,
>   And see my wealthy Andrew dock'd in sand,
>   Vailing her high top lower than her ribs
>   To kiss her burial. Should I go to church,
>   And see the holy edifice of stone,
>   And not bethink me straight of dangerous rocks,
>   Which, touching but my gentle vessel's side,
>   Would scatter all her spices on the stream,
>   Enrobe the roaring waters with my silks,

And, in a word, but even now worth this,
And now worth nothing? Shall I have the thought
To think on this; and shall I lack the thought,
That such a thing bechanc'd would make me sad?
But tell not me; I know, Antonio
Is sad to think upon his merchandise.   (I i 8)

Notice how the sea is impregnated with melancholy suggestion.
So is it in another passage, referring to human enthusiasm and
its all-too-quick extinction:

How like a younker or a prodigal
The scarfed bark puts from her native bay,
Hugg'd and embraced by the strumpet wind!
How like the prodigal doth she return,
With over-weather'd ribs and ragged sails,
Lean, rent, and beggar'd by the strumpet wind!
(II vi 14)

Such is a true Shakespearian image of life's voyages. We see
how universal is the content of our 'bark' and 'tempest' passages.
    Throughout this play we must observe the opposition of sea-
tragedy and romance, which opposition is more powerfully and
exactly significant here than in any other of these [early] plays.
The tempest–music opposition is indeed more essentially dramatic here than in former plays: the two impressions oppose each
other almost like dramatic persons. From Venice and Antonio's
melancholy we are taken eastward over seas to Love's magic
land, Belmont. Bassanio tells Antonio of the rich Portia – we
may remember that love itself is a kind of 'riches' – and her home
across the sea:

Nor is the wide world ignorant of her worth,
For the four winds blow in from every coast
Renowned suitors, and her sunny locks
Hang on her temples like a Golden Fleece;
Which makes her seat of Belmont Colchos' strond,
And many Jasons come in quest of her.   (I i 167)

Bassanio's quest is a 'sea' adventure. But we may also note that
Bassanio's journey separates him from his lover, Antonio. The
farewell is described (II viii). We may, too, observe a Venice–
Belmont contrast. Venice is, of all towns, most closely associated

with the sea, even interwoven with it; and Belmont suggests a
more airy height, a finer element. Venice is the scene of tragedy,
Belmont of love. The one is overcast with gloom – we may note
that even the masque never actually comes off; the other is a
land of music, love, and 'holy crosses'. Morocco later repeats the
idea expressed by Bassanio in his 'Jason' speech:

> The Hyrcanian deserts and the vasty wilds
> Of wide Arabia are as throughfares now
> For princes to come view fair Portia:
> The watery kingdom, whose ambitious head
> Spits in the face of heaven, is no bar
> To stop the foreign spirits, but they come,
> As o'er a brook, to see fair Portia.   (ii vii 41)

Another good example of sea-crossing in the quest of love. There
are a few points to observe here. First, the tempest–desert
association is valuable, helping us to feel tempest suggestion in
thoughts of nature's uncivilization in many contexts; next, the
Hyrcanian–tempest association recalls Macbeth's 'rugged Russian
bear', the 'arm'd rhinoceros' and 'Hyrcan tiger'. And, finally, we
may notice the metaphoric anthropomorphism whereby the sea
spits in the face of heaven: which, if visualized in human terms,
illustrates the anti-love impregnation of the tempest-image. Such
anthropomorphism is usual and may be observed elsewhere, as
when, in *Lear*, the winds are told to blow till they 'crack' their
'cheeks'. Conversely, as in *Titus Andronicus*, human beings in
grief may be imaged as sea and sky tempestuous; or, in love, as
moon and sea peacefully contemplating each other.

Antonio undertakes the venture for love's merchandise. He
loves Bassanio, and his risk is wholly a merchant's venture for
the sake of love; his love for Bassanio, Bassanio's for Portia.
The gold of love is finely associated and yet strongly contrasted
with love's gold in the Casket scene. Morocco's, Arragon's, and
Bassanio's speeches on the gold, silver, and lead caskets are most
significant. This play is full of 'riches' imagery. Such ornament

> is but the guiled shore
> To a most dangerous sea; the beauteous scarf
> Veiling an Indian beauty.   (iii ii 97)

Again the Siren idea, here given in terms of an 'Indian beauty'. Though this may at first suggest 'Indian' to have a wholly derogatory sense, we may compare the lover who 'sees Helen's beauty in a brow of Egypt' (*A Midsummer Night's Dream*, v i 11). And we remember Cleopatra. Such passages suggest, partly at least, the mystery and glamour of the East, the dangerous Indian shores of fairyland, that fairyland's too often untrustworthy and cheating lure. So merchandise, gold and silver caskets, Portia's ring, all the usual associations interthread our texture. But here they are unusually powerful, both actualized and dramatically active. Imagery is becoming the very plot itself. Twenty merchants (III ii 282) have attempted to placate Shylock. Antonio is 'a royal merchant' (III ii 242); Portia's boundless wealth is emphasized again and again; riches are scattered over the play. Shylock himself loses both his loved daughter and vast riches, 'ducats', jewels, his 'turquoise'. Love and riches are ever close. The play is full of ducats and wealth. Shylock rates his ducats and jewels above his daughter, strongly as he loves her; but Bassanio's and Portia's love is finely shown as being of an integrity that sees through the superficial brilliance of gold to the true worth within: hence Bassanio's choice of the leaden casket. These caskets are intensely symbolical. As in *Timon*, the spiritual gold of true love is contrasted with the outward gilding which decorates the false.

And there is music. Belmont is the home of love and music:

> Let music sound while he doth make his choice;
> Then, if he lose, he makes a swan-like end,
> Fading in music: that the comparison
> May stand more proper, my eye shall be the stream
> And watery death-bed for him. He may win;
> And what is music then? Then music is
> Even as the flourish when true subjects bow
> To a new-crowned monarch: such it is
> As are those dulcet sounds in break of day
> That creep into the dreaming bridegroom's ear
> And summon him to marriage.   (III ii 43)

A lovely speech, rich in typical suggestion. We should note the death and music association, the eye–stream comparison, and the 'watery death-bed': death by water made sweet in music, like Ophelia's death or like the music in which the tragedy of *Othello* dissolves in beauty. And, after the 'death' thought, the victory of love: love 'crowned' like a king, the music that awakes the sleeper, bidding him take his happiness. So Hermione 'awakes' to music in *The Winter's Tale*. The purely imaginative order reflects the progress later developed from the Tragedies to the Final Plays. So here there is a song, 'Tell me, where is fancy bred?', and music, and Bassanio wins his joy. He is like Hercules rescuing his lady from 'the sea-monster' (III ii 55–8); and if we remember that both the sea and all fierce beasts are equally symbols of mortal terror in Shakespeare we may understand the terrific significance of sea-monsters here and elsewhere, notably in *Lear*.

But Bassanio's joy is short-lived. Throughout we fear the sinister forces of tempest on which the action depends. We know, like Shylock, that the sea is dangerous:

... he hath an argosy bound to Tripolis, another to the Indies; I understand, moreover, upon the Rialto, he hath a third at Mexico, a fourth for England, and other ventures he hath, squandered abroad. But ships are but boards, sailors but men: there be land-rats and water-rats, water-thieves and land-thieves, I mean pirates, and then there is the peril of waters, winds, and rocks. ... (I iii 18)

Fears are justified:

> I reason'd with a Frenchman yesterday,
> Who told me, in the narrow seas that part
> The French and English, there miscarried
> A vessel of our country richly fraught.
>
> (II viii 27)

Again,

Salanio. Now, what news on the Rialto?
Salarino. Why, yet it lives there unchecked that Antonio hath a ship of rich lading wrecked on the narrow seas; the Goodwins, I think they call the place; a very dangerous flat and fatal, where the carcasses of many a tall ship lie buried. ...
(III i 1)

Tubal, who 'spoke with some of the sailors that escaped the

wreck' (III i 109), tells Shylock that Antonio 'hath an argosy cast
away, coming from Tripolis' (III i 105) All Antonio's ships have
failed:

> But is it true, Salanio?
> Have all his ventures fail'd? What, not one hit?
> From Tripolis, from Mexico, and England,
> From Lisbon, Barbary, and India?
> And not one vessel 'scape the dreadful touch
> Of merchant-marring rocks?
>
> (III ii 269)

'Twenty merchants' (III ii 282) sue on Antonio's behalf. But
Shylock is firm. Tempests have leagued with Shylock, both
equally forces of tragedy to be set against love, music, and Portia.
  It is significant that Shylock hates festive music:

> Lock up my doors: and when you hear the drum
> And the vile squealing of the wry-neck'd fife,
> Clamber not you up to the casements then,
> Nor thrust your head into the public street
> To gaze on Christian fools with varnished faces,
> But stop my house's ears, I mean my casements;
> Let not the sound of shallow foppery enter
> My sober house.   (II v 29)

He 'has no mind of feasting forth'. He is to be contrasted with
music and feasting. His 'music' phrases are naturally hostile:
witness his other words about when the 'bagpipe sings i' the
nose' (IV i 49) and its unpleasant effects. Now Shylock himself is
like a 'tempest'. He is the tragedy-force in the play. 'The very
tyranny and rage' of his 'spirit' (IV i 13) is a typical tempest-
impression recalling the music in *Love's Labour's Lost* that could
'ravish savage ears and plant in tyrants mild humility' (*Love's
Labour's Lost*, IV iii 348). The 'current' of his cruelty is 'unfeeling' (IV i 63–4). Again,

> I pray you, think you question with the Jew:
> You may as well go stand upon the beach
> And bid the main flood bate his usual height;
> You may as well use question with the wolf
> Why he hath made the ewe bleat for the lamb;

> You may as well forbid the mountain pines
> To wag their high tops and to make no noise,
> When they are fretted with the gusts of heaven;
> You may as well do any thing most hard,
> As seek to soften that – than which what's harder? –
> His Jewish heart.   (IV i 70)

'Tops' is a usual word in tempest-passages, applied both to waves and mountain-trees. 'Pines' are important in such passages. Here we should observe also (i) the sea, (ii) the wolf, and (iii) the winds: all associated with human cruelty, and the forces of tragedy. Here the wolf, thus enclosed by the other two, stresses the association. Elsewhere Shylock is powerfully compared to a wolf in a speech which vividly outlines the Shakespearian intuition of the beast in man:

> O, be thou damn'd, inexecrable dog!
> And for thy life let justice be accused.
> Thou almost makest me waver in my faith
> To hold opinion with Pythagoras,
> That souls of animals infuse themselves
> Into the trunks of men: thy currish spirit
> Govern'd a wolf, who, hang'd for human slaughter,
> Even from the gallows did his fell soul fleet,
> And, whilst thou lay'st in thy unhallow'd dam
> Infused itself in thee; for thy desires
> Are wolvish, bloody, starved and ravenous.
>
>   (IV i 128)

This play as certainly as, and more tragically than, the Induction to *The Taming of the Shrew*, sets the beast in man against love and music. The tempest–beast association is always important. And here both are clearly to be related to Shylock and tragedy.

Tragedy in the form of merchant-marring tempests breaks into the music of Bassanio's joy at the moment of his love-success at Belmont. But Portia, love's queen, descends from the fairyland of music and love, Belmont, into the turmoil and dust of human conflict and cruelty at Venice. She is as a being from a different world. We may observe that she, like Shakespeare's other heroines, is often associated directly with thoughts of divinity. Here, we have Portia's lovely Mercy speech, and her

pretended pilgrimage, reminding us of Helena in *All's Well*. So
she takes arms against the tragic forces of tempest and wins.

We are finally brought back to Belmont, where again we find
romance and music. Jessica and Lorenzo make love by moonlight:

> The moon shines bright; in such a night as this
> When the sweet wind did gently kiss the trees
> And they did make no noise, in such a night
> Troilus methinks mounted the Troyan walls
> And sigh'd his soul towards the Grecian tents,
> Where Cressid lay that night.   (v i 1)

Soft airs and love: a usual association, most notable of all in
Antony and Cleopatra and *Cymbeline*. Themselves happy, these
lovers yet image love's tragedies: Troilus sighing his soul out to
the gentle sigh of the wind, Thisbe who 'saw the lion's shadow'
and 'ran dismay'd away' (v i 8), and finally, Dido, parted by
cruel waters from her lover:

> In such a night
> Stood Dido with a willow in her hand
> Upon the wild sea-banks, and waft her love
> To come again to Carthage.   (v i 9)

A typical thought of love parted by water; and an inverse of our
other sea-shore and love image, wherein love beckons across
dangerous seas. The triple imagery is again important: (i) 'wind'
and 'sighs', (ii) the 'lion', and (iii) the 'sea' – an almost exact
repetition of our sea–beast–wind association just observed. Here
it is less tempestuous, the beast nobler. Twice the 'beast' is thus
sandwiched between 'sea' and 'wind', which, being the main
elements of our 'tempest' symbol, here point clearly to the close
beast–tempest association. Lorenzo calls for music to be brought
forth 'into the air', Then,

> *Lorenzo.* How sweet the moonlight sleeps upon this bank!
>   Here will we sit and let the sounds of music
>   Creep in our ears: soft stillness and the night
>   Become the touches of sweet harmony.
>   Sit, Jessica: look, how the floor of heaven
>   Is thick inlaid with patines of bright gold:
>   There's not the smallest orb which thou behold'st,

> But in his motion like an angel sings,
> Still quiring to the young-ey'd cherubins:
> Such harmony is in immortal souls;
> But, whilst this muddy vesture of decay
> Doth grossly close it in, we cannot hear it.
>
> *Enter Musicians*
> Come, ho! and wake Diana with a hymn:
> With sweetest touches pierce your mistress' ear,
> And draw her home with music.
> [*Music*
> *Jessica.* I am never merry when I hear sweet music.
> *Lorenzo.* The reason is, your spirits are attentive:
> For do but note a wild and wanton herd,
> Or race of youthful and unhandled colts,
> Fetching mad bounds, bellowing, and neighing loud,
> Which is the hot condition of their blood:
> If they but hear perchance a trumpet sound,
> Or any air of music touch their ears,
> You shall perceive them make a mutual stand,
> Their savage eyes turn'd to a modest gaze
> By the sweet power of music: therefore the poet
> Did feign that Orpheus drew trees, stones, and floods;
> Since nought so stockish, hard, and full of rage,
> But music for the time doth change his nature.
> The man that hath no music in himself,
> Nor is not mov'd with concord of sweet sounds,
> Is fit for treasons, stratagems, and spoils;
> The motions of his spirit are dull as night,
> And his affections dark as Erebus:
> Let no such man be trusted. – Mark the music.
>
> (v i 54)

Here we should observe the association of music, stillness, the moon, and love: all are elsewhere important. Stars, too, are a development of the moon idea and blend with jewel and gold imagery: 'patines of bright gold'. See, too, how the 'music of the spheres' mentioned also in *Twelfth Night* and *Pericles*, there, too, with love-suggestion, is here quaintly and beautifully taken from its Ptolemaic context and given a Copernican significance. This spheral music is heard only by 'immortal souls' – we may thus note its aptness in the paradisal vision of *Pericles* – but the universal harmony is blurred to mortal understanding. Here Portia, love's queen, is to be drawn home 'with music'. But Jessica is made sad by the too-great sweetness of music. Music thus charms the wildness of animals, a music–beast opposition; and music, similarly, can draw 'trees, stones, and floods'. Notice the tree–tempest association: it is often important. And a man who has not 'music' in him is apt to disintegrate states: since music is equally suggestive of personal love or political concord. His soul is 'dull as night' and 'dark as Erebus': hence the 'darkness' in connexion with conspiracy or murder in *Julius Caesar* and *Macbeth*. Music, stars, moonlight, and love are thus set against tempests, wild beasts, and dark conspiracy. We must ever observe the universal imagery of star, moon, and sun which blends with love and music.

So Portia returns. And in this final scene of love's victory over tragedy we should not be surprised that the melancholy Antonio, too, finds his way to Belmont, and that victorious love in Portia's person brings news of his ships' miraculous survival:

> Antonio, you are welcome;
> And I have better news in store for you
> Than you expect: unseal this letter soon;
> There you shall find three of your argosies
> Are richly come to harbour suddenly:
> You shall not know by what strange accident
> I chanced on this letter.   (v i 273)

Antonio risked all material merchandise, even the rich merchandise of his own life, for Bassanio, for love. Love's prize, in turn, gives him back his ships. It is the conquest of romance over tragedy, music and love's gold over tempests. No play more perfectly illustrates the Shakespearian feeling for merchants, riches, gold, tempests, and music entwined and interactive. These elements are here most concretely embodied in the plot, in the action. Imaginative forces conflict, and the plot is made to suit them. The play is thus highly charged with poetic power from start to finish.

SOURCE: *The Shakespearean Tempest* (1932); new edition 1953.

Mark Van Doren

THE MERCHANT OF VENICE: AN INTERPRETATION (1939)

WHEN Bassanio declares, early in the comedy of which he is so casually the hero, 'To you, Antonio, I owe the most, in money and in love' (1 i 130–1), he characterizes the world he lives in and the only world he knows. It is once more, and fully now, the gentlemen's world whose tentative capital for Shakespeare had been Verona. The capital moves to Venice; the atmosphere enriches itself until no element is lacking; and a story is found, or rather a complex of stories is assembled, which will be adequate to the golden air breathed on fair days and through soft nights by creatures whose only function is to sound in their lives the clear depths of human grace. In such a world, or at any rate in such inhabitants of it, there is no incompatibility between money and love. Shylock cannot reconcile the two; but Shylock is not of this world, as the quality of his voice, so harshly discordant with the dominant voices of the play, will inform any attentive ear.

In Belmont is a lady richly left, and Bassanio does not hesitate to say that Portia's wealth is necessary to his happiness. But it is necessary only as a condition; that she is fair and good – how much of either he has still to learn – is more than necessary, it is important. She will tell him when he has won her by the right choice of caskets that she wishes herself, for his sake, still richer than she is – not merely in money but in 'virtues, beauties, livings, friends' (III ii 158). All of which, sincerely as it is spoken, does not obscure or deny the background for this life of an enormous and happy wealth. The play opens with a conversation between gentlemen whose voices sigh and smile with thoughts of riches. Salarino cannot believe but that Antonio's mind is tossing on the gilded ocean:

> There, where your argosies with portly sail,

> Like signiors and rich burghers on the flood,
> Or, as it were, the pageants of the sea,
> Do overpeer the petty traffickers,
> That curtsy to them, do them reverence,
> As they fly by them with their woven wings.
>
> (I i 9–14)

He appears to be wrong, but his eloquence has supplied a correct symbol for these folk of whom he is one: for these arrogant yet gentle creatures whose fine clothes stream on the air of Venice and whose golden, glancing talk tosses, curtsies, and plays a constant music among their still uncorrupted thoughts.

Antonio is abstracted and sad for no reason that he knows. Shakespeare's source named a reason, but it has been suppressed in the interest of a mood the play must have. Melancholy in this world must not have in it any over-ripeness as in the case of Jaques, any wildness as in the case of Hamlet, any savagery as in the case of Timon. It must remain a grace, perhaps the distinctive grace of this life which is still young enough for satiety to mean not sourness, not spiritual disease, but a beautiful sadness of that sort which it is the highest pleasure not to explore. Much is said of satiety. Portia and Nerissa begin their scene (I ii) with talk of weariness and surfeit. But it is charming talk, unclouded by any such 'unmannerly sadness' as Portia soon criticizes in her suitor the County Palatine, who suggests 'a death's-head with a bone in his mouth'. The sadness of her class is a mannerly sadness. Antonio knows with Gratiano that all things

> Are with more spirit chased than enjoy'd.
>
> (II vi 13)

But he has not known it long enough to become other than what Bassanio calls him:

> The dearest friend to me, the kindest man,
> The best-condition'd and unwearied spirit
> In doing courtesies.   (III ii 295–7)

He wearies himself with his want-wit sadness, and thinks he wearies others; but he is not too tired for courtesies, and Bassanio's concern for him when news comes to Belmont of Shylock's insistence on the bond is deep, unspoiled, and serious. Antonio can say

> I am a tainted wether of the flock,
> Meetest for death,   (IV i 114–15)

without causing embarrassment in his hearers or incurring the charge of self-love. He is in short one of Shakespeare's gentlemen: one who wears darker clothes than his friends but knows perfectly how to wear them.

Love is the natural language of these men and women: love, and its elder brother generosity. Not generosity to Shylock, for he is of another species, and cannot receive what he will not give. But generosity to all friends, and an unmeasured love. The word love lies like a morsel of down in the nest of nearly every speech, and the noblest gestures are made in its name, Portia's surrender to Bassanio of

> This house, these servants, and this same myself
> (III ii 172)

is absolute. And so is the gift of Antonio's life to Bassanio, for there are more kinds of love here than one.

> I think he only loves the world for him,
> (II viii 50)

says Salanio, and Antonio counts on Bassanio's silent understanding of the truth. 'If your love do not persuade you to come,' he writes to him at Belmont, 'let not my letter' (III ii 323–5). Nor is there any rivalry between Antonio and Portia. It is enough for her that he is her husband's friend:

> that this Antonio,
> Being the bosom lover of my lord,
> Must needs be like my lord.   (III iv 16–18)

And it is enough for him that she is his friend's beloved:

> Commend me to your honourable wife.
> Tell her the process of Antonio's end;
> Say how I lov'd you, speak me fair in death,
> And, when the tale is told, bid her be judge
> Whether Bassanio had not once a love.
> (IV i 273–7)

Neither man knows that Portia is listening to this, but the fact that she is, and that *The Merchant of Venice* is after all a comedy, does not invalidate the mood.

The language of love is among other things intellectual. So we are not surprised to encounter abstractions in the graceful discourse of our lords and ladies. They are what make it, indeed, as graceful as it is, with its expert alternation of short and long words, its accomplished and elaborate ease such as Shylock's tongue never knows. It is natural for Portia to credit Antonio with

> a like proportion
> Of lineaments, of manners, and of spirit
> (III iv 14–15)

to that of Bassanio, 'her governor, her king'. It is as natural for her to speak of mercy as a 'quality' and an 'attribute' as it is for her to reveal upon occasion that nippiness of wit which keeps the conversation of all such people sound and sweet.

> Fie, what a question's that,
> If thou wert near a lewd interpreter!
> (III iv 79–80)

> I'll have that doctor for my bedfellow.
> (V i 233)

The intellect and the wit, and the familiarity with abstractions, have much to do with the effect of music which is so strong and pure throughout *The Merchant of Venice*. Not only do the words of the lovers maintain an unbroken, high, golden chime; but actual music is frequently in our ears.

> Let music sound while he doth make his choice;
> Then, if he lose, he makes a swan-like end,
> Fading in music.   (III ii 43–5)

So Portia commands as Bassanio broods before the caskets. And there is no clearer sign that the world is itself again when Shylock goes than the burst of melody, both verbal and performed, with which the fifth Act soars upon recovered wings. The sweet wind, the sweet moonlight, the sweet soul of Jessica melt into one singing whole with the sweet touches, the sweet harmony, the sweet power of music.

> I am never merry when I hear sweet music,
>
> (v i 69)

sighs Jessica with mannerly sadness. But that is as it should be in the world of Belmont and Venice; and there is of course Portia's wit to civilize the scene.

> He knows me as the blind man knows the cuckoo,
> By the bad voice.   (v i 112–13)

Nor are these people unaware that ultimate music is unheard. 'We cannot hear,' says Lorenzo, the harmony that is in immortal souls. Much as they love music, they love the melodies of silence more.

> Soft stillness and the night
> Become the touches of sweet harmony,
>
> (v i 56–7)

says Lorenzo now, for somewhat the same reason that Bassanio had once found the plainness of a leaden casket moving him more than eloquence (iii ii 106), and still earlier had fallen in love with Portia because of the 'fair speechless messages' he received from her eyes. Music no less than love is absolute in the world of Venice and Belmont.

Nicholas Rowe in 1709 was of the opinion that Shylock's contribution to the play made it a tragedy. 'There appears in it such a deadly Spirit of Revenge, such a savage Fierceness and Fellness, and such a bloody designation of Cruelty and Mischief, as cannot agree either with the Stile or Characters of Comedy.' As time has gone on this has come more and more to seem true. Yet it is but a seeming truth. Shylock is so alien to the atmosphere of the whole, so hostile and in his hostility so forceful, that he threatens to rend the web of magic happiness woven for the others to inhabit. But the web holds, and he is cast out. If the world of the play has not all along been beautiful enough to suggest its own natural safety from such a foe, it becomes so in a fifth Act whose felicity of sound permits no memory of ducats and bonds and long knives whetted on the heel. Comedy or not,

The Merchant of Venice by such means rescues its tone. If this is not comedy, there is no other in the play. The possibilities in Gratiano's loquacity are never developed, and the Gobbos are poor clowns.

The voice of Shylock comes rasping into the play like a file; the edge of it not only cuts but tears, not only slices but saws. He is always repeating phrases, half to himself, as misers do – hoarding them if they are good, unwilling to give them wings so that they may spend themselves generously in the free air of mutual talk.

> Three thousand ducats; well. . . .
> For three months; well. . . .
> Antonio shall become bound; well.
>
> (I iii 1–6)

They are short phrases; niggardly, ugly, curt. They are a little hoarse from their hoarding, a little rusty with disuse. And the range of their sound is from the strident to the rough, from the scratchy to the growled.

> The patch is kind enough, but a huge feeder;
> Snail-slow in profit, and he sleeps by day
> More than the wild-cat. Drones hive not with me.
>
> (II v 46–8)

The names of animals are natural to his tongue, which knows for the most part only concrete things, and crackles with reminders of brute matter. Salarino, musing of shipwrecks in the opening scene, bethinks him straight of dangerous rocks,

> Which, touching but my gentle vessel's side,
> Would scatter all her spices on the stream,
> Enrobe the roaring waters with my silks.
>
> (I i 32–4)

Shylock in the third scene rewrites Salarino's passage in his own idiom:

But ships are but boards, sailors but men; there be land-rats and water-rats, water-thieves and land-thieves, I mean pirates, and then there is the peril of waters, winds, and rocks.

> (I iii 21–5)

Land-rats and water-rats: the very sound of the words announces their malice, confesses the satisfaction with which their speaker has cursed them as they left his lips. He will go on in the play to remind us of the cur, the goat, the pig, the cat, the ass, the monkey, and the mule.

> *Tubal.* One of them showed me a ring that he had of your daughter for a monkey.
> *Shylock.* Out upon her! Thou torturest me, Tubal. It was my turquoise; I had it of Leah when I was a bachelor. I would not have given it for a wilderness of monkeys.
> (III i 123–8)

An animal itself is howling, and the emphasis upon 'wilderness' is shrill beyond the license of human rhetoric. We may feel pity for the man who remembers Leah, but the spectacle of such pain is not pleasant, the wound is animal, self-inflicted, and self-licked. 'I never heard,' says Salanio,

> a passion so confus'd,
> So strange, outrageous, and so variable.
> (II viii 12–13)

This was when Shylock ran out into the streets and declared the loss of his ducats with his daughter; but he is always strange to the play and outrageous, though in most crises he can cover his agitation with the curt voice of craft, with the insistent sound of a cold hatred.

> I'll have my bond; I will not hear thee speak.
> I'll have my bond; and therefore speak no more. . . .
> I'll have no speaking; I will have my bond.
> (III iii 12–17)

Nor is he disposed to justify his conduct by a show of reason. If he knows the language of reason he does not use it; if he knows his motives he will not name them.

> So can I give no reason, nor I will not,
> More than a lodg'd hate and a certain loathing
> I bear Antonio. (IV i 59–61)

It is by no means odd that such a man should detest music.

The favored citizens of this world love it so much that they live
only for the concord of sweet sounds, and Lorenzo can dismiss
any other kind of man as fit for treasons, stratagems, and spoils
(v i 85). Shylock is another kind of man. Music hurts his ears as
it does Malvolio's, and he is as contemptuous of merry-making,
which he calls 'shallow foppery'. A masque in the street brings
no comfort of melody; he notes only 'the vile squealing of the
wry-neck'd fife' (II v 30), and holds his ears. So must we hold
ours against so hideous a phrase; and withhold, perhaps, our
assent from the implication that any musical instrument can be a
deformed thing. Or a perverting thing, for there are men, says
Shylock in another place, who

> when the bagpipe sings i' the nose,
> Cannot contain their urine.
>
> (IV i 49–50)

That is the sort of interest he has in music, in the ridiculous
noises which dull and soft-eyed fools with varnished faces can
only pretend to believe ennobling. And that is why, since also
he is without the concord in his thoughts which love composes,
the repetitions of his speech are so lacking in resonance, so sullen
in their accent and so blighting in their tone.

Ho, no, no, no, no!   (I iii 15)

Why, there, there, there, there! A diamond gone, cost me two
thousand ducats in Frankfort! The curse never fell upon our
nation till now. I never felt it till now. Two thousand ducats in
that; and other precious, precious jewels. I would my daughter
were dead at my foot, and the jewels in her ear! Would she were
hears'd at my foot, and the ducats in her coffin! . . . I thank God,
I thank God. Is't true, is't true? . . . I thank thee, good Tubal;
good news, good news! Ha, ha! . . . Thou stick'st a dagger in
me. I shall never see my gold again. Fourscore ducats at a sitting!
Fourscore ducats! . . . I am very glad of it. I'll plague him; I'll
torture him. I am glad of it. . . . Nay, that's true, that's very
true. Go, Tubal, fee me an officer; bespeak him a fortnight
before. . . . Go, Tubal, and meet me at our synagogue; go, good
Tubal; at our synagogue, Tubal.

(III i 87–136)

That repetitions like these occur in prose is not what distinguishes them. The prose of Falstaff will contain as many with an entirely different result, with the effect indeed of a great man spending his breath freely. What distinguishes the style of Shylock is in the end, no doubt, one of its author's secrets. But we can hear the difference between him and the brethren of Antonio. And in the quality of that difference we should have no difficulty in recognizing Shylock as the alien element in a world of love and friendship, of nightingales and moonlight sleeping sweetly on a bank.

Where Shakespeare's sympathies lay it has long since been useless to inquire. His gentlemen within the code are as harsh to Shylock as Shylock is to them; however much love they have, they cannot love him. Nor has Shakespeare made the least inch of him lovely. He would seem in fact to have attempted a monster, one whose question whether a Jew hath eyes, hands, organs, dimensions, senses, affections, and passions would reveal its rhetorical form, the answer being no. Yet Shylock is not a monster. He is a man thrust into a world bound not to endure him. In such a world he necessarily looks and sounds ugly. In another universe his voice might have its properties and its uses. Here it can issue as nothing but a snarl, an animal cry sounding outrageously among the flute and recorder voices of persons whose very names, unlike his own, are flowing musical phrases. The contrast between harmony and hate, love and discord, is here complete, and Shakespeare for the time being is content to resolve it in comedy. Even in his tragedies it cannot be more complete.

Source: *Shakespeare* (1939).

E. C. Pettet

THE MERCHANT OF VENICE
AND THE PROBLEM OF USURY (1945)

> Hardness of heart hath now gotten place.
> (Wilson, *Discourse upon Usury*, 1572).

A SINGULAR feature of this markedly fairy-tale, Romantic comedy (for *The Merchant of Venice* – Shylock notwithstanding – is essentially a Romantic comedy in the general Shakespearean pattern) is that among its themes it also contains one of Shakespeare's rare considerations of a major socio-economic problem of his time. In dramatising Ser Giovanni's *Il Pecorone* he was not content simply to leave his villain as a representative, reprehensible moneylender. He seized his opportunity for a full dramatic discussion of the whole subject of usury, which, next to the agrarian question, 'provided the principal economic controversy of the sixteenth century'.[1]

There is no need here to examine this controversy in detail – to indicate the various classes and economic issues that were involved, or to distinguish sharply between usury and embryonic forms of credit, particularly as the analysis has already been lucidly made by Tawney in his Introduction to Wilson's *Discourse upon Usury*. On the other hand, it is indispensable for an understanding of *The Merchant of Venice* to know something of the usury problem as it affected the feudal aristocracy, since it was with this aspect of the question that Shakespeare chiefly concerned himself. An acquaintance of the Earl of Southampton and other 'divers of worship', who furnished him with a model for the gallants of his comedies, he was particularly drawn to a consideration of usury as it 'defaceth chivalries, beateth down nobility'.[2]

By the time Shakespeare was writing his plays the feudal aristocracy had come to feel the full pinch of the century's momentous economic developments. With wealth derived mainly from the land and with their hands tied to some extent by

conservative modes of land tenure, members of this class were
finding it extremely difficult to adjust themselves to the steep and
continuous rise in prices and to the greatly increased wealth of
the business classes. Some of them had enough sense of self-
preservation to thrust a few fingers of their own into the business-
pie,* or to become 'improving' landlords with all that meant by
way of estate reorganization and rack-renting. But these were the
exceptions: most of the feudalists tried to carry on with their
centuries-old style of life, not even realizing the wisdom of
cutting down the traditional ostentation of their class† – that
extravagance that Wilson vividly describes as 'wearing gay and
costly apparel . . . roystering with many servants more than
needed . . . mustering in monstrous great house'.

For these aristocrats, faced with the necessity of meeting the
ever-increasing expenses of their establishments, there was only
one way out – the usurer, and Tawney gives a striking account of
the indebtedness of some of the most notable figures of the last
twenty years of the sixteenth century. Sir Philip Sidney owed
£6,000, the Earl of Essex £22,000, the Duke of Norfolk
£6,000–£7,000, the Earl of Huntingdon £20,000, the Earl of
Leicester £59,000, Lord Sandys £3,100, Sir F. Willoughby
£21,000, and Sir Percival Willoughby £8,000. Others who were
heavily in debt included the Earl of Sussex, Lord Thomas
Howard, the Earl of Rutland, Lord Vaux of Harrowden, Lord
Scrope, and Shakespeare's own patron, the Earl of Southampton,
who at one time had surrendered his estates to creditors and
'scarce knows what course to take to live'. When we remember
that these sums must be multiplied at least sixfold to give them

---

* A notable instance of this is provided by the landed gentry who
took a direct part in mining and industry. Thus the Willoughby family
of Nottinghamshire supplemented its income by opening coal-mines
and setting up ironworks. (See Tawney, Introduction to Wilson's
Discourse upon Usury, p. 20).

† The Earl of Cumberland, who, largely through his extravagant
expenditure, almost exhausted his great fortune before his death, falls
into this class. On the other hand, the money he poured into privateer-
ing speculations (he had an expedition out almost every year) seems to
qualify him for the first class – even if his methods of business were
not quite orthodox!

their modern equivalent and that such a dead-weight of debt must have been felt acutely by many of the young gentry – poor relations, heirs, or hangers-on of the great feudalists – who patronized the Globe, it is easy to understand why the Elizabethan dramatists gave so much attention to the problem.

The usurers who advanced these large sums of money were not Jews, since there were few, if any, Jews in England at the time, but Englishmen of the City of London – tradesmen, merchants, and, like Milton's father, scriveners. For this class of people moneylending had become more than a surreptitious sideline. It was a major form of economic activity: it offered an attractive field for surplus capital, and, since estates were frequently demanded as security, it was a way of obtaining control of the land, either for social and political prestige, or for modern forms of agricultural exploitation, or both. Some businessmen like Audley followed an even more elaborate process, securing control of estates through usury transactions and then selling them again for a sum that reflected the increased rents they had been able to extort from their tenants.

As a result of the famous law of 1571, moneylending in England had at last become open and legal,* and, by the time Shakespeare was writing, the business of usury had been considerably expanded, while the 10 per cent interest that the 1571 Act had established as the maximum figure had become the normal, and often, when the law was circumvented, the minimum charge. Nevertheless, the medieval objection to moneylending, that it was economically bad and religiously damnable, was still strong and continued to thrive on the confusion between usury and credit facilities. For a long time pamphlets and books denouncing moneylending flowed on from the press, the most important being Wilson's *Discourse upon Usury*, first published in 1572. Another attack, worthy of note since it came out in 1595, only a year before the probable date of *The Merchant of Venice*,

---

* There had been a brief period from 1545 to 1552 when usury had been sanctioned. But, apart from this, the medieval prohibitions, monumentally re-enacted in the Statutes of 1487 and 1495, had remained in force for the greater part of the sixteenth century. [See Tawney, Introduction to Wilson, *Discourse*, p. 132. J. W.]

was Miles Mosse's *Arraignment and Conviction of Usury*, which so the Stationers' Company Register declared, contained 'proof that it [usury] is manifestly forbidden by the Word of God, and sundry reasons alleged why it is justly and worthily condemned. ... Divers causes why usury should not be practised of a Christian, especially not of an Englishman, though it could be proved that it is not simply forbidden in the Scriptures.'

Elizabethan and Jacobean literature, especially drama, is full of echoes of the controversy. For instance *The White Devil*, written upwards of twenty years after *The Merchant of Venice* and far removed in its main subject from economic issues, has no less than five obvious hits at moneylending and its consequences. There is twice the familiar moral condemnation – restrained in Flamineo's 'if there were Jews enough, so many Christians would not turn usurers', more violent in his later outburst, 'I care not, though, like Anacharsis, I am pounded to death in a mortar. And yet that death were fitter for usurers – gold and themselves to be beaten together, to make a most cordial cullis for the Devil.' When Monticelso talks of

> base rogues that undo young gentlemen
> By taking up commodities

he is alluding to a common trick of moneylenders by which they enforced their clients to accept dishonest loans in kind.* Again, in the early part of the play, there are two references to the loss of estates through mortgages: Antonelli rebukes Lodovico because

> one citizen
> Is lord of two fair manors called you master,
> Only for caviare,

while Flamineo complains of the same folly on the part of his father:

> My father proved himself a gentleman,
> Sold all 's lands, and like a fortunate fellow,
> Died ere the money was spent.

* Shakespeare has a similar reference: 'Here's young Master Rash: he's in for a commodity of brown paper and ginger, nine score and seventeen pounds, of which he made five marks, ready money.' (*Measure for Measure*, IV iii).

These quotations, which could be paralleled by numerous references from a score of Elizabethan and Jacobean plays, are typical. Almost without exception the dramatists, no doubt with an eye to the interests of their most influential patrons, condemned usury; and both in its moral and economic aspect their attitude remained conservatively medieval. An excellent summary of that attitude (and an admirable introduction to *The Merchant of Venice*) is furnished by the Preface to Wilson's *Discourse*, where he castigates 'that ugly, detestable, and hurtful sin of usury, which, being but one in grossness of name, carries many a mischief linked into it in nature, the same sin being now so rank in nature throughout all England, not in London only, that men have altogether forgotten free lending, and have given themselves wholly to live by foul gaining, making the loan of money a kind of merchandise, a thing directly against all law, against nature, and against God. And what should this mean, that instead of charitable dealing, and the use of alms (for lending is a spice thereof), hardness of heart hath now gotten place, and greedy gain is chiefly followed, and horrible extortion commonly used? I do verily believe, the end of the world is nigh at hand.'

That last sentence, re-echoed in the Dialogue by the Preacher's remark, 'It is very certain, as I take it, the world is almost at an end', may be dismissed as the extravagance of a gloomy moralist with a very clamorous bee in his bonnet. On the other hand, it may serve to remind us that the pessimism and sense of destruction reflected in Shakespeare's tragedies –

> It will come
> Humanity must perforce prey on itself,
> Like monsters of the deep –

originated to a large extent in definable and concrete social and economic conditions.

The first and third scenes of *The Merchant of Venice* clash with the discordant impact of two opposite and opposing worlds. The first sets us once more among the gay, spendthrift young gentlemen of the comedies: Bassanio is 'a scholar and a soldier', a member of the entourage of the Marquis of Montferrat, and his friends, Gratiano and Lorenzo, belong to the same class. Even Antonio is only formally a merchant: his business activities do not concern us, except in so far as (reported) they are indispensable to the plot; his obscure and mysterious melancholy, which he expressly states has nothing to do with his commercial ventures, is quite out of keeping with the ebullient optimism of the bourgeoisie,* and by his manner, conversation, and friendship he is plainly one with Bassanio.

Bassanio is obviously a type of the extravagant young gentry who, as Wilson reiterates, were the chief prey of the usurers – 'unthrift divers ways in good cheer, in wearing gay and costly apparel, in roystering with many servants more than needed, and with mustering in monstrous great house, in haunting evil company, and lashing out fondly and wastefully at cards and dice, as time served'. Bassanio makes no bones of his prodigality:

> 'Tis not unknown unto you, Antonio,
> How much I have disabled mine estate,
> By something showing a more swelling port
> Than my faint means would grant continuance:
> Nor do I now make moan to be abridged
> From such a noble rate.

Launcelot Gobbo, too, knows his man when he praises Bassanio as one 'who gives rare new liveries'. Following a time-honoured resort† of the young aristocrat hard pressed by creditors, Bassanio is going to Belmont unashamedly –

> to come fairly off from the great debts
> Wherein my time, something too prodigal,
> Hath left me gaged;

* Wilson perceived that this contemporary mood of pessimism and melancholy was most closely connected with members of the old classes. To the Preacher's dismal prophecy, already quoted, the Merchant replies shrewdly: 'What is the matter, sir? *Belike you are weary of the world?*' (*Discourse*, p. 200).

† However, L. C. Knights states (*Drama and Society in the Age of Jonson* (1937) p. 125): 'So far as can be discovered, the proportion of economic marriages increased in the sixteenth century when the merchant was anxious to be allied to blue blood, and the needy gentleman was anxious to be allied to money.'

and if there is nothing specifically Elizabethan in his hopes and motives, it is notable that, as Tawney points out,[3] seeking a loan to carry through a costly marriage was a common and typical practice of the time.

Antonio's response to Bassanio's request for help is direct and generous. In spite of his depression and the hazardous state of his various commercial ventures —

> My purse, my person, my extremest means,
> Lie all unlock'd to your occasions.

And when Bassanio, somewhat guiltily, tries to justify his request by a long-winded and casuistical argument on the retrieving of two lost arrows, Antonio cuts cleanly, and a little impatiently, through the circumlocution:

> You know me well, and herein spend but time
> To wind about my love with circumstance;
> And out of doubt you do me now more wrong
> In making question of my uttermost
> Than if you had made waste of all I have:
> *Then do but say to me what I should do*
> *That in your knowledge may by me be done,*
> *And I am prest unto it.*

This reaction of Antonio is significant not because such open-handed generosity was ever widely characteristic of the class he and Bassanio belong to, but because it introduces us to a salient economic and moral issue of the play.

In the third scene, where Bassanio endeavours to raise a loan on Antonio's credit, Shylock's earliest words remind us that we have moved to a completely different world:

Shylock. Antonio is a good man.
Bassanio. Have you heard any imputation to the contrary?
Shylock. Ho, no, no, no, no: my meaning in saying he is a
    good man, is to have you understand me that he is
    sufficient.

Those last few words of Shylock offer us the key to his values and to the values that were coming to the fore in Shakespeare's time. His 'good' and 'bad' have been simply emptied of any human or moral content: 'good' has become synonymous with 'sufficiency' (solid financial resources) and poverty is dangerously close to 'bad'.

But before we proceed any further with an analysis of this most interesting scene there is a preliminary question to be answered. Since there were few Jews in England at this time why did Shakespeare, if he was deeply concerned with the problem of usury, represent his moneylender as a Jew?

There are two closely linked answers to this question – first, that the Jews were certainly prominent in this business abroad; and, second, that Shylock, as a Jew, would give substance to the widespread feeling that usury was something alien to the national and traditional way of life. Wilson's Preacher may offer us a pointer here when he asks, 'What is the matter that Jews are so commonly hated wheresoever they come? For sooth, usury is one of the chief causes, for they rob all men they deal with, and undo them in the end. And for this cause they are hated in England.'

To return to the play: as Shylock lays his trap to catch Antonio by lending Bassanio three thousand ducats, he confesses several motives – his racial and religious antagonism towards Antonio, his desire of revenge for the personal humiliations inflicted on him in the past, and a touch of abstract hatred.* All these forces are laid bare in his first soliloquy on Antonio:

> How like a fawning publican he looks!
> I hate him for he is a Christian;
> But more for that in low simplicity
> He lends out money gratis, and brings down
> The rate of usance here with us in Venice.
> If I can catch him once upon the hip,
> I will feed fat the ancient grudge I bear him.
> He hates our sacred nation, and he rails,
> Even there where merchants most do congregate
> On me, my bargains, and my well-won thrift,
> Which he calls interest. Cursed be my tribe,
> If I forgive him!

* By this term I mean revenge without adequate motive – what Middleton Murry in his book on Shakespeare describes as 'fairy-tale hatred, of the bad for the good'. [See J. M. Murry, *Shakespeare* (1936) p. 195. J. W.]

Yet in this speech, apart from the thirst for revenge and the religious and racial hostility, another motive is prominently revealed. Most of all Shylock hates Antonio because, where to himself usury is a business, demanding interest and profit, Antonio lends money free out of Christian charity. The emphasis is on 'usance', 'thrift', and 'interest', and it is important to notice that Shylock confesses hating Antonio more for his free loans of money than for the fact that he is a Christian.

The very first words we hear from Antonio bluntly affirm his opposition to usury, though he is prepared to compromise with his convictions in order to do his friend Bassanio a good turn:

> Shylock, albeit I neither lend nor borrow
> By taking nor by giving of excess,
> Yet to supply the ripe wants of my friend
> I'll break a custom.

Shylock's reply to this is a long repetition of the Genesis story of Jacob and Laban's sheep. That story, as Shylock treats it, is indeed a rejoinder since, in showing how even in a 'natural' process of sheep-breeding increase (or profit) may be helped by enterprise and 'artificial' manipulation – and with God's blessing, he is attempting to turn upside down one of the stock arguments of the time, taken from Aristotle, against usury – namely, that because money is a 'barren' metal it cannot breed (i.e., multiply itself by interest). On this occasion Antonio hardly gets the point of the argument, and it is Shylock, when he claims that he makes his gold and silver 'breed' as fast as ewes and rams, who clinches the Aristotelian allusion. But if Antonio is slow to follow the drift of the Jacob story, he is certainly not unfamiliar with the Aristotelian objection to usury, for a little later he himself refers to it directly:

> If thou wilt lend this money, lend it not
> As to thy friends, for when did friendship take
> A breed for barren metal of his friend?

This excursion into the terminology of popular sixteenth-century controversy on moneylending should remind us that the opposition between Antonio and Shylock was not a limited or purely personal issue. Taken with his open-handed generosity in the first scene, Antonio's objection to usury, and in particular his practice of granting free loans, raises him to the level of a symbol of the whole medieval attitude, for the positive core of traditional teaching on the usury question was precisely that loans ought to be a pure act of Christian charity, without interest. What most aroused the indignation of medieval moralists against the growing practice of moneylending was, as Wilson's *Preface* makes plain, 'that men have altogether forgotten free lending', and Antonio is the hero of *The Merchant of Venice* because, through suffering and peril, he fights for the cause of disinterested generosity. That was the element of medieval morality that Shakespeare was idealizing and defending in his play, and there is some reason to believe that he was expressing a personal conviction. Child of the bourgeoisie as he was in so many of his speculative transactions, when his fellow townsman Quyny applied to him for a loan of about £150 (in modern money), he at once sent the sum, and no question of interest was raised.

By the second Act of the play, the plot has been set in motion, and henceforth it is the simple story that predominates – the mixed fairy-tale and melodrama of Antonio's entanglement in Shylock's web, his rescue in the Trial Scene by Portia's forensic skill, the choice of the caskets, and Bassanio's winning of Portia. Not surprisingly the moral and economic significance of the plot recedes into the background. But it is never entirely lost sight of, and twice Shakespeare takes care to remind us of the fundamental economic conflict between Antonio and Shylock. 'Let him look to his bond,' says Shylock: 'he was wont to call me usurer; let him look to his bond: he was wont to lend money for a Christian courtesy; let him look to his bond.' Once again the words Shylock employs lose a large part of their force if we are ignorant of the great controversy behind them: there is the allusion to traditional religious teaching in 'Christian courtesy', while Shylock's dislike for the term 'usurer' is evidence of the obloquy that still attached to the business of moneylending. Later, more nakedly, Shylock declares, 'I will have the heart of him, if he forfeit; for were he out of Venice, I can make what merchandise I will';

and Antonio also is content to explain Shylock's animosity entirely along these lines:

> He seeks my life; his reason well I know.
> I oft deliver'd from his forfeitures
> Many that have at times made moan to me;
> Therefore he hates me.

Nor is this all, for as the plot develops Shylock comes to represent the consuming sense of money-values, the 'hardness of heart' that 'now hath gotten place', in other and more terrible ways. His reaction to Jessica's elopement is, of course, not a simple one: in the fury that sends him raving through the streets there is an outraged feeling of filial disobedience, of Jessica's apostasy in marrying a Christian, and of the loss of her companionship. But, so far as the emphasis of Shakespeare's own words and phrases count for anything, what most torments Shylock is the loss of his ducats and some of his most valuable jewels. To retrieve these he would gladly see Jessica in her coffin at his feet, and he expresses this feeling in some of the most horrible lines of the play: 'I would my daughter were dead at my foot, and the jewels in her ear! would she were hearsed at my foot, and the ducats in her coffin!'*

Nevertheless, while Shylock reveals himself more and more as the child of the new 'cash-nexus', the idealized relationships of friendship and mutual service embodied in the Antonio–Bassanio world meet and ultimately overcome the challenge to them. Even in the triumph of winning Portia, Bassanio does not forget his friend, and immediately he hears of his plight comes to his aid. However, he can do nothing, since Shylock refuses to accept money payment once the settling-day of the bond is past; and it is notable that Antonio is actually rescued not by Bassanio, but by Portia, who is motivated by a sentiment of purely disinterested friendship. Antonio (whom Portia has never seen) is Bassanio's friend, a gentleman of the same class, therefore, 'being the bosom

---

* In spite of H. B. Charlton's ingenious insistence (*Shakespearian Comedy* (1938) p. 152) that this would mean burying and therefore wasting his money, I cannot agree that outraged Judaism is Shylock's strongest feeling.

lover of my Lord, Must needs be like my Lord'; and she is as uncalculating of her purse and energies to save him as Antonio was to help Bassanio in the beginning. Nothing could be more sharply in contrast with the inhuman self-interest of Shylock than this instinctive, almost blind sense of friendship, self-sacrifice, and class-loyalty.

These idealized traditional values of the aristocracy and medieval morality triumph, and the play dissolves, appropriately, in the exquisite love-scene under the moon at Belmont. But only just before this, in the Trial Scene, there are two more menacing and challenging notes of a new world. The first occurs where Shylock, having exhausted his reasons for personal hatred of Antonio, takes a fresh turn:

> You have among you many a purchas'd slave,
> Which, like your asses and your dogs and mules,
> You use in abject and in slavish parts,
> *Because you bought them:* shall I say to you,
> Let them be free, marry them to your heirs?
> Why sweat they under burdens? let their beds
> Be made as soft as yours, and let their palates
> Be season'd with such viands? You will answer:
> 'The slaves are ours'; so do I answer you.

The immediate reference of these lines is, of course, to non-European, non-Christian slaves, outside the purview even of Christian morality and ethics. At the same time it is not difficult to detect the new and ruthless doctrine of irresponsible individualism, of doing what one likes with one's own.* What one has paid for in hard cash one can use as one wishes, and if in the play that contention is defeated, in real life it was moving forward from triumph to triumph.

* There is a real-life echo of Shylock's words in the resistance of a certain Mison to the Privy Council's attempt to enforce the sale of grain at a reasonable price: 'A man named Mison declared in opposition to the action of the justices of the peace in his district: "My goods are mine own; they, nor the queen, nor the Council have to do with my goods. I will do what I like with them." But this degree of individualism was not good sixteenth-century doctrine; and Mison was fined £100, imprisoned, and forced to confess his fault.' (E. P. Cheyney, *A History of England* (1926) vol. II, pp. 10–11.

Again, there are Shylock's memorable words immediately after the Duke pronounces sentence, by which, though his life is spared, all his wealth is confiscated:

> Nay, take my life and all; pardon not that:
> You take my house when you do take the prop
> That doth sustain my house; you take my life
> When you do take the means whereby I live.

These lines have a double significance: first, and in general, they are the unrepentant outcry of one for whom Money still remains the supreme value. Now Money has gone, Life itself has gone, for Money is Life to Shylock; and it may be more than a coincidence that when Portia takes her exit a little later, after having declined a payment of three thousand ducats for her services, she uses words that contrast reminiscently with Shylock's outburst:

> He is well paid that is well satisfied;
> And I, delivering you, am satisfied,
> And therein do account myself well paid:
> My mind was never yet more mercenary.

In the second place, Shylock's words must have had a precise and concrete significance for Shakespeare's audiences, since there was still a common and deep-rooted feeling that it was something novel and morally shocking to live merely by manipulations of money. Like their Government these audiences would 'look askance at a class whose sole *raison d'être* was a single-minded pursuit of mercenary gain'.[4]

There are many details in the texture of the play whose full implication can only be appreciated when we have grasped the theme that has just been analysed. Thus Antonio's remark to Bassanio, 'The devil can cite Scripture for his purpose' (Act I, sc. iii), as well as being an immediate comment on Shylock's previous speech is almost certainly a reference to the fact that many of the apologists for usury attempted to fight traditional moralists with their own weapons – Scriptural texts. Again, Shylock's assertion that he would have to get the necessary money from Tubal reflected a characteristic trick of the moneylenders of the time. Tawney quotes an apposite story of Lord Shrewsbury. When this nobleman approached the great moneylender Sir Horatio Pallavicino for a loan of £3,000, Pallavicino alleged that he would have to secure the money from a city friend, Mr Maynard, and the miserliness of this friend (in all probability imaginary) was made the excuse for a particularly stringent arrangement by which, in return for £3,000, the Earl had to convey to Sir Horatio land worth £7,000, pay all legal and other expenses, and forfeit the land unless the mortgage was paid off in three months!

SOURCE: *Essays and Studies by Members of the English Association*, XXXI (1945) 19. Revised for inclusion in the present volume.

NOTES

1. R. H. Tawney, Introduction to Thomas Wilson's *Discourse upon Usury*, 1572 (1925) p. vii.
2. Wilson, *Discourse*, p. 366.
3. Tawney, Introduction to Wilson's *Discourse*, p. 34.
4. Ibid. p. 129.

John Palmer

SHYLOCK (1946)

SHAKESPEARE set out to write a comedy about a stage Jew involved in a grotesque story about a pound of flesh. But Shylock, to satisfy his author, must seem to act as a recognisably human being would behave in the given circumstances and Shakespeare has *humanised* him to such good purpose that this comic Jew has become, for many brilliant and sensitive critics, a moving, almost a tragic, figure. Some even go so far as to exclaim of Shylock in his anguish: O what a noble mind is here o'er-thrown!

How exactly has this come about? Why and when, if ever, does Shylock cease to be a comic character? Going to Shakespeare's text for an answer to these questions we shall perhaps find a clue not only to the nature of Shakespeare's achievement but to the process by which it is attained.

There is no better example of interplay between technical craft and creative imagination than the way in which the character of Shylock, apparently predetermined by the necessities of the story in which he figures and by the expectations of the audience to which he was presented, assumes the dimensions and habit of a character which exists freely and in its own right. Admittedly his behaviour in the play is settled in advance. But Shakespeare immediately identifies himself with the sort of person who must inevitably behave in that particular way. Shylock, setting forth upon the stage, is at once a man with hands, organs, dimensions, senses, affections, passions, and the plot to which he must conform soon appears to be no more than an opportunity for bringing him to life. The plot determined the kind of character which Shakespeare created; but the character, once created, determines everything he says or does. It is the paradox of great art that limitations arising from the nature of a given subject, the quality of the materials used and the restrictions imposed by necessary conventions merely serve to concentrate the activity of a free spirit on the business in hand. The artist with little or nothing to express complains of the discipline imposed upon him by the laws of his craft, wastes his energy in quarrelling with his tools or devotes more attention to the invention of a new technique than to the exploitation and development of an inherited tradition. Not so the man of genius. Shakespeare, taking Shylock's merry bond for a theme and accepting all the restrictions of the Elizabethan theatre, expressed himself as freely and profoundly as Beethoven when he unlocked his heart and disclosed the entire length, breadth and depth of his genius, in thirty-three variations on a merry waltz by Diabelli.

Shakespeare in presenting Shylock has so artfully combined the necessities of his plot with the revelation of a character that it is difficult, almost impossible, to say of any single incident or speech which of the two purposes is better served. The man lives in every word that he utters. He has a distinct language of his own and every syllable denotes his quality. His first words are of ducats; his introductory conversation with Bassanio might be cross-headed: Any usurer to any client: *Three thousand . . . ducats . . . For three months . . . Antonio shall become bound . . . Antonio is a good man . . . Yet his means are in supposition . . . The man is notwithstanding sufficient . . . Three thousand ducats – I think I may take his bond.* There is nothing here that seems to serve any other purpose than to present the comic Jew and to get the story under way. But the man is already alive. We shall know him again as soon as he opens his lips – a man whose words are stubborn in his mouth, in whose speech there is no ease or warmth or levity, who hammers out his phrases and can find no way of varying them once they are uttered. *Three thousand ducats . . . Antonio bound.* It is the utterance of a man whose mind is concentrated, obsessed, focussed upon a narrow range of fixed ideas. Shylock had the trick of compulsive repetition characteristic of the man in whom imagination, such as it is, forever sits on brood. It is the speech of one who is incapable of humour, whose words will always precisely fit his meaning, in whom no play or flight of fancy is possible:

Ships are but boards, sailors but men. There be land-rats and water-rats, land-thieves and water-thieves – I mean pirates. And then there is the peril of waters, winds and rocks.

Such is the eloquence of Shylock. So literal is his habit of mind that he must interrupt his recitation of the bleak hazards of trade to explain that by water-thieves, a phrase which strikes him as possibly too picturesque to be exactly understood, he means pirates. Contrast with this plain, surly, intensive style of utterance the warm, easy flow of the Venetian gentleman, Salerio, speaking to the same theme:

> My wind, cooling my broth,
> Would blow me to an ague when I thought
> What harm a wind too great might do at sea.
> I should not see the sandy hour-glass run
> But I should think of shallows and of flats,
> And see my wealthy Andrew docked in sand,
> Vailing her high-top lower than her ribs
> To kiss her burial. . . . Should I go to church
> And see the holy edifice of stone,
> And not bethink me straight of dangerous rocks,
> Which touching but my gentle vessel's side
> Would scatter all her spices on the stream,
> Enrobe the roaring waters with my silks,
> And, in a word, but even now worth this,
> And now worth nothing?

Here, then, is Shylock revealed at his first appearance in every phrase that he utters as a certain kind of man and, what is equally to the purpose, as a totally different kind of man from his Christian adversaries. His tricks of speech already project a character, unmistakeably alive, which will be recognisably true to itself in all that follows. They will recur throughout the play till they culminate in those stubborn, reiterated appeals to his bond of a man possessed by a single thought expressed in a phrase that has become almost an incantation.

Meanwhile Shakespeare must come immediately to grips with

his story of the comic Jew and the pound of flesh. He grasps the nettle firmly in an aside wherein Shylock discloses his intention and the motives behind it:

> How like a fawning publican he looks!
> I hate him for he is a Christian:
> But more for that in low simplicity
> He lends out money gratis, and brings down
> The rate of usance here with us in Venice. . . .
> If I can catch him once upon the hip,
> I will feed fat the ancient grudge I bear him. . . .
> He hates our sacred nation, and he rails,
> Even there where merchants most do congregate,
> On me, my bargains, and my well-won thrift,
> Which he calls interest. . . . Cursèd be my tribe,
> If I forgive him!

There is no hint in this speech, and there has been as yet no suggestion in the play, that Shylock has any human justification for his monstrous project. For the moment Shakespeare is satisfied with presenting his comic Jew in all the stark, ugly simplicity of the legend with which his audience was familiar. Shylock detests Antonio because he is a Christian; because he lends out money gratis and brings down the rate of usance; because he 'hates the Jews and dislikes their way of doing business'. Shylock, in this first exhibition of his malice, is a comic figure and so he remains in the passages that follow: debating of his present store; delivering the traditional patter of the moneylender about the difficulty of making up the sum required; justifying his practice of usury by citing the trick played by Jacob on Laban over the parti-coloured lambs.

Then comes the first intimation that Shakespeare, having undertaken to supply his audience with a comic Jew committed to a barbarous enterprise, not only intends to make his conduct psychologically credible but has already realised in imagination what it means to wear the star of David:

> *Shylock.* Signior Antonio, many a time and oft
> In the Rialto you have rated me
> About my moneys and my usances:
> Still have I borne it with a patient shrug,

> For suff'rance is the badge of all our tribe.
> You call me misbeliever, cut-throat dog,
> And spet upon my Jewish gaberdine,
> And all for use of that which is mine own. . . .
> Well then, it now appears you need my help:
> Go to then, you come to me, and you say,
> 'Shylock, we would have moneys' – you say so!
> You that did void your rheum upon my beard,
> And foot me as you spurn a stranger cur
> Over your threshold – moneys is your suit.
> What should I say to you? Should I not say
> 'Hath a dog money? is it possible
> A cur can lend three thousand ducats?' or
> Shall I bend low, and in a bondman's key,
> With bated breath, and whisp'ring humbleness,
> Say this:
> 'Fair sir, you spet on me on Wednesday last –
> You spurned me such a day – another time
> You called me dog: and for these courtesies
> I'll lend you thus much moneys'?

That is perhaps the most remarkable speech in the play. It suggests for the first time on any stage that the Jew has a case. The Jew, moreover, puts that case with a deadly logic, sharpened by persecution to the finest edge, and with a passion which no amount of suff'rance can conceal. It reveals a mind so intensely concentrated upon itself, so constricted in its operation, that it can only express itself in repetitions of a rhythmic, almost hypnotic, quality. *You have rated me about my moneys . . . Shylock, we would have moneys . . . moneys is your suit. . . . You call me misbeliever, cut-throat dog. . . . Hath a dog money? . . . You called me dog and, for these courtesies, I'll lend you thus much moneys. And spet upon my Jewish gaberdine. . . . You that did void your rheum upon my beard. . . . Fair sir, you spet on me on Wednesday last.*

Neither in logic nor in passion can Shylock be assailed and the Christians do not even attempt a rejoinder. Antonio, in fact, calls down upon himself the doom that awaits one side or the other in any conflict that passes the bounds of reason:

> I am as like to call thee so again,
> To spet on thee again, to spurn thee too.

If thou wilt lend this money, lend it not
As to thy friends – for when did friendship take
A breed for barren metal of his friend? –
But lend it rather to thine enemy,
Who, if he break, thou mayst with better face
Exact the penalty.

And so we come to the business of the bond. It is a difficult
moment. But note how quickly and easily it is handled. The
passages that precede it may be likened to the patter of a con-
juror who distracts the attention of his audience as he prepares
to play his master-trick. Shylock's speech and Antonio's reply
have fixed our attention on the fundamental issue of the play as
between Christian and Jew and, before we have recovered our
emotional balance sufficiently to realise what is happening, hey
presto! the thing is done:

Shylock.   Why, look you, how you storm!
    I would be friends with you, and have your love,
    Forget the shames that you have stained me with,
    Supply your present wants, and take no doit
    Of usance for my moneys, and you'll not hear me:
    This is kind I offer.
Antonio.   This were kindness.
Shylock.   This kindness will I show.
    Go with me to a notary, seal me there
    Your single bond, and, in a merry sport,
    If you repay me not on such a day,
    In such a place, such sum or sums as are
    Expressed in the condition, let the forfeit
    Be nominated for an equal pound
    Of your fair flesh, to be cut off and taken
    In what part of your body pleaseth me.
Antonio. Content, in faith – I'll seal to such a bond,
    And say there is much kindness in the Jew.

It is done, too, in a fashion which in no way detracts from the
reality of the characters or their relationship. Shylock, in for-
warding the plot, is still revealing himself as the kind of man who
will later come into court with his knife and scales. There is

nothing more sinister-comic in the whole literature of hypocrisy than the two speeches to Antonio. *This is kind I offer. . . . And in a merry sport.* Shylock kind! Shylock merry! Why, even as he makes his proposal, the secret passion that moves him is strong enough to penetrate and subdue his victim who is, as it were, hypnotised into adopting Shylock's own characteristic trick of repetition. 'This were kindness', says Antonio; 'there is much kindness in the Jew.'

The ease with which Antonio is trapped into the bond with Shylock is a good example of the way in which Shakespeare turns to advantage the limitations imposed upon him by his material. Antonio is predestined to sign a contract which will put his life at the mercy of a mortal enemy whom he has every reason to distrust. That is a tall order. Shakespeare does not evade the difficulty, but uses it to serve perhaps the most striking purpose of his play, which is to contrast the narrow, alert and suspicious character of the Jew, member of a persecuted race, with the free, careless and confident disposition of the Christian sure of his place in the sun. It is a contrast maintained in every scene of the play. Shylock in word and deed is typical, intense and precise; the Christians are impulsive, sentimental and wayward. Shylock trusts in his bond; the Christians trust to luck – whether it be Bassanio staking love and fortune on the choice of a casket or Antonio gambling on the ships which fail to come home. Shylock tells us of his 'bargains' and his 'well-won thrift', but riches fall from a window on to the head of Lorenzo. The characteristic qualities on either side are respectively those of the oppressed and the oppressor. If in Shylock we stand appalled by the warping of mind and spirit which oppression inflicts on those who suffer it, we are not less repelled by the infatuated assumption of Antonio and his friends that to them all is permitted in the best of possible worlds. The point is constantly emphasised in the minutest particulars of dialogue and incident. When Shylock, justifying his bargains, cites the case of Jacob and the particoloured lambs:

> This was a way to thrive, and he was blest:
> And *thrift* is blessing if men steal it not;

Antonio rejoins:

> This was a venture, sir, that Jacob served for –
> A thing not in his power to bring to pass,
> But swayed and fashioned by the hand of heaven.

Here, incidentally but in a nutshell, the careful husbandry of the Jew is contrasted with the careless genial improvidence of the Christian. Such touches of character, constantly repeated, not only prepare us for Antonio's easy acceptance of the bond but dispose us to swallow the whole preposterous story as entirely natural to the persons conceived.

From the sealing of the merry bond we pass to the story of Jessica. No incident in the play has so richly contributed to the transformation of Shylock, the comic Jew, into a lamentable victim of Christian bigotry and licence. This metamorphosis reached its literary climax in Heine:

I heard a voice with a ripple of tears that were never wept by eyes. It was a sob that could come only from a breast that held in it all the martyrdom which, for eighteen centuries, had been borne by a whole tortured people. It was the death-rattle of a soul, sinking down dead tired at heaven's gates. And I seemed to know the voice, and I felt I had heard it long ago when in utter despair it moaned out, then as now, 'Jessica, my girl'.[1]

On the stage it attained its theatrical climax, for those who remember it, when Henry Irving returning by the light of a lantern knocked on the door of an empty house. Where, now, is your monster with a large painted nose? This is a patriarch of Israel, wronged in his most sacred affections. Small wonder if, after this, the afflicted Jew grows blind to the quality of Christian mercy.

Alas for those who, seeking to find Shakespeare in one part only of his design, lose or pervert the whole! There is as little warrant for the voice that moaned in Heine's ear as for the Irving interpolation which made of that tragic figure beating on the door a sublime and pathetic incident to wring your hearts.

What are the facts?

Shylock, bidding farewell to his daughter, is more truly comic than at any point of the story so far reached:

> I am bid forth to supper, Jessica.
> There are my keys. But wherefore should I go?
> I am not bid for love – they flatter me.
> But yet I'll go in hate, to feed upon
> The prodigal Christian. Jessica, my girl,
> Look to my house. I am right loath to go –
> There is some ill a-brewing towards my rest,
> For I did dream of money-bags to-night.

This, then, is the voice, the death-rattle of a soul sinking down dead tired at heaven's gates. *Jessica, my girl, look to my house.* Heine, in underlining the pathos, has missed the essential quality of the scene. Shakespeare did not write '*Jessica, my girl*', but '*Jessica, my girl, look to my house*', and 'house' is the operative word. In claiming for Shylock the heartbroken misery of a loving father bereft of his child the man of sentiment loses the essential genius of the dramatist who created him. It is the house which stands at the core of Shylock's being; Jessica is no more than the daughter of the house:

> Do as I bid you, shut doors after you:
> Fast bind, fast find.

Not only the doors but the windows must be shut:

> Lock up my doors, and when you hear the drum
> And the vile squealing of the wry-neck'd fife,
> Clamber not you up to the casements then,
> Nor thrust your head into the public street
> To gaze on Christian fools with varnished faces:
> But stop my house's ears, I mean my casements,
> Let not the sound of shallow fopp'ry enter
> My sober house.*

---

* Note in this speech a delicious characteristic parenthesis. Having been betrayed into what for his precision is a flight of fancy, he instinctively corrects himself: 'Stop my house's ears, *I mean my casements*'. We have surprised him once before in this same revealing trick of speech when, after talking of water-rats and water-thieves, he felt it necessary to add: 'I mean pirates.'

Shylock, speaking of his house, is moved almost to poetry. The house is for him a living thing – *Stop my house's ears;* and the word once used, since it stands for one of the few things on which his mind is passionately centred, must be repeated – '*Let not the sound of shallow fopp'ry enter my sober house.*' And that word will be heard again:

> Nay, take my life and all, pardon not that.
> You take my house, when you do take the prop
> That doth sustain my house.

Shylock's farewell to Jessica, which established him for Heine as a tragic figure, leaves him still comic in the play that Shakespeare wrote. Shakespeare has done no more in this scene – but how much it is – than humanise the stage qualities of the comic Jew. Every stroke aims at our sense of comedy. 'Thou shalt not gormandise, as thou hast done with me,' he tells Lancelot who is quitting him to serve Bassanio, and, in bidding farewell to this 'huge feeder', he exhibits a malevolence which, like all fixed ideas in a living creature, is at the same time ludicrous and terrible:

> Drones hive not with me.
> Therefore I part with him, and part with him
> To one that I would have him help to waste
> His borrowed purse.*

Is Shylock, mourning his daughter's flight, any less comic than Shylock bidding his daughter to shut his doors and windows? A careful study of the scene with Salerio and Tubal provokes conclusions profoundly disconcerting to the heirs of the romantic tradition. It is supremely comic in itself and Shakespeare deliberately contrived in advance that the comic element should prevail over its emotional implications. Far from intending us to sympathise with an afflicted father, he has emphasised before the event that Shylock's affection is abnormally possessive and, in depicting the Jew's reaction to her flight, he subordinates even

---

* Let anyone who is disposed to over-sentimentalise Shylock's relations with his daughter ponder his sly warning: *Perhaps I will return immediately.* Distrusting her obedience he cautions her that he may be back sooner than she expects.

this self-centred affection to the fury of a man of property upon whose well-won thrift an unspeakable outrage has been committed. *My own flesh and blood to rebel.* . . . *I say, my daughter is my own flesh and blood.* This chimes perfectly with 'Jessica, my girl, look to my house.' His daughter, his own flesh and blood, has abandoned his house and 'she is damned for it'. She has made off, too, with his jewels and his ducats. There was no need for Shakespeare to introduce this incident at all. It detracts from the pleasure which his audience is clearly intended to take in the sweet infidel who holds a candle to her shames and it encourages romantics and realists alike to take a very poor view of Bassanio's friend, Lorenzo. Heine, as we have seen, would have given Lorenzo fifteen years in the penitentiary. But Shakespeare had other fish to fry. Jessica gilds herself with Shylock's ducats so that Shylock may reveal himself more effectively as an essentially comic character:

> *Shylock.* How now, Tubal! what news from Genoa? hast thou found my daughter?
> *Tubal.* I often came where I did hear of her, but cannot find her.
> *Shylock.* Why there, there, there, there – a diamond gone, cost me two thousand ducats in Frankfort – the curse never fell upon our nation till now, I never felt it till now – two thousand ducats in that, and other precious, precious jewels. I would my daughter were dead at my foot, and the jewels in her ear! would she were hearsed at my foot, and the ducats in her coffin! No news of them? Why, so – and I know not what's spent in the search: why, thou loss upon loss! the thief gone with so much and so much to find the thief, and no satisfaction, no revenge, nor no ill luck stirring, but what lights o' my shoulders, no sighs but o' my breathing, no tears but o' my shedding. [*he weeps*]

That is admittedly a rather terrible scene. But it is undeniably comic, the victim growing more ludicrous as he becomes more poignantly enslaved to his obsession; and the passage that follows in which Shylock alternately rages at the thought of Jessica squandering his ducats and rejoices to hear of Antonio's losses at sea, brings the comedy to a climax. Shylock's responses to Tubal are like the jerking reflexes of a marionette. They give him just that appearance of a human automaton which is one of the most characteristic effects of pure comedy. Nevertheless it is this scene from which the romantic tradition of Shylock is mainly derived. For it contains the great speech, so often read and quoted with too little regard for its context, which has misled so many critics into praising Shakespeare as a champion of tolerance and humanity where they might more pertinently have admired his genius as a dramatist and his imaginative intimacy with all sorts and conditions of men:

> *Shylock.* Hath not a Jew eyes? Hath not a Jew hands, organs, dimensions, senses, affections, passions? fed with the same food, hurt with the same weapons, subject to the same diseases, healed by the same means, warmed and cooled by the same winter and summer, as a Christian is? If you prick us, do we not bleed? if you tickle us, do we not laugh? if you poison us, do we not die?

That sounds like a plea for charity. Taken in its context, however, it is something less, and at the same time something more. Shylock's theme is not charity but revenge. He will have Antonio's flesh, if only to bait fish withal:

> He hath disgraced me and hindered me half a million, laughed at my losses, mocked at my gains, scorned my nation, thwarted my bargains, cooled my friends, heated mine enemies — and what's his reason? I am a Jew.

and he concludes:

> If a Jew wrong a Christian, what is his humility? Revenge. If a Christian wrong a Jew, what should his sufferance be by Christian example? Why, revenge. The villainy you teach me, I will execute, and it shall go hard but I will better the instruction.

Thus, what is commonly received as Shylock's plea for tolerance is in reality his justification of an inhuman purpose. That does not, however, lessen, but rather increase its significance. The most dreadful consequence of injustice is that it degrades not only the oppressor but the oppressed. Shakespeare is concerned to present only the human truth of a situation which he has accepted for the purpose of his play. Shylock, since his motives must be more humanly comprehensible, is presented as a natural product of Christian intolerance, but he does not thereby cease to be a comic character or become an advocate of the humaner virtues. There is something grotesque even in his pleading. *If you tickle us, do we not laugh?* Shakespeare was not here concerned – he never is concerned – with pleading a case in morality. He was presenting Shylock as Shylock lived in his imagination and, in so doing, he showed us how a dramatist, intent only upon his vision, incidentally achieves a moral effect wider in scope and more profound in its implications than a dramatist who consciously devotes himself to an ethical purpose. The comically distorted image of Shylock the Jew is in effect a more telling indictment of Christian oppression, though Shakespeare was not primarily concerned with that aspect of the matter, than the fictitiously sentimentalised presentment of the character created for modern playgoers by Edmund Kean and his successors. Many fine plays have been written by dramatists which expressly indict man's inhumanity to man, but no work of art created with an express political or moral intention is in the last resort so effective, even in the attainment of its purpose, as a work of art which achieves excellence in the form and spirit proper to itself. Critics and actors who, to enhance Shakespeare's hypothetical message, do their best to make Shylock humanly impressive and invite our commiseration for the ruins of a noble nature are likely to discover in the end that they have not only spoiled a comedy but defeated their own object and impaired the moral effect of the play.

Shakespeare is now ready – and his audience, too – for the confrontation in court by which his comedy will stand or fall. His task was to get the maximum dramatic effect out of an intrinsically improbable situation. So well did he succeed that the scene is theatrically one of the most effective ever put upon the stage. It is, at the same time, a scene which, owing to the skill with which the playwright solved his technical problems and brought his characters imaginatively to life as dramatic persons, has moral implications which exceed the author's immediate purpose. Critics tend to ignore the technical achievement and make too much of the implications, finding here a noble plea for Christian charity or there an exposure of Christian barbarity. The court scene is frequently read or produced as though its prime purpose and title to fame were Portia's very adequate but by no means outstanding discourse upon the quality of mercy, whereas, in fact, that speech is merely one of many in which Shakespeare exploits the dramatic possibilities of the situation.*

Shylock, in this scene, achieves his discomfiture by the very qualities which distinguish him most conspicuously as a comic character. He digs with his own hands the pit into which we know that he will most assuredly fall and supplies his enemies with the very weapons by which he is defeated. From the moment in which he enters the court, he stands inexorably upon the letter of the law. The Duke, when the case is opened, entreats him to glance an eye of pity on the losses of Antonio. But Shylock has sworn to have his bond. The Duke asks how he can hope for mercy if he renders none. But Shylock has no need of mercy; Antonio's flesh is dearly bought, 'tis his and he will have it. Portia, finding the bond correct, declares that the Jew must be merciful. But Shylock admits no such compulsion; and, when Portia, echoing the Duke, urges that men should be merciful as they hope for mercy, he exclaims: 'My deeds upon my head, I crave the law.' When Portia begs him to take the money and to forgo the pound of flesh, he charges her by the law to proceed to judgment; he stays upon his bond. The flesh must be cut from the merchant's breast – nearest his heart. So says the bond – those are the very words. Portia asks for a surgeon. But Shylock can find no mention of a surgeon. Is it so nominated in the bond?

Thus, speech by speech, Shakespeare prepares for the moment when Shylock's own insistence upon the letter of the law will be turned against him and when his repudiation of charity will bring its own retribution. Portia's speech on the question of mercy is dramatically merely an item in the comic process.

---

* The dramatic significance of this speech lies in its inconsistency with the behaviour of the Christians who applaud it. From this point of view it may be regarded as a striking example of the way in which Shakespeare's habit of presenting things as they are constantly reveals the irony of character and circumstance.

Note, too, how Shylock increases his own discomfiture –
again it is the comic process – by accepting Portia in advance as
a worthy representative of the law by which he stands. Portia has
been scolded by some critics for keeping the wretched Antonio
and his friends on tenterhooks. Surely it was most unkind to
bring the poor merchant to the point of baring his breast for the
knife when she had it in her power at any moment to shatter the
whole case against him.* Shakespeare, by lending verisimilitude
to this impossible scene, has again betrayed his commentators
into applying to it the standards of normal behaviour. He sees to
it, as a craftsman, that the scene shall be played for all it is worth
and that Shylock shall in every particular turn the tables on
Shylock. The Jew is self-entrapped not only into supplying the
Christian advocate with a plausible justification for strictly rendering the letter of the law against him but into finding for his
enemies the very words with which they taunt him in his over-
throw. *Most rightful judge! Most learned judge! A Daniel come
to judgment!* Portia, proceeding to extremes against Antonio,
earns these praises from Shylock in order that they may in poetic
justice be used against him. Her behaviour throughout the scene
is conditioned by the part which Shakespeare requires her to play
in achieving the comic catastrophe.

Shylock is never more Shylock than when he bears the full
burden of this incredible scene. He has the same tricks of speech,
the same obsessions, the same compulsive habits of thought and
expression. The clear stubborn logic of his mind still enables him
to confound his enemies by justifying his own practice from
Christian example. He has rated Christian hypocrisy – *How like
a fawning publican he looks!* He has declared that the Jew, equally
with the Christian, knows how to revenge a wrong and can even
better the instruction. He now turns in court on the men who

* Mr M. J. Landa in a searching study of the Shylock myth is provoked into a notable outburst on the inhuman conduct of Portia in the
trial scene: 'She plays cat and mouse . . . hypocrite to boot.' All this,
and much more, equally unanswerable, just shows what happens when
we allow ourselves to be misled by Shakespeare's theatrical skill into
praising or blaming his characters for conduct which, however true
and appropriate in its setting, fails to conform with our standard
notions of a good companion. (*The Shylock Myth*, 1942, 36–7)

counsel mercy and try to argue him out of his rights with the same unanswerable logic:

> You have among you many a purchased slave,
> Which, like your asses and your dogs and mules,
> You use in abject and in slavish parts,
> Because you bought them – shall I say to you,
> Let them be free, marry them to your heirs?
> Why sweat they under burthens? Let their beds
> Be made as soft as yours, and let their palates
> Be seasoned with such viands? You will answer,
> 'The slaves are ours.' So do I answer you –
> The pound of flesh, which I demand of him,
> Is dearly bought, *'tis mine*, and I will have it.

On his own ground, which he claims to share with his persecutors, Shylock is impregnable. He knows, none better, that Christian society is *not* based on the mercy for which the Duke and Portia so ingenuously plead. He asks no more than that the Christians shall apply to his case the principles whereby their own affections and affairs are ruled. A man may do what he will with his own. Antonio's flesh is his, legally acquired and dearly bought, and, if he likes to use it to bait fish withal, that is entirely his affair:

> You'll ask me why I rather choose to have
> A weight of carrion flesh than to receive
> Three thousand ducats: I'll not answer that!
> But say it is my humour, is it answered?
> What if my house be troubled with a rat,
> And I be pleased to give ten thousand ducats
> To have it baned? what, are you answered yet?

He has successfully contrived a situation which enables him to do for once what they are in the habit of doing every day of their lives and he means to make good use of it.

Shylock, carrying his hatred to extremes, exposes the injustice and ferocity of the social institutions from which it springs. He appeals to the twin laws of retribution and property on which the society in which he lives is based. Nothing is further from Shakespeare's mind than to convey a lesson. But the lesson is there, product of a perfectly balanced and sensitive mind intent upon the dramatic presentation of human realities. The debated question whether Shakespeare writing certain passages of *The Merchant of Venice* was pleading for toleration or indicting Christian hypocrisy, exalting equity above the law or divine mercy above human justice, does not arise. He presents a situation in which all these issues are involved, characters in which their effects are displayed, arguments appropriate to the necessary incidents and persons of the comedy; and leaves it to his critics to draw the indictment or convey the apology. His purpose was to write a comedy and he is never more intent on this purpose than in the scene whose moral implications have excited so much interest among those who study the play in the light of their own ethical and social standards. Shylock eagerly producing the bond for Portia's inspection – the bond which is to prove his own undoing – is undeniably comic. So is Shylock examining the bond to verify that the flesh must be cut from Antonio nearest his heart. So is Shylock looking in vain for any mention of a surgeon. So is Shylock applauding the wisdom of the judge who is about to ruin him. So, above all, is Shylock promptly asking for the return of his money when he realises that his claim to Antonio's flesh will not be allowed.

And behind all this obvious comedy is the indifferent irony of the comic spirit which, in presenting the human realities of a situation, necessarily exposes the blindness of human beings to their own inconsistencies: Portia, singing the praises of mercy when she is about to insist that the Jew shall have the full rigours of justice according to the strict letter of the law; Antonio, congratulating himself on his magnanimity in the very act of imposing on his enemy a sentence which deprives him of everything he values; Christian and Jew mutually charging one another with an inhumanity which is common to both parties.

How Shylock, imagined by Shakespeare as a comic figure and sustaining his comic character to the last, was yet able to become a depositary of the vengeance of his race (Hazlitt), the ruins of a great and noble nature (Hudson) and the most respectable person in the play (Heine) is now perhaps sufficiently evident. The question when and how, if ever, Shylock ceases to be comic answers itself as we read the play. To the question when? the answer, if we bear in mind that Shakespeare's comedy springs from imaginative sympathy and not from intellectual detachment, is: never for an instant. The question how? should not therefore arise. But alas for logic and the categories! No-one can remain wholly insensible to the emotional impact of the play. The imaginative effort expended by Shakespeare in making his Jew a comprehensibly human figure has imparted to him a vitality that every now and then stifles laughter and freezes the smile on our lips. If these passages are rightly handled by the actor or accorded their just place and value by the reader, the comedy remains intact. If, on the contrary, these passages are thrown into high relief and made to stand out of their context, the comedy is destroyed. Heine maintained that Shakespeare *intended* to write a comedy but was too great a man to succeed.[2] This comes very near the truth, but what really happened was something rather more subtle and difficult to describe. Shakespeare took the comic Jew for a theme, and wrote a true comedy. But it was a comedy after his own pattern and desire – a comedy in which ridicule does not exclude compassion, in which sympathy and detachment are reconciled in the irony which is necessarily achieved by the comic spirit in a serene presentation of things as they are.

SOURCE: Abridged from an essay in *Comic Characters of Shakespeare* (1946).

NOTES

1. Heinrich Heine, *Shakespeare's Maidens and Women* in *Works* trans. C. G. Leland, 10 vols (1891) I 401. J. W.
2. See p. 29. J. W.

M. C. Bradbrook

MORAL THEME AND ROMANTIC STORY (1951)

MODERN humanitarianism has run riot on Shylock; like Falstaff, with whom he has little else in common, he is held to be wronged in the end. Though the abuse of Bassanio's fortune-hunting, Antonio's manners and the Duke's notion of mercy has abated a little of recent years, there is still a tendency to overwork that phrase:

> Out upon her, thou torturest me, *Tuball*, It was my Turkies, I had it of *Leah* when I was a Batchelor: I would not haue giuen it for a wildernesse of Monkies.

Such an admission of conjugal fidelity is almost held to outweigh a taste for judicial murder.

But Shylock is in search of Revenge. So indeed was Barabas, and they have the same excuse:

> I learn'd in *Florence* how to kisse my hand,
> Heaue up my shoulders when they call me dogge,
> And ducke as low as any bare-foot Fryar,
> Hoping to see them starue upon a stall,
> Or else be gather'd for in our Synagogue;
> That when the offring-Bason comes to me,
> Euen for charity I may spit intoo't.
>
> (Jew of Malta, II, 784–890)

> Shall I bend low and in a bond-mans key
> With bated breath and whispring humblenesse,
> Say this: Faire sir, you spet on me on Wednesday
>   last;
> You spurn'd me such a day: another time
> You cald me dog: and for these curtesies
> Ile lend you thus much moneys.
>
> (I iii 124–30)

Revenge, even in the most extenuating circumstances, was for the Elizabethan a crime; Shylock's injuries were not *per se* any further justification than Edmund's grievance of illegitimacy, or the predisposition to vice which his crooked birth gave Richard III. Nothing less monstrous than the theatre's prize bogyman, linked in the popular mind with Machiavelli and the Devil in an infernal triumvirate, would serve for the villain of a romantic comedy. Were he less diabolic, Shylock would not be tolerable. It might be said of Shylock, as Swinburne said of Mary of Scots:

> Surely you were something better
> Than innocent!

A human Shylock, devoted to Jessica, smarting under what Antonio can do in the way of spitting on his gabardine, is something less than Shakespeare's. Still less can he be looked on as an embodiment of the Rise of Capitalism, Shakespeare's protest against the new money economy.[1] Naturally Shakespeare used his feeling about 'the breed of barren metal' – later to be used to more potent effect in *Timon* – but only as a similitude, shadowing in a baser manner the theme of his play; which is very plainly set forth as Justice and Mercy;[2] the law and love that is the fulfilling of the law, the gold of Venice, and the gold of Belmont.

Shylock, in so far as he stands for anything, stands for the Law: for the legal system which, to be just to all in general, must only approximate to justice in particular cases. Shylock's creed is an eye for an eye, and in a later play Shakespeare set out the measure to be meted in the name of strict justice. The Bible would be sufficient lead to the identification of a Jew with legal concepts of justice, and for the opposition of the Old Law to the New. Portia's famous speech is the most purely religious utterance in the canon – the most directly based upon Christian teaching, with its echoes of the Lord's Prayer, the Christian doctrine of salvation, and the words of *Ecclesiasticus*, xxxv 20:

Mercy is seasonable in the time of affliction, as clouds of rain in the time of drouth.

As addressed to a Jew, the argument loses its cogency, but it is intended rather as contrast to Shylock's

> What iudgement shall I dread doing no wrong? . . .
> I stand for iudgement, answer, Shall I haue it?
>
> (IV i 89 ff)

As in so many trial scenes of the Elizabethan drama, the pleading is addressed directly to the audience; it is exposition. In Shylock's and Portia's case it is also self-revelation; but it is the peculiar virtue of this play, and of the later *Measure for Measure*, that the characters are at the same time fully human, and symbolic or larger than human. Shakespeare has achieved here what he failed to do in *All's Well that Ends Well* and written a 'moral play' – that is a play in which the lively image of a general truth is embodied with such decorum and in so fitting a form that it has all the immediacy, the 'persuasion' as the Elizabethans would say, of a particular instance.

> Hath not a *Jew* eyes? hath not a Jew hands, organs, dementions, senses, affections, passions, fed with the same foode, hurt with the same weapons, subiect to the same diseases, healed by the same meanes, warmed and cooled by the same Winter and Summer as a Christian is? . . .
>
> (III i 63 ff)

This is so powerful a plea, ending as it does with an echo of Barabas,

> The villanie you have taught me I will execute, and it shall goe hard but I will better the instruction

that it produces a natural rush of sympathy, and Salarino is given no answer. But of course the answer is provided later:

> My deedes upon my head.
>
> (IV i 206)

It is the sentence which drew down the Curse upon his race:

> Then answered all the people and said, His blood be on us and on our children.
>
> (St Matthew XXVII 25)

So when Portia asks him to have a surgeon ready lest Antonio bleed to death, Shylock says:

> It is not nominated in the bond?
> *Portia.* It is not so exprest: but what of that?
> Twere good you do so much for charitie.
> *Shylock.* I cannot finde it, tis not in the bond.

(IV i 260)

There is a sense in which Shylock has not the eyes that a Christian has – the sense which Gloucester implies when he says:

> I stumbled when I saw.

The doctrine of grace and the second birth of baptism, the new man and regeneration were such commonplaces that Portia's allusion to the 'sceptred sway' which is 'enthroned in the hearts of Kings' would suffice as reminder of the inward and outward kingdom, and the inward and outward senses. Gratiano has already made a cruder statement of Shylock's privation, but Gratiano here plays much the part that Emilia does at the end of *Othello*: by his vehement and violent assertion of the truth he relieves the tension, while in a kind of exasperated crescendo continuing to work up the excitement.

> O be thou damn'd inexecrable dogge,
> And for thy life let iustice be accus'd:
> Thou almost mak'st me waver in my faith;
> To hold opinion with *Pythagoras*,
> That soules of Animals infuse themselves
> Into the trunkes of men. Thy currish spirit
> Gouern'd a wolfe, who hang'd for humane slaughter,
> Euen from the gallowes did his fell soule fleet;
> And whilst thou layest in thy unhallowed dam,
> Infus'd itself in thee: For thy desires
> Are woluish, bloody, steru'd and rauenous.

(IV i 128–38)

This is Metamorphosis in its tragic vein: 'O tyger's hart wrapt in a woman's hide'. Humanity lapsing back into the beast was to become one of the central themes of *King Lear*.*

* Not only Margaret but Tamora in *Titus Andronicus* is called a tiger on a good many occasions. The use of symbolism from animals in

> If that the heauens doe not their visible spirits
> Send quickly downe to tame these vild offences,
> It will come
> Humanity must perforce pray on it self
> Like monsters of the deepe.

(IV ii 46—50)

It is no belittlement of Shakespeare's achievement to say that in Shylock he has drawn a man lapsing into beast. The personal responsibility of Shylock for his horrible state is very small; it is the result of his wrongs, his birth and his creed. But to remove all guilt from him on this account, and to treat him as a sympathetic criminal would not have occurred to any Elizabethan. Few would have had Shakespeare's insight and awareness of the natural case to be made out for Shylock's revenge; but that case, and the figure of Shylock himself, is very much weakened if his crime is seen as anything less than damnable. The present generation has been taught by bitter examples that persecution breeds criminals, and sometimes criminals of so violent and perverted a nature that their only end, in a world that does not believe in the efficacy of forcible baptism, would seem to be despair. The concentration camps of Nazi Germany bred many heroes and martyrs but also a few Shylocks.

The legal quibble by which Portia saves Antonio is triumphantly and appropriately a quibble. Any sounder argument would be giving Shylock less than his deserts. The bare letter of the law nooses him; and mercy takes the form of another legal instrument. The deed of gift balances the 'merry bond'.

The whole play is built upon contrasts of this sort. The original story and Marlowe's stage Jew require stronger counterweights than the heroine of *Il Pecorone* provided. Portia and Belmont are Shakespeare's creation; the casket story, which he added to his original, stands in precise and symbolic contrast to the story of the bond. In this play Shakespeare makes more direct

---

King Lear has often been commented on, e.g. by Miss Spurgeon and Wilson Knight. The relation of the 'wolf' in this speech to the execution of Lopez the Jewish physician — if such a reference were intended — does not seem to me in any way to preclude the larger significance being there as well.

use than anywhere else of dramatic *impresa*: the bold physical contrasts of the Jew with his curving knife and the boy-Portia in doctor's gown. The splendours of the Doge's court and the moonlight of Belmont would probably be outdone as sheer pageantry on the Elizabethan stage by the highly symbolic casket scenes.

The Prince of Morocco who comes first wearing 'the shadowed liuerie of the burnished sun' is described as 'Morochus a tawnie Moore all in white'. He has the accents of Tamburlaine:

> By this Symitare
> That slew the Sophie and a Persian Prince
> That won three fields of Sultan Solyman . . .
>
> (II i 24–6)

and ruled by his planet Sol, he chooses the Golden Casket with its motto, 'Who choses me shall gaine what men desire', in a speech that deliberately recalls Tamburlaine's praise of Zenocrate:

> The Hircanion deserts, and the vaste wildes
> Of wide Arabia are as throughfares now
> For princes come to view fair *Portia*.
>
> (II vii 41–3)

The answer is a death's head. Mortality conquers those who like Tamburlaine are more 'bold' than 'wise' (II vii 71).

The Prince of Arragon is a Spaniard, incarnation of Pride. He chooses silver which promises 'as much as he deserves'. The answer is a fool's head; and unlike Morocco, he is not only dismissed but rebuked by Portia; his wisdom only makes him a 'deliberate fool' (II ix 80).

Bassanio chooses the lead casket: 'Who chooseth me must giue and hazard all he hath'. The hazards of love in this venture are Antonio's; Bassanio invited him to hazard (chance) a second arrow after the first, and the hazards (dangers) of the venture are no less than his life. The scene of Bassanio's choosing is made into a tapestry picture by Portia's magnificent 'augmentation':

> Now he goes,
> With no lesse presence but with much more loue
> Than yong *Alcides* when he did redeeme
> The virgine tribute paid by howling Troy
> To the Sea-monster: I stand for sacrifice,

The rest aloof are the Dardanian wiues
With bleared visages come forth to view
The issue of th' exploit.

(III ii 53–60)

The heightened language (almost with a touch of Hamlet's First
Player), the tableau, the soft music whose significance Portia has
explained so fully, are all designed to isolate this moment, the
turning point of the story – the song, warning Bassanio against
the fancy (or love) that is 'engendered in the eyes'. His dangerous hazard brings him to a moment of blind and naked choice:
and his choice is based on negatives. He will not take the *seeming*
beauty. The speech of his choice echoes a theme which was to
recur in the tragedies, and even before the tragedies, was to
appear with almost tragic significance.

To work so much morality out of a pretty fairy tale may
appear too much like breaking a butterfly upon a wheel; but the
fairy-tale quality of the story serves to keep these significances
unemphatic, not to obliterate them. Some such technique, but
far subtler, was to be used in the final plays. To ignore the moral
significance of the casket story – familiar commonplace morality,
but the Elizabethans enjoyed the familiar and doted on the commonplace – is to ignore the main counterbalance to Shylock. He
is symbolic in an all but tragic manner: these scenes are symbolic in an all but fairy-tale manner. The thrust of the opposing
stresses maintains the arch of the narrative.

Portia, whose sunny locks hang on her temples like a golden
fleece, whose suitors come from all corners of the earth to woo
her, is set against the wealth of Venice, the mart where all the
trade of east and west flows in. Antonio's argosies sail to Mexico,
England, Tripoli, Lisbon, Barbary and India. The pledge and
bond of matrimony – which is both a sacrament and a legal
contract – is set against the bond of the Jew and Antonio's pledge
of his flesh. Bassanio has won all, for with the ring Portia gives
power as

her Lord, her Governour, her King.
Myself and what is mine, to you and yours
Is now conuerted.

(III ii 166–8)

The exchange of property is an exchange of the very self, which leaves Bassanio confused, as his powers recognize the voice of their sovereign* in Portia's voice.

The rings which are exchanged reappear in the final scene as the pledge of this bond. It is as parody of the trial scene that the final episode becomes something more than a jest out of the Hundred Merry Tales. The gold of the rings is not the gold which Shylock deals in, and to which Portia and Antonio are both so superbly indifferent, which Bassanio has rejected in the casket scene, and which the unthrift Lorenzo acquires in so light-fingered a fashion. It is the gold of Belmont, and in parting from the ring, for Antonio's sake, Bassanio has supplied some backing for his second choice, made in the trial scene:

> Antonio, I am married to a wife,
> Which is as deare to me as life it selfe,
> But life it selfe, my wife, and all the world,
> Are not with me esteem'd aboue thy life.
> I would loose all, I sacrifice them all
> Heere to this deuill, to deliuer you.
>
> (IV i 283 ff)

So that in the dispute between husband and wife, Antonio reasonably intervenes, with the offer of a new and even more reckless bond, though of the kind that may not be registered in law.

> I once did lend my bodie for thy wealth,
> Which but for him that had your husbands ring
> Had quite miscarried. I dare be bound againe,
> My soule upon the forfeit, that your Lord
> Will neuer more break faithe aduisedly.
>
> (V i 249–53)

The pretty jests about cuckoldry are far from modern taste (like the jests which Diana makes with Lafeu and the King at the end of *All's Well* over Hellen's ring). Yet it is as hopelessly anachronistic to boggle at them as to treat Bassanio as a fortune-hunter. He is luck and young love personified, given as much

* By exchange of sovereignties, Portia and Bassanio have reached that happy state depicted in the sonnets under the figure of exchanged hearts.

character as the object of Portia's and Antonio's devotion
requires; but, like Bertram though without any of the condemnation that Bertram receives, he is there to be the *object* of
devotion, and he must look and move his part. I have seen it
suggested that if his feelings for Antonio are all that he proclaims,
he has only to run Shylock through with his rapier in the open
court and stand to the consequences. Let anyone try to write a
play on these lines. *The Merchant of Venice* is in the best sense
artificial; Portia's successful disguise, the nature of the bond
itself, the set pleas of Justice and Mercy are all artifice, designed
not to make the story slighter but to control, direct and focus the
emphasis upon the theme or 'cause' of the play. Every piece of
artifice is there for a purpose, and a purpose which an imaginative
reading discloses readily enough. For *The Merchant of Venice* is
not a subtle play; it is a recklessly bold and obvious sort of
play. The symbolism is almost blatant, the violence of the contrasts almost glaring. It can be turned about and viewed from
many aspects; the personal relationship between Antonio and
Bassanio – which is mostly Antonio's – is so familiar from elsewhere in the Works that the only danger is lest the connexion
with the sonnets should be pressed too far.[3] The reproachful
sonnets should not be invoked. Nor must the economics of the
situation be taken on economic lines. In an age when economic
treatises could be written by city merchants in the form of
allegory and called *St George for England*,* there would have
been little danger of misunderstanding, even from those members of Shakespeare's audience who smelt most strongly of ink

---

* Gerrard de Malynes, *St George for England, allegorically described*
(1601). Those who regard Portia as the economic motive personified
would do well to study this extraordinary little work. The virgin who
is the King's Treasure is threatened by a horrible dragon called Foenus
Politicum, whose two wings are Usura palliata and Usura explicata,
and rescued by St George, who is the King's authority. The praise of
the Virgin begins in accents that are not unfamiliar: 'Hide, *Absalon*
thy clear gilt tresses, and you *Hester*, your meekness and beauty,
giving place to the Virgin and noble creature: neither you, *Lucrece*
and *Polyxene*, *Dido*, *Laodamia* or *Tisbe*, that have brought your love
so dear. . . .' Later it takes another strain: 'She is the rose of the field
and the lily of the valley. . . .'

and counters. For the groundlings he had provided a magnificent villain, some exciting scenes of pageantry and a tale which might have been authorized by their grandam. For the young gentlemen of the Inns of Court, he had provided some lovely speeches of wooing and some of morality and good life; for everyone the contrast between Justice and Mercy, gold and love, embodied in figures of so winning a grace that the critics talk of them as if they lived. It is the first of Shakespeare's plays which invites the moral judgments of real life in this way.

SOURCE: *Shakespeare and Elizabethan Poetry* (1965).

NOTES

1. See E. C. Pettet, '*The Merchant of Venice* and the Problem of Usury', in *Essays and Studies by Members of the English Association*, XXXI (1945) 19. [See pp. 100–13 above. J. W.]

2. The point has been made by Nevill Coghill, who examines the play from this point of view in 'The Governing Idea: Essays in the Interpretation of Shakespeare', in *Shakespeare Quarterly* I (1948).

3. Kenneth Muir and S. O'Loughlin, in *The Voyage to Illyria*, have dealt with this subject tactfully and sensitively. The comparison of Bassanio with Bertram is, I think, an extremely interesting one.

Harold C. Goddard

THE THREE CASKETS (1951)

I

THE social world of Venice and more especially of Belmont centres around pleasure. It is a golden world – a gilded world we might better say. It is a world of luxury and leisure, of idle talk and frivolity, of music and romance. It has the appearance of genuine grace and culture. Except for a few scenes, the average production of *The Merchant of Venice* leaves an impression of bright costumes, witty conversations, gay or dreamy melody, and romantic love. Gold is the symbol of this world of pleasure. But what is under this careless ease? On what does it rest for foundation? The answer is – on money. Or, if you will, on the trade and commerce that bring the money, and on the inheritance that passes it along. Now this world of trade and commerce, as it happens, does not resemble very closely the world that its profits purchase. Its chief symbol in the play is silver, which in the form of money is the 'pale and common drudge 'tween man and man'. When the Prince of Arragon opens the silver casket, he finds, within, the portrait of a blinking idiot and verses telling him that he is a fool who has embraced a shadow in mistake for sub-stance.

But there is something even worse than money under the sur-face of this social world. Exclusiveness – and the hypocrisy exclusiveness always involves, the pretense that that which is excluded is somehow less real than that which excludes. When the Prince of Morocco opens the golden casket he finds not a fool's head, as Arragon finds, but a Death's head – so much deadlier than money is the moral degradation that money so often brings. 'All that glisters is not gold'.

Dimly, in varying degrees, these Venetians and Belmontese reveal an uneasiness, a vague discontent, an unexplained sense of something wrong. This note, significantly, is sounded in the very first words of four or five of the leading characters.

> In sooth, I know not why I am so sad,

says Antonio in the first line of the play. 'By my troth, Nerissa, my little body is aweary of this great world,' are Portia's first words. 'Our house is hell,' Jessica announces in her opening speech. And we wonder what cruelty her father has been guilty of, until she goes on to explain that the hell she refers to is tediousness. Melancholy, weariness, tedium – the reiteration of the note cannot be coincidence. And the other characters confirm the conjecture. Over and over they give the sense of attempting to fill every chink of time with distraction or amusement, often just words, to prevent their thinking. Bassanio makes his bow with a greeting to Salanio and Salarino:

> Good signiors both, when shall we laugh? say when?

and Gratiano (after a reference to Antonio's morose appearance, from which he takes his cue) begins:

> Let me play the fool!
> With mirth and laughter, let old wrinkles come,
> And let my liver rather heat with wine
> Than my heart cool with mortifying groans.

Gratiano's cure for care is merriment and torrents of talk. He is not the only one in Venice who 'speaks an infinite deal of nothing'. Launcelot Gobbo, the 'witsnapper', is merely a parody and reduction to the absurd of the loquaciousness that infects the main plot as well as the comic relief. Lorenzo condemns as fools those of higher station who, like Launcelot, 'for a tricksy word defy the matter', and then proceeds in his very next speech to defy it in the same way. We can feel Shakespeare himself wearying of 'wit' – the verbal gold that conceals paucity of thought – and it would scarcely be far-fetched to find a prophecy of his great taciturn characters, like Cordelia and Virgilia, in the declaration: 'How every fool can play upon the word! I think the best grace of wit will shortly turn into silence, and discourse grow commendable in none only but parrots'.

What is the trouble with these people and what are they trying to hide? Why should the beautiful Portia, with all her adorers, be bored? Nerissa, who under her habit as waiting-maid has much wisdom, hits the nail on the head in *her* first speech in answer to Portia's: 'For aught I see, they are as sick that surfeit with too much as they that starve with nothing.' What these people are trying to elude is their own souls, or, as we say today, the Unconscious.

Now Shylock is a representative of both of the things of which we have been speaking: of money, because he is himself a money-lender, and of exclusion, because he is the excluded thing. Therefore the Venetian world makes him their scapegoat. They project on him what they have dismissed from their own consciousness as too disturbing. They hate him because he reminds them of their own unconfessed evil qualities. Down the ages this has been the main explanation of racial hatred and persecution, of the mistreatment of servant by master. Our unconsciousness is our foreign land. Hence we see in the foreigner what is actually the 'foreign' part of ourselves.

Grasp this, and instantly a dozen things in the play fall into place, and nearly every character in it is seen to be one thing on the outside and another underneath – so inherent, so little mere adornment, is the casket theme. It ramifies into a hundred details and into every corner of the play.

II

Bassanio is a good example to begin with. He fools the average reader and, especially if the play is conventionally cast and handsomely mounted, the average spectator, as completely as the dashing movie star does the matinee girl. Is he not in love with the rich heroine?

Bassanio admits that he has posed as wealthier than he is and has mortgaged his estate

> By something showing a more swelling port
> Than my faint means would grant continuance.

And Antonio abets the deception. As a youth, says Bassanio,

when I lost one arrow, I shot another in the same direction and often retrieved both. So now. Lend me a little more to make love to a lady who has inherited a fortune (and who has beauty and virtue) and with good luck I will repay you (out of her wealth) both your new loan and your old ones:

> I have a mind presages me such thrift.

This is not exactly in the key of *Romeo and Juliet.*

If this seem an ungracious way of putting it, note that Bassanio himself describes it as a 'plot' to get clear of his debts. But when the young spendthrift is handsome, we forgive him much. In watching the development of the love affair it is easy to forget its inception. And yet, when Bassanio stands in front of the golden casket, clad in the rich raiment that Antonio's (i.e. Shylock's) gold has presumably bought, and addresses it,

> Therefore, thou gaudy gold,
> Hard food for Midas, I will none of thee,

we feel that if Shakespeare did not intend the irony it got in in spite of him. No, gold, I'll have none of thee, Bassanio declares (whether he knows it or not), except a bit from Antonio-Shylock to start me going, and a bit from a certain lady 'richly left' whose dowry shall repay the debts of my youth and provide for my future. Beyond that, none.

> *Who chooseth me must give and hazard all he hath.*

It is almost cruel to recall the inscription on the casket Bassanio picked in the light of what he *received* from Shylock and of what he let Antonio *risk* in his behalf.

If it be objected that this is subjecting a fairy tale to the tests of realistic literature, the answer is that it is not the first time that a fairy tale has been a fascinating invention on the surface and the hardest fact and soundest wisdom underneath. Ample justice has been done by his admirers to Bassanio's virtues. It is the economic aspect of his career that has been understressed. Like a number of others in this play the source of whose income will not always bear inspection, like most of us in fact, he was not averse to receiving what he had not exactly earned. Bassanio is the golden casket. He gained what many men desire: a wealthy wife.

III

Antonio's case is a bit subtler than Bassanio's but even more illuminating. Why is Antonio sad?

Shakespeare devotes a good share of the opening scene of the play to a discussion of that question.

> In sooth, I know not why I am so sad.
> It wearies me; you say it wearies you;
> But how I caught it, found it, or came by it,
> What stuff 'tis made of, whereof it is born,
> I am to learn;
> And such a want-wit sadness makes of me,
> That I have much ado to know myself.

Salanio and Salarino confirm his changed appearance and suggest that he is anxious over his argosies. But Antonio brushes that aside. His ventures are not in one bottom trusted nor all his wealth committed to the present enterprise:

> Therefore, my merchandise makes me not sad.

He denies, too, the charge that he is in love. So Salarino, baffled, concludes that it is a matter of temperament. Antonio was just born that way. But this explains nothing and his altered looks give it the lie.

Commentators have commonly either sidestepped the problem or explained Antonio's melancholy as a presentiment of the loss of his friend Bassanio through marriage. That may have accentuated it at the moment, but Antonio has had barely a hint of what is coming when the play opens, while his depression has all the marks of something older and deeper. It is scarcely too much to say that he is a sick man. Later, at the trial, when the opportunity of sacrificing himself is presented, his sadness becomes almost suicidal:

> I am a tainted wether of the flock,
> Meetest for death. The weakest kind of fruit
> Drops earliest to the ground; and so let me.

> You cannot better be employ'd, Bassanio,
> Than to live still, and write mine epitaph.

Only something fundamental can explain such a sentimental welcome to death. The opening of the play is an interrogation three times underscored as to Antonio's sadness.

Later, a similar question is propounded about another emotion of another character: Shylock and his thirst for revenge. Now Shylock is a brainier man than Antonio, and his diagnosis of his own case throws light on Antonio's. The Jew gives a number of reasons for his hatred. Because Antonio brings down the rate of usury in Venice. Because he hates the Jews. Because he rails on Shylock in public. Because he is a hypocrite. Because he is a Christian. Because he has thwarted the Jew's bargains. Because he has heated his enemies. Because he has cooled his friends. And so on, and so on. An adequate collection of motives, one would say. Yet not one of them, or all together, sufficient to account for his passion. They are rationalizations, like Iago's reasons for his plot against Othello, or Raskolnikov's for his murder of the old woman in *Crime and Punishment*. And Shylock comes finally to recognize that fact. In the court scene when the Duke asks his reason for his mad insistence on the pound of flesh, Shylock says he can and will give no reason other than 'a certain loathing I bear Antonio'. A certain loathing! It matches exactly the certain sadness of Antonio.

But it matches another emotion of Antonio's even more closely. If Shylock loathes Antonio, Antonio has a no less savage detestation of Shylock. His hatred is as 'boundless' as was Juliet's love. It appears to be the one passion that like a spasm mars his gentle disposition, as a sudden squall will ruffle the surface of a placid lake.

> A kinder gentleman treads not the earth,

says Salarino, and so Antonio impresses us except in this one relation. When Shylock complains,

> Fair sir, you spet on me on Wednesday last;
> You spurn'd me such a day; another time
> You call'd me dog,

we might think it the hallucination of a half-maddened mind. But does Antonio deny the charge? On the contrary he confirms it:

> I am as like to call thee so again,
> To spit on thee again, to spurn thee too.

That from this paragon of kindliness! It is not enough to say that in those days everybody hated the Jews, for that leaves unexplained why the gentlest and mildest man in the play is the fiercest Jew-baiter of them all. As far as the record goes, he outdoes even the crude and taunting Gratiano. Oh, but Shylock is a usurer, it will be said, while Antonio is so noble that the mere mention of interest is abhorrent to him. Why, then, does not Antonio state his objection to it like a rational being instead of arguing with kicks and saliva? Why is he so heated, as well as so noble?

Unless all signs fail, Antonio, like Shylock, is a victim of forces from far below the threshold of consciousness. What are they?

Shakespeare is careful to leave no doubt on this point, but, appropriately, he buries the evidence a bit beneath the surface: Antonio abhors Shylock because he catches his own reflection in his face.

'What! Antonio like Shylock!' it will be said. 'The idea is preposterous. No two men could be more unlike.' They are, in many respects. But extremes meet, and in one respect they are akin. It is Antonio's unconscious protest against this humiliating truth that is the secret of his antipathy. 'Wilt thou whip thine own faults in other men?' cries Timon of Athens. Shakespeare understood the principle, and he illustrates it here.

The contrast between Shylock and Antonio is apparently nowhere more marked than in the attitude of the two men toward money. Shylock is a usurer. So strong is Antonio's distaste for usury that he lends money without interest. But where does the money come from that permits such generosity? From his argosies, of course, his trade. For, after all, to what has Antonio dedicated his life? Not indeed to usury. But certainly to money-making, to profits. And profits, under analysis, are often only 'usury' in a more respectable form. Appearance and reality again.

Shakespeare seizes one of the most exciting moments of the play (when the dramatic tension is so high that nobody will notice) to drive home this truth, the instant when Portia, disguised as a Young Doctor of Laws, enters the courtroom.

> Which is the merchant here and which the Jew?

she inquires in almost her first words. All she wants, of course, is to have defendant and plaintiff identified. But the Shakespearean overmeaning is unmistakable. Merchant and Jew! Noble trader of Venice and despicable money-changer, at what poles they appear to stand! Yet – which is which? (Editors who punctuate the line

> Which is the merchant here? And which the Jew?

miss the point.)

Nor is the distinction between merchant and moneylender the only one, the poet implies, that may be difficult at times to draw. As if to prepare us for Portia's Delphic line, Shakespeare has Gratiano anticipate it in cruder form with respect to Gentile and Jew. Jessica, in boy's clothes, is about to elope with Lorenzo:

> I will make fast the doors, and gild myself
> With some more ducats, and be with you straight.
> *(Exit above)*

That 'gild', with its clear allusion to the golden casket, not to mention the familiar symbolism of the descent from above, gives us in one word the moral measure of this girl who crowns her deception and desertion of her father by robbing him. As the young thief comes down, Gratiano cries in delighted approval

> Now, by my hood, a Gentile, and no Jew.

Gratiano is thinking of the fascinating boldness of this saucy boy-girl. She's too good to be a Jew, he says, she's one of us. But Shakespeare has not forgotten the stolen ducats. That unusual oath, 'by my hood', is enough to suggest that there is something under cover here. Is it her dashing air or her hard heart that entitles Jessica to the name of Gentile? The poet does not say. But he clearly asks. Plainly Jew and Gentile are not to him separate species with distinct virtues and vices. Morocco makes a like point when he says his blood will be found as red as that of the fairest blonde from the north. And Shylock, when he asks, 'If you prick us, do we not bleed?' Under the skin, all men are brothers.

And here an interesting fact should be recorded. On 22 July 1598, James Roberts entered in the Stationers' Register *The Marchaunt of Venyce or otherwise called the Jewe of Venyce*. Here is testimony that already in Shakespeare's own day the public was puzzled by the title of the play and had substituted for, or added to, the author's another title more expressive of what seemed to be its leading interest and central figure. The world did not have to wait for Kean and Irving to discover its 'hero'. Yet the poet knew what he was about when he named it.

> Which is the merchant here and which the Jew?

The public needed two titles. Shakespeare is content with two-in-one.

Now Shylock, with his incisive mind, grasps very early this resemblance of Antonio's vocation to his own. Apparently it first strikes him with full force on the occasion when Antonio backs Bassanio's request for a loan. Knowing of old the merchant's antipathy to interest, Shylock is astonished:

> Methought you said you neither lend nor borrow
> Upon advantage.

Antonio admits it is not his habit.

> When Jacob graz'd his uncle Laban's sheep,

Shylock begins. Jacob? What has Jacob to do with it?

> And what of him? Did he take interest?

Antonio inquires.

> No; not take interest; not, as you would say,
> Directly interest.

That 'directly'! It is necessary to get the tone as well as the word. The sarcasm of it is the point. There are more ways than one of taking interest, it says. There are many tricks of the trade, many ways of thriving, as Jacob knew in the old days. *And as certain others know nowadays.* But Antonio, quite unaware in his self-righteousness of the fact that he is himself the target, thinks the story Shylock goes on to tell of how Jacob increased his wages by a sly device is told to justify the taking of interest, whereas what the Jew is saying, if a bit less bluntly, is: Look a bit closer, Antonio, and you will see that your profits amount to the same thing as my interest. We are in the same boat.

Antonio, though unaware that he is hit, does scent some danger lurking in the story and insists on a distinction essential to his self-respect:

> This was a venture, sir, that Jacob serv'd for;
> A thing not in his power to bring to pass,
> But sway'd and fashion'd by the hand of heaven,

and, still puzzled over the point of Shylock's illustration, he adds:

> Was this inserted to make interest good?
> Or is your gold and silver ewes and rams?

'I cannot tell,' answers Shylock, 'I make it breed as fast.'

'Your example turns against you, Shylock!' is what Antonio implies. Rams and ewes are very different from silver and gold. It is right and proper that they should multiply, but it is against nature for barren metal to. Antonio's speech is an example of how a man may say one thing with his tongue and quite another with his soul. It is the word 'venture' that gives him away. The very term he had applied to his own argosies ('My ventures are not in one bottom trusted')! It is these and not Jacob's lambs that are really troubling him, and his 'sway'd and fashion'd' confirms the conjecture, the one an allusion to the winds of heaven as certainly as the other is to the hand of heaven. But this unconscious introduction of the argosies into the argument, by way of self-defense, is fatal to Antonio's contention. For when it comes to generation, cargoes generally resemble gold and silver far more nearly than they do ewes and rams. In so far as they do, Aristotle's famous argument against interest proves to be equally cogent against profits. Antonio and Shylock are still in the same boat.

But Antonio, blind as ever, turns to his friend and says:

> Mark you this, Bassanio,
> The devil can cite Scripture for his purpose.
> An evil soul, producing holy witness,
> Is like a villain with a smiling cheek,
> A goodly apple rotten at the heart.
> O, what a goodly outside falsehood hath!

Considering Antonio's reputation for virtue (what are the smiling villain and goodly apple but the golden casket?), the speech is a moral boomerang if there ever was one. He very conveniently forgets that he no more produced the treasures with which his argosies are loaded than Shylock did his ducats – treasures which he himself boasts a few speeches further on will bring in within two months 'thrice three times the value of this bond'. Antonio's business is thriving. Usury? God forbid! 'Not, as *you* would say, directly interest.'

This does not mean that Antonio is a hypocrite. Far from it. Who does not know an Antonio – a man too good for money-making who has dedicated his life to money-making? Antonio was created for nobler things. And so he suffers from that home-sickness of the soul that ultimately attacks everyone who 'consecrates' his life to something below his spiritual level. Moreover, Antonio is a bachelor, and his 'fie, fie!' in answer to Salanio's bantering suggestion that he is in love may hint at some long-nourished disappointment of the affections. Antonio has never married, and he is not the man to have had clandestine affairs. So he has invested in gentle friendship emotions that nature intended should blossom into love. But however tender and loyal, it is a slightly sentimental friendship, far from being an equivalent of love. Both it and the argosies are at bottom opiates. Those who drown themselves in business or other work in order to forget what refuses to be forgotten are generally characterized by a quiet melancholy interrupted occasionally by spells of irritation or sudden spasms of passion directed at some person or thing that, if analyzed, is found to be a symbol of the error that has spoiled their lives.

Therefore, my merchandise makes me not sad.

By his very denial Antonio unwittingly diagnoses his ailment
correctly. This surely is the solution of the opening conundrum
of the play, and anger at himself, not a conventional anti-
Semitism of which Antonio could not conceivably be guilty, is
the cause of his fierce and irrational outbursts against Shylock.
Antonio is the silver casket. He got as much as he deserved:
material success and a suicidal melancholy.

IV

Why did Shylock offer Antonio a loan of three thousand ducats
without interest?

On our answer to that crucial question, it is scarcely too much
to say, our conception of the Jew and our interpretation of the
play will hinge.

The superficial reader or auditor will think this is complicating
what is a simple matter. He has probably heard the outcome of
the bond story before he ever picks up the book or enters the
theatre, or, if not, is the willing victim of an actor who has.
Where, he will ask, is there any problem? Shylock is a villain.
He is out from the first for bloody revenge. Doesn't he say so,
in an aside, the moment Antonio enters his presence?

> If I can catch him once upon the hip,
> I will feed fat the ancient grudge I bear him.

What could be plainer than that? The Jew foresees (as does the
actor of his part) that Antonio will not be able to pay on the
appointed day, and so slyly and cruelly, traps the merchant into
signing the bloody bond under the pretense that he is joking.

Unfortunately the text contradicts in a dozen places this easy
assumption that the Jew is a sort of super-Iago. . . . But apart
from this, the idea that as intelligent a man as Shylock could have
deliberately counted on the bankruptcy of as rich a man as
Antonio, with argosies on seven seas, is preposterous. And if
anyone would cite to the contrary his speech about land-rats and
water-rats, waters, winds, and rocks, the answer is that that is
the merest daydreaming, the sheerest wishful thinking. The bond
whatever else it is, is more of the same. It does indeed reveal a

hidden desire on Shylock's part to tear out Antonio's heart. but that is a power-fantasy pure and simple. It is like a child's 'I'll kill you!' Such things are at the opposite pole from deliberate plans for murder, even judicial murder.

Shylock's offer to take no interest for his loan was obviously as unexpected to him as it was to Bassanio and Antonio. Just thirty-six lines before he makes it he was considering the rate he should charge:

> Three thousand ducats; 'tis a good round sum.
> Three months from twelve; then, let me see; the rate –

Then comes the well-known speech beginning

> Signior Antonio, many a time and oft
> In the Rialto you have rated me . . .

(a significant pun, by the way, on the word 'rate'). 'You spat upon me, kicked me, called me dog' is the gist of what he says, 'and for these courtesies you now expect me to lend you money?'

'No!' cries Antonio, stung by the justice of Shylock's irony. 'I want no courtesy or kindness. Friends take no interest from friends. Let this transaction be one between enemies, so that, if I forfeit, you can exact the penalty with a better conscience, and so that I' (he does not say it, but who can doubt that he thinks it?) 'may retain my right to spit on you.'

How to the heart Antonio is hit is revealed by the stage direction which Shakespeare, as so often, skilfully inserts in the text.

> Why, look you, how you storm!

cries Shylock. Antonio's anger is as good as a confession, but, clad in the pride of race and virtue, he does not realize it. How the tables are now turned, how the relation between the two is reversed! Hitherto, Antonio has always been the superior, Shylock the inferior. It is not just that the borrower, being the beggar, is always below the lender. That is a trifle here. The significant thing is that the man who loses his temper is below the man who keeps his self-control. A small man meets anger with anger. A big man meets it with augmented patience and self-restraint. Does Shylock show himself great or small in the situation? And if great, is it genuine greatness of heart, or only the counterfeit greatness of intelligent self-interest?

It is just here that he makes his offer to forget the past, to supply Antonio's wants, as a friend would, without interest. . . . It is clear that he had it in him, however deep down, to be humane, kindly, and patient, and his offer to Antonio of a loan without interest seems to have been a supreme effort of this submerged Shylock to come to the surface. If so, here is the supreme irony of this ironical play. If so, for a moment at least, the Jew was the Christian. The symbolism confirms the psychology: Shylock was the leaden casket with the spiritual gold within.

v

Portia, too, like so many of the others in this play, is not precisely all she seems to be. Indeed, what girl of her years, with her wealth, wit, and beauty, could be the object of such universal adulation and come through unscathed? In her uprush of joy when Bassanio chooses the right casket there is, it is true, an accent of the humility that fresh love always bestows, and she speaks of herself as 'an unlesson'd girl, unschool'd, unpractis'd'. There the child Portia once was is speaking, but it is a note that is sounded scarcely anywhere else in her role. The woman that child has grown into, on the contrary, is the darling of a sophisticated society which has nurtured in her anything but unselfconsciousness. Indeed, it seems to be as natural to her as to a queen or princess to take herself unblushingly at the estimate this society places on her.

> *Who chooseth me shall gain what many men desire.*
> Why, that's the lady: all the world desires her;
> From the four corners of the earth they come . . .

says Morocco. And tacitly Portia assents to that interpretation of the inscription on the golden casket. She mocks half a dozen of her suitors unmercifully in the first scene in which we see her, and it never seems to occur to her that any man who could would not choose her. Yet it is not easy to imagine Hamlet choosing her, or Othello, or Coriolanus. (Nor Shakespeare himself, I feel like adding.)

> *Who chooseth me shall get as much as he deserves.*
> I will assume desert,

says Arragon. Portia, likewise, quietly assumes that she somehow deserves the attention and sacrifices of these crowding suitors. Perhaps she does. Yet we cannot help wishing she did not know it, though we scarcely blame her for thinking what everyone around her thinks.

But if Portia is willing to let her suitors take any risk in her pursuit in the spirit of the third inscription,

> *Who chooseth me must give and hazard all he hath,*

there is nothing to indicate that life has ever called on her to sacrifice even a small part of all she has, and when the man of her choice attains her, though she modestly wishes that for his sake she were a thousand times more fair, she also wishes significantly that she were ten thousand times more rich. Bassanio pronounces her

> nothing undervalu'd
> To Cato's daughter, Brutus' Portia.

But it is hard to think Shakespeare would have thought the comparison a happy one. Both Portias were good women. But, granted that, how could they be more different? If it is a question of the poet's later heroines, another comes to mind. When the Prince of Morocco goes out after having chosen the wrong casket, Portia dismisses him and innumerable other uninspected suitors with the line:

> Let all of his complexion choose me so.

Who is judging now by the outside? And we remember Desdemona's

> I saw Othello's visage in his mind.

In view of her father's scheme for selecting her husband, no one will blame Portia for giving Bassanio several hints on the choice of the right casket. Because of her declared intention not to be forsworn, we give her the benefit of the doubt and assume the hints were unconscious ones.* Indeed, the fact that she uses the word 'hazard' (from the inscription on the leaden casket), not only before Bassanio chooses but before Morocco and Arragon do, all but proves that the suspense and peril of the choice fascinate her at the moment hardly less than her passion for Bassanio. She is not the only girl who has been excited by the adventure of getting married, as well as by being in love with her future husband. Contrast her with Juliet, who did give and hazard all she had for love, and you feel the difference.

This is not to suggest that Portia ought to have been a Juliet, or a Desdemona, and still less that Shakespeare should have made her anything other than she is. Given his sources, it is easy to see why Portia had to be just what she is.

The casket motif, the court scene, and the ring incident taken together comprise a good share of the story. Each of them is intrinsically spectacular, histrionic or theatrical – or all three in one. Each is a kind of play within a play, with Portia at the centre or at one focus. The casket scenes are little symbolic pageants; the court scene is drama on the surface and tragedy underneath; the ring incident is a one-act comedy complete in itself. What sort of heroine does all this demand? Obviously one with the temperament of an actress, not averse to continual limelight. Portia is exactly that.

When she hears that the man who helped her lover woo and win her is in trouble, her character and the contingency fit each other like hand and glove. Why not impersonate a Young Doctor of Laws and come to Antonio's rescue? It is typical of her that at first she takes the 'whole device', as she calls it, as a kind of prank. Her imagination overflows with pictures of the opportunities for acting that her own and Nerissa's disguise as young

* Who selected the song that is sung while Bassanio meditates we shall never know. It of course gives away the secret. And in that connection there is a point I have never happened to see noted. The verses inside the golden casket begin with a rhyme on long *o* (gōld); those inside the silver casket on a rhyme on short *i* (this). The song sung while Bassanio is making up his mind begins with a rhyme on short *e* (bred). But *bred* (as someone has pointed out) is a full rhyme with *lead*!

men will offer, of the innocent lies they will tell, the fun they will have, the fools they will make of their husbands. The tragic situation of Antonio seems at the moment the last thing in her mind, or the responsibility of Bassanio for the plight of his friend. The fact that she is to have the leading role in a play in real life eclipses everything else. There is more than a bit of the stage-struck girl in Portia.

And so when the curtain rises on Act IV, Shakespeare the playwright and his actress-heroine, between them, are equipped to give us one of the tensest and most theatrically effective scenes he had conceived up to this time. What Shakespeare the poet gives us, however, and what it means to Portia the woman, is something rather different. What possessed Portia to torture not only Antonio but her own husband with such superfluous suspense? She knew what was coming. Why didn't she let it come at once? Why didn't she invoke immediately the law prescribing a penalty for any alien plotting against the life of any citizen of Venice instead of waiting until she had put those she supposedly loved upon the rack? The only possible answer is that she wanted a spectacle, a dramatic triumph with herself at the centre. The psychology is identical with that which led the boy Kolya in *The Brothers Karamazov* to torture his sick little friend Ilusha by holding back the news that his lost dog was found, merely in order to enjoy the triumph of restoring him to his chum at the last moment in the presence of an audience. In that case the result was fatal. The child died from the excitement.

To all this it is easy to imagine what those will say who hold that Shakespeare was first the playwright and only incidentally poet and psychologist. 'Why, but this is just a play!' they will exclaim, half-amused, half-contemptuous, 'and a comedy at that! Portia! It isn't Portia who contrives the postponement. It is Shakespeare. Where would his play have been if his heroine had cut things short or failed to act exactly as she did?' Where indeed? Which is precisely why the poet made her the sort of woman who would have acted under the given conditions exactly as she did act. That was his business: not to find or devise situations exciting in the theatre (any third-rate playwright can do that) but to discover what sort of men and women would

behave in the often extraordinary ways in which they are represented as behaving in such situations in the stories he inherited
and selected for dramatization.

VI

And so Portia is given a second chance. She is to be tested again.
She has had her legal and judicial triumph. Now it is over will she
show to her victim that quality which at her own divine moment
she told us 'is an attribute to God himself'? The Jew is about to
get his deserts. Will Portia forget her doctrine that mercy is
mercy precisely because it is not deserved? The Jew is about to
receive justice. Will she remember that our prayers for mercy
should teach us to do the deeds of mercy and that in the course of
justice none of us will see salvation? Alas! she will forget, she
will not remember. Like Shylock, but in a subtler sense, she who
has appealed to logic 'perishes' by it.

Up to this point she has been forward enough in arrogating
to herself the function of judge. But now, instead of showing
compassion herself or entreating the Duke to, she motions Shylock to his knees:

Down therefore and beg mercy of the Duke.

'Mercy'! This beggar's mercy, though it goes under the same
name, has not the remotest resemblance to that quality that drops
like the gentle rain from heaven. Ironically it is the Duke who
proves truer to the true Portia than Portia herself.

Duke. That thou shalt see the difference of our spirits,
    I pardon thee thy life before thou ask it.

And he suggests that the forfeit of half of Shylock's property to
the state may be commuted to a fine.

Ay, for the state; not for Antonio,

Portia quickly interposes, as if afraid that the Duke is going to
be too merciful, going to let her victim off too leniently. Here,
as always, the aftermath of too much 'theatrical' emotion is a
coldness of heart that is like lead. The tone in which Portia

has objected is reflected in the hopelessness of Shylock's next words:

> Nay, take my life and all! Pardon not that!
> You take my house when you do take the prop
> That doth sustain my house. You take my life
> When you do take the means whereby I live.

Portia next asks Antonio what 'mercy' he can render. And even the man whom Shylock would have killed seems more disposed than Portia to mitigate the severity of his penalty: he is willing to forgo the half of Shylock's goods if the Duke will permit him the use of the other half for life with the stipulation that it go to Lorenzo (and so to Jessica) at his death. But with two provisos: that all the Jew dies possessed of also go to Lorenzo-Jessica and that

> He presently become a Christian.

Doubtless the Elizabethan crowd, like the crowd in every generation since including our own, thought that this was letting Shylock off easily, that this *was* showing mercy to him. Crowds do not know that mercy is wholehearted and has nothing to do with halves or other fractions. Nor do crowds know that you cannot make a Christian by court decree. Antonio's last demand quite undoes any tinge of mercy in his earlier concessions.

Even Shylock, as we have seen, had in him at least a grain of spiritual gold, of genuine Christian spirit. Only a bit of it perhaps. Seeds do not need to be big. Suppose that Portia and Antonio, following the lead of the seemingly willing Duke, had watered this tiny seed with that quality that blesses him who gives as well as him who takes, had overwhelmed Shylock with the grace of forgiveness! What then? The miracle, it is true, might not have taken place. Yet it might have. But instead, as if in imitation of the Jew's own cruelty, they whet their knives of law and logic, of reason and justice, and proceed to cut out their victim's heart. (That that is what it amounts to is proved by the heartbroken words,

> I pray you give me leave to go from hence.
> I am not well.)

Shylock's conviction that Christianity and revenge are synonyms is confirmed. 'If a Christian wrong a Jew, what should his sufferance be by Christian example? Why, revenge.' The unforgettable speech from which that comes, together with Portia's on mercy, and Lorenzo's on the harmony of heaven, make up the spiritual argument of the play. Shylock asserts that a Jew is a man. Portia declares that man's duty to man is mercy – which comes from heaven. Lorenzo points to heaven but laments that the materialism of life insulates man from its harmonies. A celestial syllogism that puts to shame the logic of the courtroom.

That Shakespeare planned his play from the outset to enforce the irony of Portia's failure to be true to her inner self in the trial scene is susceptible of something as near proof as such things can ever be. As in the case of Hamlet's

A little more than kin, and less than kind,

the poet, over and over, makes the introduction of a leading character seemingly casual, actually significant. Portia enters *The Merchant of Venice* with the remark that she is aweary of the world. Nerissa replies with that wise little speech about the illness of those that surfeit with too much (an observation that takes on deeper meaning in the retrospect after we realize that at the core what is the trouble with Portia and her society is boredom). 'Good sentences and well pronounced,' says Portia, revealing in those last two words more than she knows. 'They would be better if well followed,' Nerissa pertinently retorts. Whereupon Portia, as if gifted with insight into her own future, takes up Nerissa's theme:

If to do were as easy as to know what were good to do, chapels had been churches, and poor men's cottages princes' palaces. It is a good divine that follows his own instructions: I can easier teach twenty what were good to be done, than be one of the twenty to follow mine own teaching.

If that is not a specific preparation for the speech on mercy and what follows it, what in the name of coincidence is it? The words on mercy were good sentences, well pronounced. And far more than that. But for Portia they remained just words in the sense that they did not teach her to do the deeds of mercy. So, a few seconds after we see her for the first time, does Shakespeare let her pass judgment in advance on the most critical act of her life. For a moment, at the crisis in the courtroom, she seems about to become the leaden casket with the spiritual gold within. But the temptation to gain what many men desire – admiration and praise – is too strong for her and she reverts to her worldly self. Portia is the golden casket.

SOURCE: Abridged from an essay in *The Meaning of Shake-speare*, 2 vols (1963).

John Russell Brown

LOVE'S WEALTH AND THE JUDGEMENT OF *THE MERCHANT OF VENICE* (1957)

It may seem *malapropos* to talk about romantic love in terms of buying and selling, leaseholds, merchandise, and bargains, but in each of the early comedies, and in many other plays and poems, Shakespeare wrote of love as of a kind of wealth in which men and women traffic.

Of all the comedies, *The Merchant of Venice* is the most completely informed by Shakespeare's ideal of love's wealth.[1] Each of Portia's suitors has to choose one of three caskets and he who chooses the one which contains a portrait of Portia, wins her as his bride. Each casket is of a different metal and each bears a motto: one of gold reads 'Who chooseth me shall gain what many men desire', one of silver reads 'Who chooseth me shall get as much as he deserves', and one of lead reads 'Who chooseth me must give and hazard all he hath'. Morocco, the type of those who make their choice in love for the sake of what they will 'gain', chooses gold and finds inside a skull – a reminder that death must cancel all such gain; Arragon, who presumes to take what 'he deserves', finds a fool's head; Bassanio who is willing to 'give and hazard', who does not mind the quality of the casket if he finds Portia within it, chooses lead and wins the bride of his choice. It could not be otherwise if love's true wealth, unlike commercial wealth, should be 'in bounty' cherished, if 'giving', not 'gaining' or 'getting', is essential to love. And so by these contrasts, clearly and formally, the wooing of Portia is related to Shakespeare's ideal.

As in *The Comedy of Errors* and *The Shrew*, this ideal is contrasted with a frankly commercial wealth, but here Shakespeare has broadened his theme. Previously commerce has been presented, in contrast to love, as concerned solely with possession and gain; now Shakespeare shows that it can involve personal relationships as well. Both Shylock and Antonio get their livelihood by commerce, but Antonio is ready to submit the rights of commerce to the claims of love; he lends freely to his friend Bassanio without security, although he has squandered previous loans and although it involves risking his own life by giving a bond to Shylock for a pound of his flesh. This is to 'give and hazard'. In contrast, Shylock, the Jew, demands his rights; repeatedly he claims his due according to the bond (cf. iv i 37, 87, 139, 242, 253 and 259, etc.), and sees no reason to relent:

> What judgement shall I dread, doing no wrong? . . .
> The pound of flesh which I demand of him,
> Is dearly bought; 'tis mine and I will have it.
> If you deny me, fie upon your law!
> There is no force in the decrees of Venice.
> I stand for judgement: answer; shall I have it?
>
> (iv i 89–103)

Shylock stands 'for law' (iv i 142): he disregards the plea for mercy because it has no 'compulsion' and he will not provide a surgeon to stop Antonio's wounds because there is no stipulation to that effect in the bond. He is content to cry:

> My deeds upon my head! I crave the law,
> The penalty and forfeit of my bond.
>
> (iv i 202–3)

In Shylock's eyes, this is to 'get what he deserves'. Both he and Antonio may be judged by the mottoes on the caskets.

The contrast between these two is emphasized much earlier in the play in a discussion about usury. As Antonio enters to negotiate the bond, Shylock discovers his hatred in an aside:

> I hate him for he is a Christian,
> *But more* for that in low simplicity
> He lends out money gratis and brings down
> The rate of usance here with us in Venice. . . .
>
> (i iii 43–6)

Shylock lends only for what he can gain, Antonio for the sake of friendship; he makes this clear to Shylock:

> If thou wilt lend this money, lend it not
> As to thy friends; for when did friendship take
> A breed for barren metal of his friend?
> But lend it rather to thine enemy,
> Who, if he break, thou mayst with better face
> Exact the penalty.   (I iii 133–8)

This issue is maintained throughout the play. When Antonio is in prison because he cannot repay the loan, Shylock taunts him with 'This is the fool that lent out money gratis' (III iii 2; see also III i 50–2). Such generosity restricts the exercise of Shylock's rights and, as Antonio recognizes, is the main cause of his malice:

> I oft deliver'd from his forfeitures
> Many that have at times made moan to me;
> Therefore he hates me.
>
>   (III iii 22–4)

It is sometimes argued that Shylock's affairs are so far removed in kind from the affairs of the lovers at Belmont, that the play falls into two parts. But, in one way the play is very closely knit, for, besides contrasting Shylock with Antonio, the discussion about usury is yet another contrast between him and Portia and Bassanio. Shakespeare saw love as a kind of usury, and so in their marriage Bassanio and Portia put Nature's bounty to its proper 'use', Shylock practises a usury for the sake of gain and is prepared to enforce his rights; the lovers practice their usury without compulsion for the joy of giving:

> That use is not forbidden usury
> Which happies those that pay the willing loan.
>   (Sonnet VI)

As soon as Bassanio has chosen the right casket, being ready to 'give and hazard all', Portia knows love's 'increase':

> O love,
> Be moderate; allay thy ecstasy;
> In measure rein thy joy; scant this *excess*.
> I feel too much thy blessing: make it less,
> For fear I surfeit.
>   (III ii 111–15)

Antonio has already used the word 'excess' meaning 'usury' (I iii 62–3) and remembering Juliet's:

> . . . my true love is *grown* to such *excess*
> I cannot *sum up* sum of half my *wealth* . . .
>
> (*Romeo and Juliet*, II vi 33–4)

the same sense seems to be required here. Bassanio's first reaction is to wonder at the beauty of the portrait which he finds inside the casket, then he finds a scroll ('The continent and summary of my *fortune*') which tells him to '*claim*' his lady with 'a loving kiss'; at this point he uses yet another commercial image:

> A gentle scroll. Fair lady, by your leave;
> I *come by note*, to *give* and to *receive*.
>
> (III ii 140–1)

To 'come by note' meant to present one's bill or I.O.U.,[2] Bassanio has 'ventured' all and can now claim his 'fortune'. But as every bill in the commerce of love implies both giving and receiving, he is ready 'to give *and* to receive'; these are the conditions of love's usury and so it is fitting that their 'bargain' (III ii 195) should be 'confirm'd, sign'd, ratified' (III ii 149) with an interchange of kisses.

The comparison of the two usuries is part of a more general comparison of commerce and love which is likewise maintained throughout the play. From the beginning Bassanio's quest has been described in commercial terms; indeed, he might have equal claim with Antonio and Shylock for the title of *The Merchant of Venice*. To Antonio he outlines his plans as a means of getting 'clear of all the debts' he owes (I i 134), trying, with little success, to present his intention of paying court to Portia as a good business proposition. Antonio tells him that all this is unnecessary, that such values are inappropriate to friendship, and thereupon Bassanio changes his tone, praising Portia in the 'innocence' (I i 145) of his love: she is indeed rich, and –

> . . . she is fair *and*, fairer than that word,
> Of wondrous virtues. . . .
>
> (I i 162–3)

He '*values*' her as Cato's daughter, renowned for constancy and virtue, and her 'sunny locks' are as the '*golden* fleece' for which Jason ventured. The comparison with the golden fleece is particularly significant, for the phrase was used of the fortunes for which merchants ventured; Drake, for example, was said to have returned from his voyage round the world bringing 'his golden fleece'.[3] In Bassanio's description of Portia there is a curious, but, to those who trade in love, a natural, confusion of her wealth, beauty, and virtue; all these comprise her wealth in love. In Bassanio's eyes she has all perfections, and, amazed by them, he sees no obstacle to his fortune:

> I have a mind presages me such *thrift*,
> That I should questionless be *fortunate*!
>
> (I i 175–6)

When Bassanio has chosen the right casket, and comes 'by note, to give and to receive', Portia responds in similarly commercial terms:

> You see me, Lord Bassanio, where I stand,
> Such as I am: though for myself alone
> I would not be ambitious in my wish,
> To wish myself much better; yet, for you
> I would be trebled twenty times myself;
> A thousand times more fair, ten thousand times
> More rich. . . .
>
> (III ii 150–6)

Portia desires greater wealth only for Bassanio's sake:

> That only to stand high in your *account*,
> I might in virtues, beauties, livings, friends,
> *Exceed account*. . . .
>
> (III ii 157–9)

She cannot possess enough of this kind of wealth to enable her to give as generously as she would wish:

> . . . but the *full sum* of me
> Is sum of something, which, to *term in gross*,
> Is an unlesson'd girl. . . .
>
> (III ii 159–61)

Bassanio's willingness to give and hazard is answered by Portia's giving, and the contract of love is complete. So the willing, generous and prosperous transactions of love's wealth are compared and contrasted with Shylock's wholly commercial transactions in which gain is the object, enforcement the method, and even human beings are merely things to be possessed.

Normally in Shakespeare's early narrative comedies, hero and heroine are betrothed at the end of the very last scene of the play where there is little time for the expression of sentiment; *The Merchant of Venice* is the major exception to this, presenting Portia's modest, eager, rich-hearted committal to Bassanio in the third Act. In consequence, Shakespeare is not only able to show how love's wealth is risked, given, and multiplied, but also how it is possessed. At the end of Portia's speech of self-giving, she 'commits' herself to Bassanio:

> . . . to be directed,
> As from her lord, her governor, her king.
>
> (III ii 166–7)

All her wealth is made over as if it were a commercial possession:

> Myself and what is mine to you and yours
> Is now *converted*: but now I was the lord
> Of this fair mansion, master of my servants,
> Queen o'er myself; and even now, but now,
> This house, these servants and this same myself
> *Are yours*, my lord: I *give* them with this ring. . . .
>
> (III ii 168–73)

Bassanio is told never to part with the ring, and in his confused joy, he can only swear that he will keep it for life. The story of Portia and Bassanio is by no means complete at this point; love is not like merchandise, it is not simply a question of possessor and possessed.

This is at once apparent: when news comes that Shylock is about to enforce the penalty to which his bond entitles him, Portia finds she has yet more to give; she is ready to forgo wealth and delay her marriage rights, and she urges Bassanio to leave for Venice before nightfall. A line sums up her response:

> Since you are *dear bought*, I will love you *dear*.
>
> (III ii 316)

Pope relegated this to the foot of the page in his edition on the grounds that its commercial attitude was unworthy of Shakespeare, but 'dear' is used in the double sense of 'expensively' and 'with great affection'; the line, in fact, expresses Portia's willingness to continue to give joyfully in love. In the commerce of love, giving is the secret of keeping as well as of gaining.

Under this impulse, Portia herself goes to Venice and, disguised as a lawyer, defeats Shylock's claims. For this service she refuses payment:

> He is well paid that is well satisfied;
> And I, delivering you, am satisfied
> And therein do *account* myself well *paid*:
> My mind was never yet more *mercenary*.
>
> (IV i 415–18)

Not recognizing Portia in the young lawyer, Antonio and Bassanio cannot know how deeply he is satisfied, how 'dearly' he has given; they do not know that he has acted with love's bounty. Portia chooses to bring this to their knowledge by the trick of asking Bassanio for the ring she gave him at their betrothal. At first he refuses because of his vow, but when he is left alone with Antonio, his love for this friend persuades him to send the ring to the young lawyer. This twist in the plot is resolved in the last Act, and still further illustrates the kind of possession which is appropriate for love's wealth.

The act begins with music, and talk of ancient loves and of the harmony of the spheres, but when Portia, Bassanio, and Antonio enter, all harmony seems threatened by a quarrel over the ring of gold, the symbol of possession. They now talk about unfaithfulness, adultery, and cuckoldry. Bassanio's story is most unplausible and he is in a difficult position; as Portia protests with mock seriousness:

> What man is there so much unreasonable,
> If you had pleased to have defended it
> With any terms of zeal, wanted the modesty
> To urge the thing held as a ceremony? . . .
> I'll die for't but some woman had the ring.
>
> (V i 203–8)

Bassanio can only say that he was unable to refuse the one

> ... that had held up the very life
> Of my dear friend. . . .
> I was beset with shame and courtesy;
> My honour would not let ingratitude
> So much besmear it.
>
> (v i 214–19)

But when Antonio interjects that he is willing to 'be bound again', with his 'soul upon the forfeit', that Bassanio will 'never more break faith advisedly' (v i 251–3), Portia returns the ring and perplexity is soon resolved. And Bassanio is soon pardoned, for he has erred only through generosity to his friend. The whole episode is a light-hearted reminder that Portia has saved Antonio's life, and that the claim of generosity must always rank as high as that of possession.

The bawdy talk, which the misunderstandings provoke, also serves an important purpose; hitherto Bassanio and Portia have conducted their courtship and love in unsensual terms, almost as if the body was always a quietly acquiescing follower of the mind and spirit, but the manner in which they weather the disagreement about the ring shows that their love is appropriate to the world as well as to Belmont, the 'beautiful mountain' of a fairy-tale. The wealth of love, although it exists in the free giving of both parties to the contract and is possessed by neither one of them, has yet to be kept safe and guarded: so the blunt, unromantic Gratiano who has been as merrily fooled by Nerissa as Bassanio has been by Portia, finishes the play:

> Well, while I live I'll fear no other thing
> So sore as keeping safe Nerissa's ring.
>
> (v i 306–7)

After the ring episode, we know that Bassanio and Portia will be equally wise. If *The Merchant of Venice* is seen as a play about Shakespeare's ideal of love's wealth, this last Act is a fitting sequel to the discord of the trial scene where love and generosity confront hatred and possessiveness; it suggests the way in which love's wealth may be enjoyed continually.

The central theme of love's wealth is amplified in many other details which may seem irrelevant on casual inquiry. So Jessica's story has its contribution; she escapes with Lorenzo from behind the locked doors of Shylock's house, squanders the Venetian wealth she has stolen in joyful celebration, and then finds peace and happiness with her '*unthrift* love' (v i 16) in the garden of Belmont. If her reckless prodigality is a fault, it is a generous one and an understandable excess after the restriction of her father's precept of

> Fast bind, fast find;
> A proverb never stale in *thrifty* mind.
>
> (II v 54–5)

She has her due place at Belmont. And Launcelot Gobbo earns his place there by joining Bassanio's household; Shylock may have good reason for calling him an '*unthrifty* knave' (I iii 177) but we also recognize Launcelot's good sense in counting it a fine fortune

> To leave a *rich* Jew's service, to become
> The follower of so *poor* a gentleman.
>
> (II ii 156–7)

The ideal of love's wealth which relates and contrasts Shylock and Antonio, and Shylock and Portia and Bassanio, also informs the contrasts and relationships between the subsidiary narrative plots; in the final scene the easily responsive love of Jessica and Lorenzo, the bolder love of Gratiano and Nerissa, and Launcelot's unseeing pleasure in his master's good fortune, all contribute to the judgement on life which is implicit in the play as a whole.

The reservations which must be made before Jessica, Gratiano, and Launcelot fit into the general pattern illustrate an important quality of the play. Shakespeare has not simply contrived a contrast of black and white, a measured interplay of abstract figures with every detail fitting neatly into a predetermined pattern; the lovers are not all paragons and Shylock's cry for revenge is not without a 'kind of wild justice'. Judged against Shakespeare's ideal of love's wealth we cannot doubt on which side our sympathies should rest, but such final harmony is only established after we have judged, as in life, between mixed motives and imperfect responses. Even when the central theme has been recognized, *The Merchant of Venice* is not an 'easy' play; it presents an action to which we must respond as to a golden ideal, and also as to a human action.

We have already noticed Shakespeare's achievement of this double purpose in dialogue; for example, when Portia gives herself to Bassanio Shakespeare has not provided a well-rounded expression of generosity in love for her to utter; her speech also embodies modesty, eagerness, and a gathering confidence, feelings that in a human context must attend such generosity. Action and dialogue are allied to the same end; so Shakespeare presented Bassanio's ill-judged attempt to justify his venture in commercial terms and followed that by his confused description of Portia's wealth, at first formal, then quickening, glowing, almost boasting, and, finally, blindly confident. Such technique does not simply present a theoretical ideal of love's adventurer, but a human being, fearful and eager, inspired and embarrassed as he realizes the possibilities of love's wealth. In human terms his is a difficult role, for he must feel the confusion of one who asks:

> . . . how do I hold thee by thy *granting*?
> And for that *riches* where is my deserving?
>   (Sonnet LXXXVII)

For the role of Bassanio the 'humanizing' of action and dialogue has been so thorough that its ideal implications are in some danger of being obscured. Some critics have discounted the embarrassment of love's largess and, because of his round-about approach to Antonio, have called Bassanio a heartless 'fortune-hunter' – and in doing so they have failed to see the balance and judgement of the play as a whole.

Shylock is in greatest danger of causing such misinterpretation. This is truly surprising, for in order to bring generosity and possessiveness into intense conflict Shakespeare has made him perpetrate the outrageous deeds of some fantastic villain whom we might expect to see punished without compunction. Moreover Shylock is a Jew and therefore, for an Elizabethan audience, one of an exotic, fabulous race to whom cunning, malice, and cruelty were natural satisfactions; Jews lived obscurely in Shakespeare's London, but in literature and popular imagination they were monstrous bogeys from strange, far-off places and times, fit only to be reviled or mocked.[4] Shakespeare exploited both Shylock's irrational, or devilish, motivation and the outrage of his action, but he has presented him in such a way that an audience can find itself implicated in his inhuman demands. Shakespeare seems to have done everything in his power to encourage this reaction. Our revulsion from Shylock's hatred and cruelty is mitigated by the way in which his opponents goad and taunt him; we might suppose that he was driven to excessive hatred only through their persecution. Shakespeare also arranged that he should voice his grievances and plead his case in the play's most obviously lively and impassioned dialogue. This treatment is so successful that when Shylock tries to justify his murderous purpose, some critics have believed that he is making a grand, though tortured, plea for human tolerance. But to go to such lengths of sympathy for Shylock is to neglect the contrasts and comparisons implicit in the play as a whole; we must judge his actions against a purposefully contrasted generosity in love as portrayed by Antonio, Portia, Bassanio, and others. Indeed we may guess that it was in order to make this contrast lively and poignant that Shakespeare has laboured to implicate us in Shylock's hatred, frustration, and pain.

The outcome of the comparison cannot be long in question for judged by Shakespeare's ideal of love's wealth as expressed here and in other comedies, the sonnets and *Romeo and Juliet*, we cannot doubt that Shylock must be condemned. However lively Shylock's dialogue may be, however plausibly and passionately he presents his case, however cruelly the lovers treat him, he must still be defeated, because he is an enemy to love's wealth and its free, joyful, and continual giving; in opposition to this he has 'contrived' against the very life (IV i 360) of Antonio, the 'fool that lent out money gratis'.

But this judgement cannot be made lightly; the mirror that Shakespeare held up to nature was unsparing in its truth, and, by presenting his ideal in human terms, he has shown that those who oppose the fortunes of lovers are apt to get more than justice as punishment at their hands. It is Shylock's fate to bring out the worst in those he tries to harm: the 'good Antonio' shows unfeeling contempt towards him, the light-hearted Salerio and Solanio become wantonly malicious when they meet him, and Portia, once she has turned the trial against him, wounds him still further with sarcastic humour. The trial scene shows that the pursuit of love's wealth does not necessarily bring with it a universal charity, a love which reaches even to one's enemies. The balance is fairly kept, for Antonio and the Duke magnanimously spare Shylock's life and this is thrown into relief by the irresponsible malice of Gratiano.

Shakespeare does not enforce a moral in this play – his judgement is implicit only – but as the action ends in laughter and affection at Belmont we know that each couple, in their own way, have found love's wealth. We know too that their happiness is not all that we would wish; as they make free with Shylock's commercial wealth, we remember that they lacked the full measure of charity towards one who, through his hatred and possessiveness, had got his choice of that which he deserved. *The Merchant of Venice* presents in human and dramatic terms Shakespeare's ideal of love's wealth, its abundant and sometimes embarrassing riches; it shows how this wealth is gained and possessed by giving freely and joyfully; it shows also how destructive the opposing possessiveness can become, and how it can cause those who traffic in love to fight blindly for their existence.

Because such judgements are not made explicit in the play, we, as an audience in the theatre, may never become consciously aware of them; we would almost certainly fail in our response if, during performance, our whole attention was given to recognizing and elucidating such judgements. But, consciously or unconsciously, they were in Shakespeare's mind as he wrote the play and helped to control its shape, its contrasts, relationships and final resolution, and to direct and colour the detail of its dialogue; and it therefore follows that as we respond to the action and dialogue on the stage, as we follow with spontaneous interest and delight, these judgements will, consciously or unconsciously, impress themselves on our minds; they are the pattern of the dance that we are appreciating and in which, imaginatively, we participate. To understand that dance, to hold it more fully in our memory, we must also learn to appreciate its pattern; to understand the full beauty and truth of Shakespeare's comedy we must become conscious of the ideals and implicit judgements that inform it.

SOURCE: *Shakespeare and his Comedies* (1962).

NOTES

1. The following section uses and develops some ideas which I first published in my Arden edition of *The Merchant of Venice* (1955).
2. Halliwell pointed this out in his edition of 1856.
3. G. Whitney, *Emblems* (1586) C2. See *Merchant of Venice*, III ii 242–4, and the Arden edition, p. lv, for further examples.
4. Cf C. J. Sisson, in *Essays and Studies* XXIII (1938) 38–51, and J. L. Cardozo, *The Contemporary Jew in the Elizabethan Drama* (Amsterdam, 1925). It has been argued that Shylock offered his loan in genuine friendship, but Shakespeare has gone out of his way to inform us that, before Jessica eloped and before he had news of Antonio's losses, Shylock had hoped to take 'Antonio's flesh' (III ii 289); see also I iii 48.

C. L. Barber

THE MERCHANTS AND THE JEW
OF VENICE (1959)

The Merchant of Venice, as its title indicates, exhibits the bene-
ficence of civilized wealth, the something-for-nothing which
wealth gives to those who use it graciously to live together in a
humanly knit group. It also deals, in the role of Shylock, with
anxieties about money, and its power to set men at odds. Our
econometric age makes us think of wealth chiefly as a practical
matter, an abstract concern of work, not a tangible joy for
festivity. But for the new commercial civilizations of the Renaissance, wealth glowed in luminous metal, shone in silks, per-
fumed the air in spices. Robert Wilson, already in the late
eighties, wrote a pageant play in the manner of the moralities,
Three Lords and Three Ladies of London, in which instead of
Virtues, London's Pomp and London's Wealth walked gor-
geously and smugly about the stage.[1] Despite the terrible suffer-
ings some sections of society were experiencing, the 1590's were
a period when London was becoming conscious of itself as
wealthy and cultivated, so that it could consider great commercial
Venice as a prototype. And yet there were at the same time traditional suspicions of the profit motive and newly urgent anxieties
about the power of money to disrupt human relations.[2] Robert
Wilson also wrote, early in the eighties, a play called *The Three
Ladies of London*, where instead of London's Wealth and Pomp
we have Lady Lucar and the attitude towards her which her
name implies. It was in expressing and so coping with these
anxieties about money that Shakespeare developed in Shylock a
comic antagonist far more important than any such figure had
been in his earlier comedies. His play is still centered in the cele-
brants rather than the intruder, but Shylock's part is so fascinating
that already in 1598 the comedy was entered in the stationers'

register as 'a book of the Merchant of Venice, or otherwise called the Jew of Venice'. Shylock's name has become a byword because of the superb way that he embodies the evil side of the power of money, its ridiculous and pernicious consequences in anxiety and destructiveness. In creating him and setting him over against Antonio, Bassanio, Portia, and the rest, Shakespeare was making distinctions about the use of riches, not statically, of course, but dynamically, as distinctions are made when a social group sorts people out, or when an organized social ritual does so. Shylock is the opposite of what the Venetians are; but at the same time he is an embodied irony, troublingly like them. So his role is like that of the scapegoat in many of the primitive rituals which Frazer has made familiar, a figure in whom the evils potential in a social organization are embodied, recognized and enjoyed during a period of licence, and then in due course abused, ridiculed and expelled.

The large role of the antagonist in *The Merchant of Venice* complicates the movement through release to clarification: instead of the single outgoing of *A Midsummer Night's Dream*, there are two phases. Initially there is a rapid, festive movement by which gay youth gets something for nothing, Lorenzo going masquing to win a Jessica gilded with ducats, and Bassanio sailing off like Jason to win the golden fleece in Belmont. But all this is done against a background of anxiety. We soon forget all about Egeus' threat in *A Midsummer Night's Dream*, but we are kept aware of Shylock's malice by a series of interposed scenes, and no sooner is the joyous triumph accomplished at Belmont than Shylock's malice is set loose. It is only after the threat he poses has been met that the redemption of the prodigal can be completed by a return to Belmont.

The key question in evaluating the play is how this threat is met, whether the baffling of Shylock is meaningful or simply melodramatic. Certainly the plot, considered in outline, seems merely a prodigal's dream coming true: to have a rich friend who will set you up with one more loan so that you can marry a woman both beautiful and rich, girlishly yielding, and masterful; and on top of that to get rid of the obligation of the loan because the old money bags from whom your friend got the money is proved to be so villainous that he does not deserve to be paid back! If one adds humanitarian and democratic indignation at anti-semitism, it is hard to see, from a distance, what there can be to say for the play: Shylock seems to be made a scapegoat in the crudest, most dishonest way. One can apologize for the plot, as Middleton Murry and Granville-Barker do, by observing that it is based on a fairy-story sort of tale, and that Shakespeare's method was not to change implausible story material, but to invent characters and motives which would make it acceptable and credible, moment by moment, on the stage.[3] But it is inadequate to praise the play for delightful and poetic incoherence. Nor does it seem adequate to say, as E. E. Stoll does, that things just do go this way in comedy, where old rich men are always baffled by young and handsome lovers, lenders by borrowers.[4] Stoll is certainly right, but the question is whether Shakespeare has done something more than merely appeal to the feelings any crowd has in a theatre in favor of prodigal young lovers and against old misers. As I see it, he has expressed important things about the relations of love and hate to wealth. When he kept to old tales, he not only made plausible protagonists for them but also, at any rate when his luck held, he brought up into a social focus deep symbolic meanings. Shylock is an ogre, as Middleton Murry said, but he is the ogre of money power. The old tale of the pound of flesh involved taking literally the proverbial metaphors about money-lenders 'taking it out of the hide' of their victims, eating them up. Shakespeare keeps the unrealistic literal business, knife-sharpening and all; we accept it, because he makes it express real human attitudes:

> If I can catch him once upon the hip,
> I will feed fat the ancient grudge I bear him.*
>
> (I iii 47–8)

* It is striking that, along with the imagery of the money-lender feeding on his victims, there is the complementary prohibition Shylock mentions against eating with Christians; Shakespeare brings alive a primitive anxiety about feasting *with* people who might feast *on* you. And when Shylock violates his own taboo ('But yet I'll go in hate, to feed upon / The prodigal Christian' (II v 14–15)) it is he who is caught upon the hip!

So too with the fairy-story caskets at Belmont: Shakespeare makes Bassanio's prodigal fortune meaningful as an expression of the triumph of human, social relations over the relations kept track of by accounting. The whole play dramatizes the conflict between the mechanisms of wealth and the masterful, social use of it. The happy ending, which abstractly considered as an event is hard to credit, and the treatment of Shylock, which abstractly considered as justice is hard to justify, *work* as we actually watch or read the play because these events express relief and triumph in the achievement of a distinction.

To see how this distinction is developed, we need to attend to the tangibles of imaginative design which are neglected in talking about plot. So, in the two first scenes, it is the seemingly incidental, random talk that establishes the gracious, opulent world of the Venetian gentlemen and of the 'lady richly left' at Belmont, and so motivates Bassanio's later success. Wealth in this world is something profoundly social, and it is relished without a trace of shame when Salerio and Salanio open the play by telling Antonio how rich he is:

> Your mind is tossing on the ocean;
> There where your argosies with portly sail –
> Like signiors and rich burghers on the flood,
> Or, as it were, the pageants of the sea –
> Do overpeer the petty traffickers,
> That curtsy to them, do them reverence,
> As they fly by them with their woven wings.
>
> (I i 8–14)

Professor Venezky points out that Elizabethan auditors would have thought not only of the famous Venetian water ceremonies but also of 'colorfully decorated pageant barges' on the Thames or of 'pageant devices of huge ships which were drawn about in street shows'.[5] What is crucial is the ceremonial, social feeling for wealth. Salerio and Salanio do Antonio reverence just as the petty traffickers of the harbour salute his ships, giving way to leave him 'with better company' when Bassanio and Gratiano arrive. He stands at ease, courteous, relaxed, melancholy (but not about his fortunes, which are too large for worry), while around him

moves a shifting but close-knit group who 'converse and waste
the time together' (III iv 12), make merry, speak 'an infinite deal
of nothing' (I i 114), propose good times: 'Good signiors, both,
when shall we laugh? say, when?' (I i 66). When Bassanio is
finally alone with the royal merchant, he opens his mind with

> To you, Antonio,
> I owe the most, in money and in love.
>
> (I i 130–1)

Mark Van Doren, in his excellent chapter on this play, notes how
these lines summarize the gentleman's world where 'there is no
incompatibility between money and love'.[6] So too, one can add,
in this community there is no conflict between enjoying Portia's
beauty and her wealth: 'her sunny locks / Hang on her temples
like a golden fleece'. When, a moment later, we see Portia mock-
ing her suitors, the world suggested is, again, one where standards are urbanely and humanly social: the sad disposition of the
county Palatine is rebuked because (unlike Antonio's) it is
'unmannerly'. Yet already in the first scene, though Shylock is
not in question yet, the anxiety that dogs wealth is suggested.
Salerio's mind moves from attending church – from safety, comfort and solidarity – through the playful association of the 'holy
edifice of stone' with 'dangerous rocks', to the thought that the
sociable luxuries of wealth are vulnerable to impersonal forces:

> rocks,
> Which, touching but my gentle vessel's side,
> Would scatter all her spices on the stream,
> Enrobe the roaring waters with my silks. . . .
>
> (I i 31–4)

The destruction of what is cherished, of the civic and personal,
by ruthless impersonal forces is sensuously immediate in the
wild waste of shining silk on turbulent water, one of the magic,
summary lines of the play. Earlier there is a tender, solicitous
suggestion that the vessel is the more vulnerable because it is
'gentle' – as later Antonio is gentle and vulnerable when his
ships encounter 'the dreadful touch/ Of merchant-marring rocks'
(III ii 270–1) and his side is menaced by a 'stony adversary' (IV i 4).

When Shylock comes on in the third scene, the easy, confident flow of colourful talk and people is checked by a solitary figure and an unyielding speech:

Shylock. Three thousand ducats — well.
Bassanio. Ay, sir, for three months.
Shylock. For three months — well.
Bassanio. For the which, as I told you, Antonio shall be bound.
Shylock. Antonio shall become bound — well.
Bassanio. May you stead me? Will you pleasure me? Shall I know your answer?
Shylock. Three thousand ducats for three months, and Antonio bound.

(I iii 1–10)

We can construe Shylock's hesitation as playing for time while he forms his plan. But more fundamentally, his deliberation expresses the impersonal logic, the mechanism, involved in the control of money. Those *well*'s are wonderful in the way they bring bland Bassanio up short. Bassanio assumes that social gestures can brush aside such consideration:

Shylock. Antonio is a good man.
Bassanio. Have you heard any imputation to the contrary?
Shylock. Ho, no, no, no, no! My meaning in saying he is a good man, is to have you understand me that he is sufficient.

(I iii 12–17)

The laugh is on Bassanio as Shylock drives his hard financial meaning of 'good man' right through the center of Bassanio's softer social meaning. The Jew goes on to calculate and count. He connects the hard facts of money with the rocky sea hazards of which we have so far been only picturesquely aware: 'ships are but boards'; and he betrays his own unwillingness to take the risks proper to commerce: 'and other ventures he hath, squand'red abroad'.

> . . . I think I may take his bond.
Bassanio. Be assur'd you may.

Shylock. I will be assur'd I may; and, that I may be assured,
    I will bethink me.

(I iii 28–31)

The Jew in this encounter expresses just the things about money
which are likely to be forgotten by those who have it, or presume
they have it, as part of a social station. He stands for what we
mean when we say that 'money is money'. So Shylock makes an
ironic comment – and *is* a comment, by virtue of his whole tone
and bearing – on the folly in Bassanio which leads him to confuse
those two meanings of 'good man', to ask Shylock to dine, to use
in this business context such social phrases as 'Will you *pleasure*
me?' When Antonio joins them, Shylock (after a soliloquy in
which his plain hatred has glittered) becomes a pretender to
fellowship, with an equivocating mask:

Shylock.   This is kind I offer.
Bassanio. This were kindness.
Shylock.   This kindness will I show.

(I iii 143–4)

We are of course in no doubt as to how to take the word 'kindness' when Shylock proposes 'in a merry sport' that the penalty
be a pound of Antonio's flesh.

In the next two Acts, Shylock and the accounting mechanism
which he embodies are crudely baffled in Venice and rhapsodi-
cally transcended in Belmont. The solidarity of the Venetians
includes the clown, in whose part Shakespeare can use conventional blacks and whites about Jews and misers without asking
us to take them too seriously:

To be ruled by my conscience, I should stay with the Jew my
master, who (God bless the mark) is a kind of devil. . . . My
master's a very Jew.

(II ii 24–5, III)

Even the street urchins can mock Shylock after the passion which
'the dog Jew did utter in the streets':

      Why, all the boys in Venice follow him,
      Crying his stones, his daughter, and his ducats.

(II viii 23–4)

But the accounting mechanism which has been left behind by Bassanio and Portia has gone on working, back at Venice, to put Antonio at Shylock's mercy, and the anxiety it causes has to be mastered before the marriage can be consummated,

> For never shall you lie by Portia's side
> With an unquiet soul.
>
> (III ii 305–6)

Historical changes in stock attitudes have made difficulties about Shylock's role as a butt, not so much in the theatre, where it works perfectly if producers only let it, but in criticism, where winds of doctrine blow sentiments and abstractions about. The Elizabethans almost never saw Jews except on the stage, where Marlowe's Barabas was familiar. They did see *one*, on the scaffold, when Elizabeth's unfortunate physician suffered for trumped-up charges of a poisoning plot. The popular attitude was that to take interest for money was to be a loan shark – though limited interest was in fact allowed by law. An aristocrat who like Lord Bassanio ran out of money commanded sympathy no longer felt in a middle-class world. Most important of all, suffering was not an absolute evil in an era when men sometimes embraced it deliberately, accepted it as inevitable, and could watch it with equanimity. Humanitarianism has made it necessary for us to be much more thoroughly insulated from the human reality of people if we are to laugh at their discomfiture or relish their suffering. During the romantic period, and sometimes more recently, the play was presented as a tragi-comedy, and actors vied with one another in making Shylock a figure of pathos. I remember a very moving scene, a stock feature of romantic productions, in which George Arliss came home after Bassanio's party, lonely and tired and old, to knock in vain at the door of the house left empty by Jessica. How completely unhistorical the romantic treatment was, E. E. Stoll demonstrated overwhelmingly in his essay on Shylock in 1911, both by wide-ranging comparisons of Shylock's role with others in Renaissance drama and by analysis of the *optique du théâtre*.[7]

To insert a humanitarian scene about Shylock's pathetic homecoming prevents the development of the scornful amusement

with which Shakespeare's text presents the miser's reaction in
Solanio's narrative:

> I never heard a passion so confus'd,
> So strange, outrageous, and so variable,
> As the dog Jew did utter in the streets.
> 'My daughter! O my ducats! O my daughter!
> Fled with a Christian! O my Christian ducats! ...'
>
> (II viii 12–16)

Marlowe had done such a moment already with Barabas hugging
in turn his money bags and his daughter – whom later the Jew
of Malta poisons with a pot of porridge, as the Jew of Venice later
wishes that Jessica 'were hears'd at my foot, and the ducats in her
coffin' (III i 93–4). But the humanitarian way of playing the part
develops suggestions that are *also* in Shakespeare's text:

> I am bid forth to supper, Jessica.
> There are my keys. But wherefore should I go?
> I am not bid for love; they flatter me.
> But yet I'll go in hate, to feed upon
> The prodigal Christian.
>
> (II v 11–15)

Shakespeare's marvelous creative sympathy takes the stock role
of Jewish usurer and villain and conveys how it would feel to be
a man living inside it. But this does not mean that he shrinks from
confronting the evil and the absurdity that go with the role; for
the Elizabethan age, to understand did not necessarily mean to
forgive. Shylock can be a thorough villain and yet be allowed to
express what sort of treatment has made him what he is:

> You call me misbeliever, cutthroat dog,
> And spet upon my Jewish gaberdine,
> And all for use of that which is mine own.
> (I iii 112–14)

We can understand his degradation and even blame the Antonios
of Venice for it; yet it remains degradation:

> Thou call'dst me dog before thou hadst a cause;
> But, since I am a dog, beware my fangs.
> (III iii 6–7)

Shylock repeatedly states, as he does here, that he is only finishing what the Venetians started. He can be a drastic ironist, because he carries to extremes what is present, whether acknowledged or not, in their silken world. He insists that money is money – and they cannot do without money either. So too with the rights of property. The power to give freely, which absolute property confers and Antonio and Portia so splendidly exhibit, is also a power to refuse, as Shylock so logically refuses:

> You have among you many a purchas'd slave,
> Which, like your asses and your dogs and mules,
> You use in abject and in slavish parts,
> Because you bought them. Shall I say to you,
> 'Let them be free, marry them to your heirs! ...'
> > You will answer,
> 'The slaves are ours.' So do I answer you.
> The pound of flesh which I demand of him
> Is dearly bought, 'tis mine, and I will have it.
>
> > (IV i 90–100)

At this point in the trial scene, Shylock seems a juggernaut that nothing can stop, armed as he is against a pillar of society by the principles of society itself: 'If you deny me, fie upon your law! ... I stand for judgement. Answer. Shall I have it?' Nobody does answer him here, directly; instead there is an interruption for Portia's entrance. To answer him is the function of the whole dramatic action, which is making a distinction that could not be made in direct, logical argument.

Let us follow this dramatic action from its comic side. Shylock is comic, so far as he is so, because he exhibits what should be human, degraded into mechanism. The reduction of life to mechanism goes with the miser's wary calculation, with the locking up, with the preoccupation with 'that which is mine own'. Antonio tells Bassanio that

> My purse, my person, my extremest means
> Lie all unlock'd to your occasions.
>
> > (I i 138–9)

How open! Antonio has to live inside some sort of rich man's melancholy, but at least he communicates with the world through outgoing Bassanio (and, one can add, through the commerce which takes his fortunes out to sea). Shylock, by contrast, who breeds barren metal, wants to keep 'the vile squeeling of the wry-neck'd fife' out of his house, and speaks later, in a curiously revealing, seemingly random illustration, of men who 'when the bagpipe sings i'th'nose, / Cannot contain their urine' (IV i 49–50). Not only is he closed up tight inside himself, but after the first two scenes, we are scarcely allowed by his lines to feel with him. And we never encounter him alone; he regularly comes on to join a group whose talk has established an outside point of view towards him. This perspective on him does not exclude a potential pathos. There is always potential pathos, behind, when drama makes fun of isolating, anti-social qualities. Indeed, the process of *making fun of* a person often works by exhibiting pretensions to humanity so as to show that they are inhuman, mechanical, not validly appropriate for sympathy. With a comic villain such as Shylock, the effect is mixed in various degrees between our responding to the mechanism as menacing and laughing at it as ridiculous.

So in the great scene in which Solanio and Salerio taunt Shylock, the potentiality of pathos produces effects which vary between comedy and menace:

> *Shylock.* You knew, none so well, none so well as you, of my
> daughter's flight.
> *Salerio.* That's certain. I, for my part, knew the tailor that
> made the wings she flew withal.
>
> (III i 27–30)

Shylock's characteristic repetitions, and the way he has of moving ahead through similar, short phrases, as though even with language he was going to use only what was his own, can give an effect of concentration and power, or again, an impression of a comically limited, isolated figure. In the great speech of self-justification to which he is goaded by the two bland little gentlemen, the iteration conveys the energy of anguish:

– and what's his reason? I am a Jew. Hath not a Jew eyes? Hath not a Jew hands, organs, dimensions, senses, affections, passions? fed with the same food, hurt with the same weapons, subject to

the same diseases, healed by the same means, warmed and cooled
by the same winter and summer as a Christian is? If you prick us,
do we not bleed? If you tickle us, do we not laugh? If you poison
us, do we not die? And if you wrong us, shall we not revenge?
If we are like you in the rest, we will resemble you in that.

(III i 60–71)

Certainly no actor would deliver this speech without an effort at
pathos; but it is a pathos which, as the speech moves, converts
to menace. And the pathos is qualified, limited, in a way which is
badly falsified by humanitarian renderings that open all the stops
at 'Hath not a Jew hands, etc. . . .' For Shylock thinks to claim
only a *part* of humanness, the lower part, physical and passional.
The similar self-pitying enumeration which Richard II makes
differs significantly in going from 'live with bread like you' to
social responses and needs, 'Taste grief, / Need friends' (*Richard
II*, III ii 175–6). The passions in Shylock's speech are conceived
as reflexes; the parallel clauses draw them all towards the level of
'tickle . . . laugh'. The same assumption, that the passions and
social responses are mechanisms on a par with a nervous tic,
appears in the court scene when Shylock defends his right to
follow his 'humor' in taking Antonio's flesh:

> As there is no firm reason to be rend'red
> Why he cannot abide a gaping pig,
> Why he a harmless necessary cat,
> Why he a woollen bagpipe – but of force
> Must yield to such inevitable shame
> As to offend himself, being offended;
> So can I give no reason, nor I will not,
> More than a lodg'd hate and a certain loathing
> I bear unto Antonio. . . .

(IV i 52–61)

The most succinct expression of this assumption about man is
Shylock's response to Bassanio's incredulous question:

> *Bassanio.* Do all men kill the things they do not love?
> *Shylock.* Hates any man the thing he would not kill?

(IV i 66–7)

There is no room in this view for mercy to come in between

'wrong us' and 'shall we not revenge?' As Shylock insists, there
is Christian example for him: the irony is strong. But the mechanism of stimulus and response is only a part of the truth. The
reductive tendency of Shylock's metaphors, savagely humorous
in Iago's fashion, goes with this speaking only the lower part of
the truth. He is not cynical in Iago's aggressive way, because as
an alien he simply doesn't participate in many of the social ideals
which Iago is concerned to discredit in self-justification. But the
two villains have the same frightening, ironical power from
moral simplification.

In the trial scene, the turning point is appropriately the
moment when Shylock gets caught in the mechanism he relies on
so ruthlessly. He narrows everything down to his roll of parch-
ment and his knife: 'Till thou canst rail the seal from off my
bond . . .' (IV i 139). But two can play at this game:

> as thou urgest justice, be assur'd
> Thou shalt have justice more than thou desir'st.
>
> (IV i 315–16)

Shylock's bafflement is comic, as well as dramatic, in the degree
that we now see through the threat that he has presented, recognizing it to have been, in a degree, unreal. For it is unreal to
depend so heavily on legal form, on fixed verbal definition, on
the mere machinery by which human relations are controlled.
Once Portia's legalism has broken through his legalism, he can
only go on the way he started, weakly asking 'Is that the law?'
while Gratiano's jeers underscore the comic symmetry:

> A Daniel still say I, a second Daniel!
> I thank thee, Jew, for teaching me that word.
>
> (IV i 340–1)

The turning of the tables is not, of course, simply comic,
except for the bold, wild and 'skipping spirit' of Gratiano. The
trial scene is a species of drama that uses comic movement in slow
motion, with an investment of feeling such that the resolution is
in elation and relief colored by amusement, rather than in the
evacuation of laughter. Malvolio, a less threatening kill-joy intruder, is simply laughed out of court, but Shylock must be ruled

out, with jeering only on the side lines. The threat Shylock offers is, after all, drastic, for legal instruments, contract, property are fundamental. Comic dramatists often choose to set them hilariously at naught; but Shakespeare is, as usual, scrupulously responsible to the principles of social order (however factitious his 'law' may be literally). So he produced a scene which exhibits the limitations of legalism. It works by a dialectic that carries to a more general level what might be comic reduction to absurdity. To be tolerant, because we are all fools; to forgive, because we are all guilty – the two gestures of the spirit are allied, as Erasmus noted in praising the sublime folly of following Christ. Shylock says before the trial 'I'll not be made a soft and dull-ey'd fool' by 'Christian intercessors' (III iii 14–15). Now when he is asked how he can hope for mercy if he renders none, he answers: 'What judgement shall I dread, doing no wrong?' As the man who will not acknowledge his own share of folly ends by being more foolish than anyone else, so Shylock, who will not acknowledge a share of guilt, ends by being more guilty – and more foolish, to judge by results. An argument between Old Testament legalism and New Testament reliance on grace develops as the scene goes forward. (Shylock's references to Daniel in this scene, and his constant use of Old Testament names and allusions, contribute to the contrast.) Portia does not deny the bond – nor the law behind it; instead she makes such a plea as St Paul made to his compatriots:

> Therefore, Jew,
> Though justice be thy plea, consider this –
> That, in the course of justice, none of us
> Should see salvation. We do pray for mercy,
> And that same prayer doth teach us all to render
> The deeds of mercy.
>
> (IV i 197–202)

Mercy becomes the word that gathers up everything we have seen the Venetians enjoying in their reliance on community. What is on one side an issue of principles is on the other a matter of social solidarity: Shylock is not one of the 'we' Portia refers to, the Christians who say in the Lord's Prayer 'Forgive us our

debts as we forgive our debtors.' All through the play the word
Christian has been repeated, primarily in statements that enforce
the fact that the Jew is outside the easy bonds of community.
Portia's plea for mercy is a sublime version of what in less
intense circumstances, among friends of a single communion, can
be conveyed with a shrug or a wink:

Dost thou hear, Hal? Thou knowest in the state of innocency
Adam fell; and what should poor Jack Falstaff do in the days of
villany?

> (*I Henry IV*, iii iii 185–8)

Falstaff, asking for an amnesty to get started again, relies on his
festive solidarity with Hal. Comedy, in one way or another, is
always asking for amnesty, after showing the moral machinery of
life getting in the way of life. The machinery as such need not be
dismissed – Portia is very emphatic about not doing that. But
social solidarity, resting on the buoyant force of a collective life
that transcends particular mistakes, can set the machinery aside.
Shylock, closed off as he is, clutching his bond and his knife,
cannot trust this force, and so acts only on compulsion:

> *Portia.*   Do you confess the bond?
> *Antonio.* I do.
> *Portia.*   Then must the Jew be merciful.
> *Shylock.* On what compulsion must I? Tell me that.
> *Portia.* The quality of mercy is not strain'd;
>   It droppeth as the gentle rain from heaven
>   Upon the place beneath. It is twice blest –
>   It blesseth him that gives, and him that takes.
>
> (IV i 181–7)

It has been in giving and taking, beyond the compulsion of
accounts, that Portia, Bassanio, Antonio have enjoyed the
something-for-nothing that Portia here summarizes in speaking
of the gentle rain from heaven.

I must add, after all this praise for the way the play makes its
distinction about the use of wealth, that *on reflection*, not when
viewing or reading the play, but when thinking about it, I find
the distinction, as others have, somewhat too easy. While I read
or watch, all is well, for the attitudes of Shylock are appallingly

inhuman, and Shakespeare makes me feel constantly how the Shylock attitude rests on a lack of faith in community and grace. But when one thinks about the Portia–Bassanio group, not in opposition to Shylock but alone (as Shakespeare does not show them), one can be troubled by their being so very very far above money:

> What, no more?
> Pay him six thousand, and deface the bond.
> Double six thousand and then treble that. . . .
> (III ii 298–300)

It would be interesting to see Portia say no, for once, instead of always yes. One can feel a difficulty too with Antonio's bland rhetorical question:

> when did friendship take
> A breed of barren metal of his friend?
> (I iii 134–5)

Elizabethan attitudes about the taking of interest were unrealistic: while Sir Thomas Gresham built up Elizabeth's credit in the money market of Antwerp, and the government regulated interest rates, popular sentiment continued on the level of thinking Antonio's remark reflects. Shakespeare's ideal figures and sentiments are open here to ironies which he does not explore. The clown's role just touches them when he pretends to grumble.

> We were Christians enow before, e'en as many as could well live by one another. This making of Christians will raise the price of hogs.
> (III v 23–6)

. . . Shakespeare could no doubt have gone beyond the naïve economic morality of Elizabethan popular culture, had he had an artistic need. But he did not, because in the antithetical sort of comic form he was using in this play, the ironical function was fulfilled by the heavy contrasts embodied in Shylock.

About Shylock, too, there is a difficulty which grows on reflection, a difficulty which may be felt too in reading or performance. His part fits perfectly into the design of the play, and yet he is so alive that he raises an interest beyond its design. The figure of

Shylock is like some secondary figure in a Rembrandt painting, so charged with implied life that one can forget his surroundings. To look sometimes with absorption at the suffering, raging Jew alone is irresistible. But the more one is aware of what the play's whole design is expressing through Shylock, of the comedy's high seriousness in its concern for the grace of community, the less one wants to lose the play Shakespeare wrote for the sake of one he merely suggested.

SOURCE: Abridged from an essay in *Shakespeare's Festive Comedy* (1959).

NOTES

1. Printed together with *The Three Ladies of London*, in Robert Dodsley, *A Select Collection of Old Plays*, ed. W. C. Hazlitt, 15 vols (1874–6) VI.

2. A very useful background for understanding *The Merchant of Venice* is provided by L. C. Knights, *Drama and Society in the Age of Jonson* (1937) and by the fundamental social history which Mr Knights used as one point of departure, R. H. Tawney's *Religion and the Rise of Capitalism* (New York, 1926).

3. John Middleton Murry, *Shakespeare* (New York, 1936) pp. 154–7; Harley Granville-Barker, *Prefaces to Shakespeare* (Princeton, 1946–7) I 335–6.

4. *Shakespeare Studies* (New York, 1927) pp. 293–5.

5. Alice S. Venezky, *Pageantry on the Elizabethan Stage* (New York, 1951) p. 172.

6. See p. 91 above. J. W.

7. In *Shakespeare Studies*.

Graham Midgley

THE MERCHANT OF VENICE:
A RECONSIDERATION (1960)

THE PROBLEM of *The Merchant of Venice* has always been its unity, and most critical discussions take this as the centre of their argument, asking what is the relative importance of its two plots and how Shakespeare contrives to interweave them into a unity; the two plots being the Shylock plot and what is called the love or romance plot. Is the play, we are asked to decide, primarily a love comedy, as most of Shakespeare's mature comedies are, in which the story of the Jew and his bond is but a necessary cog in a more important machine, or is the play a study of the personality of the Jew, with the love-story merely a useful way of engineering the entry of Antonio into the dreadful bond? Moreover, where does Shakespeare mean our sympathies to lie – with the Jew as an oppressed and persecuted sufferer forced to vengeance by the heartless society which surrounds him, or with the ladies and gentlemen of Venice who so splendidly thwart the machinations of the diabolic Jew? If we insist in analysing the play with these two plots as our central consideration, we find ourselves in trouble. We find Shakespeare working out a remarkably steady alternation of scene between Venice and Belmont and then, as if to cap this alternating structure, giving the whole of Act IV to Venice and the trial scene, and the whole of Act V to Belmont, with Shylock apparently forgotten. Whatever else he might do, Shakespeare does not throw away his fifth Act and, if we are working on the Shylock–lovers pattern, it would appear that the farewell and lasting impression on the audience, which the fifth Act can give, is meant by Shakespeare to be, not the end of Shylock and the misery of his defeat, but the love theme, the happiness of the united lovers and the lyrical beauty of Belmont by moonlight. Shylock is forgotten completely by the lovers beneath the stars, and the main theme is the triumph of love. If this is the truth, then Shylock has been allowed to become far too imposing a figure in the previous four Acts of the play (where he should have been little more than the equivalent of such characters as Don John or Malvolio in the other love comedies), and this fifth Act is a desperate attempt to redress a lost balance. If, on the other hand, we accept Shylock as the central point of interest, the play collapses beautifully but irrelevantly in a finely-written Act given over to a secondary theme. It is possible to show, however, that the construction becomes more meaningful if we accept an entirely different theme and two different points of interest. If we do this, the problem of divided interest between Shylock and the lovers becomes an irrelevant one, or at least relevant in a different way, and the play becomes something far more interesting than a fairy tale with unfortunate deeper intrusions, or a tragic downfall of a Jew, disfigured by lovers' adventures and tedious casket scenes.

Other critics have faced up to the problem, but their solutions are not completely convincing. At the one extreme is the critic who rejects any serious consideration of the play as beside the point, like Granville-Barker to whom the play was a 'fairy tale' and who saw 'no more reality in Shylock's bond and the Lord of Belmont's will than in Jack and the Beanstalk'.[1] Professor Nevill Coghill wishes us to interpret the play as an allegory of 'Justice and Mercy, of the Old Law and the New', with the trial scene as the central point of the debate and the last Act the act of reconciliation, where we find 'Lorenzo and Jessica, Jew and Christian, Old Law and New, united in love; and their talk is of music, Shakespeare's recurrent symbol of harmony'.[2] Some see the theme as one of contrast between seeming and reality or, as Professor C. S. Lewis, between the *values* of Bassanio and Shylock, 'between the crimson and organic wealth in his veins, the medium of nobility and fecundity, and the cold, mineral wealth in Shylock's counting house'.[3] Professor J. W. Lever contrasts love which 'comprehends the generous give and take of emotion, the free spending of nature's bounty, and the increase of progeny through marriage', with usury which, he writes, is the 'negation of friendship and community'.[4] Sir E. K. Chambers, with an attractive simplicity, found a conflict between Love and Hate, Shylock representing Hate and Antonio and Portia embodying Love.[5] Most of these solutions are only partial, most of them failing to explain great parts of the play's subject matter and attitude. All of them are trying to find a synthesis of a wrong opposition.

I would suggest that the two focal points of the play are Shylock and, not the lovers or the romance theme, but Antonio, and that the world of love and marriage is not opposed by Shylock, but rather paralleled by Venetian society as a whole, social, political and economic. The scheme of the play is, if I may reduce it to ratio terms: As Shylock is to Venetian society, so is Antonio to the world of love and marriage. The relationship of these two to these two worlds is the same, the relationship of an outsider. The play is, in effect, a twin study in loneliness. The fact that these two outcasts, these two lonely men, only meet in the cruel circumstances they do, adds an irony and pathos to the play which lift it out of the category of fairy tale or romance. Indeed, seen from any angle, *The Merchant of Venice* is not a very funny play, and we might gain a lot if, for the moment, we ceased to be bullied by its inclusion amongst the Comedies. This thesis has much to offer in our understanding of the play. It reinstates Antonio to a position in the play more commensurate with the care and interest Shakespeare seems to have shown in his creation (and the play is, after all, called *The Merchant of Venice*): it does not force us into having to condemn Shylock if we accept the values of the love world, for it offers us different oppositions and asks us to make different moral judgements, different in kind as well as direction: and finally, it seems to make more impressive sense of the construction of the play, especially of Acts IV and V.

An examination of the characters of Shylock and Antonio as parallel studies is a preliminary task which should throw light on the reconsideration of the play as a whole.

Examinations of Shylock have too often been obscured by a scholarly heap of secondary considerations arising from the fact that he is a Jew. It is surprising how much of the work on *The Merchant of Venice* turns out on inspection to be on the lines of 'The Jew in Elizabethan England', 'The Elizabethan Jew in

Drama', or 'The Jew in Elizabethan Drama'. We are urged, in seeing the play, not to forget that the audience had probably never seen a Jew; we are reminded that this is an Elizabethan play and that Shakespeare could count on a stock response to a Jew figure, shaped by age-old memories of the Hugh of Lincoln and baby-killing kinds; we are advised not to be influenced by our reactions to anti-Semitism in our own day into making a sentimental figure out of Shylock which Shakespeare could never have understood. Comparisons with Marlowe's Jew are made, and the body of the unfortunate Dr Lopez is always exhumed as an important exhibit. To work through this mass of material is to feel at once that the play is being smothered, and when, for example, one is asked to accept as superbly clever hypocrisy a speech of Shylock's which rings with obvious sincerity and feeling, one begins to rebel and return to the play and what the play says. In my opinion it is not of much importance that Shylock is a Jew, and all the 'background work' on Jews and Judaism strikes me as quite irrelevant. The important thing is that he is a Jew in a Gentile society, that all he is and all he holds dear is alien to the society in which he has to live. He is an alien, an outsider, tolerated but never accepted. His being a Jew is not important in itself: what is important is what being a Jew has done to his personality. He is a stranger, proud of his race and its traditions, strict in his religion, sober rather than miserly in his domestic life, and filled with the idea of the sanctity of the family and family loyalty. Around him is the society of Venice, a world of golden youth, richly dressed, accustomed to luxury, to feasting, to masking, of a comparatively easy virtue and of a religious outlook which, though orthodox, hardly strikes one as deep, a society faithful and courteous in its own circle and observing a formal politeness of manner and address, but quite insufferable to those outside its own circle, where Shylock is so obviously placed. By that society Shylock is treated as dirt. Antonio never denies the treatment he has given this proud man:

> Signior Antonio, many a time and oft
> In the Rialto you have rated me
> About my moneys and my usances:
> Still have I borne it with a patient shrug,

> For suffrance is the badge of all our tribe.
> You call me misbeliever, cut-throat dog,
> And spit upon my Jewish gaberdine,
> And all for use of that which is mine own.
>
> (I iii 101)

Antonio's only response is:

> I am as like to call thee so again,
> To spit on thee again, to spurn thee too.
> If thou wilt lend this money, lend it not
> As to thy friends; for when did friendship take
> A breed of barren metal?
>
> (I iii 125)

And all the repressed humiliation and sense of injustice which lies beneath Shylock's proud and patient bearing, bursts out in:

He hath disgraced me and hindered me half a million; laughed at my losses, mocked at my gains, scorned my nation, thwarted my bargains, cooled my friends, heated mine enemies; and what's the reason? I am a Jew. Hath not a Jew eyes? hath not a Jew hands, organs, dimensions, senses, affections, passions? fed with the same food, hurt with the same weapons, subject to the same diseases, healed by the same means, warmed and cooled by the same summer and winter, as a Christian is? If you prick us, do we not bleed? if you tickle us, do we not laugh? if you poison us, do we not die?

(III i 48)

With this side of the man in mind, let us follow him swiftly through the play.

Our first meeting with him is in the arranging of the bond. He is faced with insolent rudeness on the part of those who come in fact to beg a favour, with the peremptory snaps of Bassanio:

Ay sir, for three months. . . .
May you stead me? will you pleasure me? shall I know your answer?
Your answer to that. . . .

(I iii 2)

He is drawn into a discussion on usury, attacked for lending

money on interest, and the only reply to his quite sensible
defence is Antonio's supercilious:

> Mark you this, Bassanio,
> The devil can cite scripture for his purpose,
> An evil soul, producing holy witness,
> Is like a villain with a smiling cheek,
> A goodly apple rotten at the heart.
> O what a goodly outside falsehood hath!
>
> (I iii 93)

Shylock is stirred to remind Antonio, in words already quoted,
of his former cruel behaviour to him, to call attention to the
almost forgotten fact that Antonio *is* begging a favour, but he is
again rejected by Antonio with cold scorn. Can we blame him
if a scheme of revenge forms in his mind?

Later Lorenzo elopes with Jessica, the two of them rejoicing
callously in the tricking and robbing of the Jew. Jessica's elopement, added by Shakespeare to his source, is no mere romantic
addition, but the crucial point in Shylock's development. In this
deed a blow is struck at all that Shylock holds dear, his pride of
race, the sober decency of his household life and the dear sanctity of the family and family bonds. The mixing of ducats with
his daughter in his cries of despair is because his ducats, as his
daughter, are part of his family pride, the only bulwarks against
the general scorn of the society he lives in as he exclaims later
when his estates are ordered to be confiscated:

> Nay, take my life and all; pardon not that:
> You take my house when you do take the prop
> That doth sustain my house; you take my life
> When you do take the means whereby I live.
>
> (IV i 370)

When he first appears in the court his mood is not one of rage
or mad vindictiveness: rather of cold and controlled intent on revenge. He speaks quietly, deliberately and logically, but quite un-
wavering in his intent. Against the calm insults of the Duke and
the more hysterical reviling of Gratiano, he maintains this calm:

> Repair thy wit, good youth, or it will fall
> To cureless ruin.   (IV i 141)

And behind this calm front, the burning sorrow of Jessica's shame is still there:

> The pound of flesh which I demand of him
> Is dearly bought.   (IV i 99)

Dearly bought by Jessica's shame, surely, for which he holds Antonio scapegoat, rather than the miserable 3,000 ducats. There we may leave Shylock for the moment, postponing a fuller discussion of the trial scene until Antonio, the dramatic antagonist of Shylock, is also established as his spiritual companion, adrift like him in a hostile society.

Antonio is in no way rejected externally or consciously by the people he has to live with. He is respected, rich, with easy access to economic, legal and social circles, and Venice is always on his side. His loneliness is within and not without, as Shylock's. Antonio is an outsider because he is an unconscious homosexual in a predominantly, and indeed blatantly, heterosexual society. Against such a statement I am aware that a great amount of scholarly opposition could be mustered, studies of friendship in Renaissance thought and Elizabethan literature, evidence of an extremer vocabulary of endearment between men than could be used nowadays without risk of misunderstanding, studies of Shakespeare's sonnets and the theme of friendship there. All this may be very true, but my first bare formulation stands. The fact which strikes one above all about Antonio is his all-absorbing love of Bassanio, his complete lack of interest in women – in a play where this interest guides the actions of all the other males – and his being left without a mate in a play which is rounded off by a full-scale mating dénouement. Moreover, his relationship with Bassanio has very special facets which need a special interpretation. We first meet Antonio in a state of deep melancholy – not the pretty heigh-ho sadness of Portia which is (purposefully?) to be contrasted with it in the next scene – but a deeper and completely unaffected melancholy:

> In sooth, I know not why I am so sad,
> It wearies me, you say it wearies you;
> But how I caught it, found it, or came by it,
> What stuff 'tis made of, whereof it is born,

> I am to learn;
> And such a want-wit sadness makes of me,
> That I have much ado to know myself.
>
> (I i 1–7)

It is soon established that its cause is not worry over his business affairs, and the first clue comes in the exchange with Solanio:

> *Solanio.* Why then you are in love.
> *Antonio.*   Fie! Fie!   (I i 46)

This is more than a simple contradiction or negative. There is a reproach here either for something being mentioned which ought not to be mentioned – Antonio thinking Solanio refers to his love for Bassanio – or for something being mentioned which Antonio finds repugnant to his nature – thinking Solanio suggests some love-affair with a woman. Whichever it may be, Antonio, a few lines later, perfectly sums up his place in the society in which he moves:

> I hold the world but as the world, Gratiano,
> A stage, where every man must play a part,
> And mine a sad one.
>
> (I i 77–9)

The cause of this sadness which Antonio has refused to acknowledge even to himself is revealed as soon as Antonio and Bassanio are alone together, for Antonio's first words are:

> Well, tell me now what lady is the same
> To whom you swore a secret pilgrimage.
>
> (I i 119)

It was, apparently, Bassanio's first mention of the possibility of his wooing and marriage some time previously, which had cast Antonio into this gloomy sadness. This is not, I think, a forcing of the text, for all the previous writing about Antonio has been to establish that sadness, to stress its apparent causelessness, except in that inexplicably angry 'Fie! Fie!' Now, added to this, comes this sudden rush to the heart of the matter, where Antonio seeks to know more of the thing which has ruined his happiness, and then, knowing, he does the only thing his love can do, sacri-

ficing himself as fully as possible for his beloved. The description
of the parting of these two brings out these motives in Antonio
quite clearly:

> I saw Bassanio and Antonio part,
> Bassanio told him he would make some speed
> Of his return: he answered, 'Do not so,
> Slubber not business for my sake, Bassanio,
> But stay the very riping of the time,
> And for the Jew's bond which he hath of me –
> Let it not enter in your mind of love:
> Be merry, and employ your chiefest thoughts
> To courtship, and such fair ostents of love
> As shall conveniently become you there.'
> And even there (his eye being big with tears),
> Turning his face, he put his hand behind him,
> And with affection wondrous sensible
> He wrung Bassanio's hand, and so they parted.
>
> (II viii 36)

Solanio's reaction is clearly meant to be ours:

> I think he only loves the world for him.

Perhaps that is why, knowing Bassanio was going, Antonio
could say earlier:

> I hold the world but as the world, Gratiano,
> A stage where every man must play a part,
> And mine a sad one.

We are not to see Antonio again until disaster has overtaken him,
his fortune gone and his death at the hands of the Jew for his
friend's sake apparently inevitable. His attitude to that fate and
what he makes of it have been neglected in criticism, which has
concentrated its interest on Shylock and Portia, relegating
Antonio to the rank of another bystander. The first piece of
evidence is the letter which he sends to Bassanio:

Sweet Bassanio, my ships have all miscarried, my creditors
grow cruel, my estate is very low, my bond to the Jew is forfeit,
and (since in paying it, it is impossible that I should live) all
debts are clear'd between you and I, if I might but see you at my

death: notwithstanding, use your pleasure – if your love do not persuade you to come, let not my letter.

(III ii 314)

The last words indicate Antonio's mood. The death is, in a way, welcome, for it is his greatest, if his last, opportunity to show his love, and to escape from the world where his part is a sad one. This is why he never questions Shylock's claim, never fights against the outrage of it. Death he accepts – as long as Bassanio is there:

> These griefs and losses have so bated me
> That I shall hardly spare a pound of flesh
> To-morrow to my bloody creditor.
> Well, gaoler, on – pray God Bassanio come
> To see me pay his debt, and then I care not.

(III iii 32–6)

In the trial scene his attitude is of resignation, and almost of an eagerness for death:

> Let me have judgment, and the Jew his will.

(IV i 83)

> Most heartily I do beseech the court
> To give the judgment.

(IV i 238–9)

and there are two important exchanges with Bassanio, the first when Bassanio tries to encourage Antonio with hope and big words, and Antonio replies in terms which only make sense if they refer to a bigger problem in his life than the immediate legal one:

> I am a tainted wether of the flock,
> Meetest for death – the weakest kind of fruit
> Drops earliest to the ground, and so let me;
> You cannot better be employ'd, Bassanio,
> Than to live still and write mine epitaph.

(IV i 114–18)

What would have been, but for Portia's intervention, his last farewell to Bassanio is a wonderful drawing-together of all the

threads which make up the complex character and motives of
Antonio at this point:

> Give me your hand, Bassanio, fare you well,
> Grieve not that I am fall'n to this for you:
> For herein Fortune shows herself more kind
> Than is her custom: it is still her use
> To let the wretched man outlive his wealth,
> To view with hollow eye and wrinkled brow
> An age of poverty: from which ling'ring penance
> Of such misery doth she cut me off.
> Commend me to your honourable wife,
> Tell her the process of Antonio's end,
> Say how I lov'd you, speak me fair in death:
> And when the tale is told, bid her be judge
> Whether Bassanio had not once a love:
> Repent but you that you shall lose your friend
> And he repents not that he pays your debt.
> For if the Jew do cut but deep enough,
> I'll pay it instantly with all my heart.
>
> (IV i 261–77)

Death is welcome in that it cuts short what would be a wretched
existence; it is also welcome as a final and supreme expression
of love which Antonio can leave with Bassanio, which he
impresses on him and cannot help contrasting with that other
love which is always at the back of his mind when he speaks to
Bassanio, the love for Portia. Bassanio's reply could not be
nearer to what Antonio longs to hear:

> Antonio, I am married to a wife
> Which is as dear to me as life itself,
> But life itself, my wife, and all the world,
> Are not with me esteem'd above thy life.
> I would lose all, ay sacrifice them all
> Here to this devil, to deliver you.
>
> (IV i 278–83)

But we know that Bassanio speaks for the nonce. Portia speaks
the real truth of the world which is to conquer:

> Your wife would give you little thanks for that
> If she were by to hear you make the offer.

And so the trial scene moves to its climax and resolution, and from now on Antonio hardly speaks, with the result that, reading the play, we tend to forget him – a mistake which leads to a maimed interpretation of the fifth Act.

What now remains to be done is to look again at the play as a whole, accepting these two interpretations of Shylock and Antonio, to see how it achieves a unity and meaning denied it by the Shylock–romance antithesis.

The parallel between Shylock and Antonio is the framework of the play. Both are not fully at home in the society in which they are forced to live, for different reasons. Shylock is accepted only because of his wealth and economic usefulness: otherwise in all the things which a man needs for happiness with his fellows, friendship, respect, social intercourse, sympathy, co-operation, he is denied and spurned. Antonio has all these things, but the thing he most desires is denied him, again by the society around him, not denied to him as violently as to Shylock, because Antonio's lack is secret and personal, and those around him neither know nor understand that in fact he lacks anything. Yet for all these differences, there is the basic kinship in the Jew and the Merchant, the kinship of loneliness.

Each, then, has to make a gesture against being overwhelmed, and each has to make it through the channel open to him or dear to him. The Jew makes his offer of friendship, he tries to escape from his isolation by means of the only common link between himself and his enemies, his wealth. Antonio makes his gesture of sacrifice in entering upon the bond, through the only thing which really means anything to him, his love.

Each makes his gesture and each is defeated, for as the people around Shylock violently and cruelly reply to his gesture with renewed attacks on his home and beliefs, finally overcoming him completely through the congregated social and legal powers of that society, at the same time they condemn Antonio to the loneliness his death would have ended. The violence of the defeat differs, of course, as the very positions of Shylock and Antonio differ. Shylock's fate is more violent and cruel because he outwardly opposes a whole society and outrages its pride and its code: Antonio's fate is private and quiet, as his opposition and loneliness are private and quiet. But their defeat is nevertheless a common one, and each is left holding an empty reward, each is left with cold comfort. Shylock is stripped of half of his wealth, the one thing which gave him standing in Venice, and is given in return the formal badge of entrée, to become a member of the society in which he has always been an outcast – he is to be made a Christian. The hollowness of the gesture and its real meaninglessness are obvious in the words of the play:

> *Duke.*　　　　　　　　Get thee gone, but do it.
> *Gratiano.* In christ'ning shalt thou have two godfathers, –
> 　　Had I been judge, thou shouldst have had ten more
> 　　To bring thee to the gallows, not to the font.
>
> 　　　　　　　　　　　　　　(IV i 393–6)

Antonio is rewarded with the return of his ships and money, and his receiving of this news is marked by such a flat unexcitement that we realise he speaks the whole truth and nothing more nor less, when he tells Portia:

> 　　Sweet lady, you have given me life and living;
> 　　For here I read for certain that my ships
> 　　Are safely come to road.
>
> 　　　　　　　　　　　　(v i 286–8)

'Life and living' in a world where he is destined to play a part, and that a sad one. The defeat of Shylock has been in a way the cause of his defeat, for it has deprived him of the one great gesture of love which would have ended his loneliness and crowned his love with one splendid act. Now he is left with his wealth and his loneliness, surrounded by the lovers and received by Portia at Belmont with words as full of warmth and feeling as those receiving Shylock into the fold of the Church:

> 　　Sir, grieve you not, – you are welcome notwithstanding.

The climax of this parallel which is built up throughout the play, is reached in the parallel action of Act IV and Act V. Act IV covers the rejection and defeat of Shylock, quite explicitly, quite completely. It also covers the defeat of Antonio, but not so explicitly, and Act V is needed to bring out fully and unmistakably what has actually been done to him before the Duke and the court. In Act IV all the powers which oppose Shylock are drawn together into the court room, the glittering youth of Venice, with their friendship and solidarity, and above all the Duke and the magnificoes, embodiments of the law and social code which has rejected Shylock all his life, which, in bitter revenge, he now tries to use for his own ends, but which will turn and destroy him. Shylock is doomed and the net closes round him quite inescapably. He is thrust out from the court as he has always been thrust out, and the visual symbol is more powerful than any reading can be – the Duke on his throne, the magnificoes in all the haughty pomp and robes of state, the gentlemen and ladies grouped together hand in hand or arm in arm, a great, splendid and friendly phalanx filling one side of the stage, while at the other, beaten and alone, the Jew leaves the stage. Antonio's Act is still to come, and I would stress it as his Act, though he hardly speaks, rather than an attempt to restore the play safely to the romance comedy world from which it seemed to have been in danger of escaping – the interpretation forced on us if we accept the old reading of the play. Now it is not the state, the law, the social solidarity of Venice which is built up into the symbol of the rejecting power. The Act opens with:

> The moon shines bright. In such a night as this,
> When the sweet wind did gently kiss the trees,
> And they did make no noise, in such a night
> Troilus methinks mounted the Trojan walls,
> And sigh'd his soul towards the Grecian tents
> Where Cressid lay that night.

(v i 1)

and this lyrical note of romance sets the key for the whole Act:

> How sweet the moonlight sleeps upon this bank!

(v i 54)

Against this background move the lovers, Lorenzo and Jessica, lying entranced in the moonlight, Portia hastening back to her husband, Nerissa to hers – even Launcelot has found a dark-skinned lover. The talk is all of husbands and wives, of reunion, of welcomes home, of going to bed – for with three pairs of happy united lovers, this night is to see the consummation of their marriages. Antonio is welcomed to Belmont, but welcome him as they may, he is alone, and the words of welcome are formal and polite, spoken by people who have more important things to think about:

> Sir, you are very welcome to our house:
> It must appear in other ways than words,
> Therefore I scant this breathing courtesy . . .
> Sir, grieve you not, – you are welcome notwithstanding.

And then he is forgotten. Again one needs to see the scene to realise this fully. From the moonlit garden into the glow of the candle-lit house the lovers pass two by two, Portia with her Bassanio, Lorenzo with his Jessica, and lastly, rushing to their bed, Gratiano and Nerissa – and Antonio is left behind to walk from the stage alone, the stage to which he had likened his world, where he must play a part, and that a sad one. Visually one cannot escape the parallel between the lonely Shylock creeping from the stage, leaving the triumphant ranks of Venice, and this lonely Antonio walking from the stage, following without joy the triumphant pairs of lovers. The sad irony of the whole play is that these two never really meet. Indeed, they are pitched *against* each other, each retiring defeated into his own loneliness again, while Venice goes about its business, and the nightingales of Belmont serenade three happy marriage beds.

SOURCE: *Essays in Criticism*, X (1960), 119–33.

NOTES

1. *Prefaces to Shakespeare*, Second Series (1930) p. 67.
2. 'The Governing Idea', in *Shakespeare Quarterly* I (1948) 9–17.
3. 'Hamlet: the Prince or the Poem', in *Proceedings of the British Academy* (1942) p. 146.
4. *Shakespeare Quarterly* III (1952) 383.
5. *Shakespeare: a survey* (1925) p. 112.

Sigurd Burckhardt

THE MERCHANT OF VENICE:
THE GENTLE BOND (1962)

THE danger of literary source-hunting is that it abets our natural tendency to discount things we believe we have accounted for. The source, once found, relieves us of the effort to see what a thing *is*; we are satisfied with having discovered how it got there. Shakespeare's plots – especially his comedy plots – have generally been at a discount; we have been content to say that the poet took his stories pretty much as he found them and then, as the phrase goes, 'breathed life' into them, enriched them with his subtle characterizations and splendid poetry. That the dramatist must make his plot into the prime metaphor of his meaning – this classical demand Shakespeare was magnanimously excused from, the more readily because by the same token we were excused from the labour of discovering the meaning of complex and 'improbable' plots.

But with the plot thus out of the way, other problems often arose. *The Merchant of Venice* is a case in point. Audiences persist in feeling distressed by Shylock's final treatment, and no amount of historical explanation helps them over their unease. It is little use telling them that their attitude toward the Jew is anachronistic, distorted by modern, un-Elizabethan opinions about racial equality and religious tolerance. They know better; they know that, in the play itself, they have been made to take Shylock's part so strongly that his end seems cruel. Nor does it do them much good to be told that Shakespeare, being Shakespeare, 'could not help' humanizing the stereotype villain he found in his sources; Richard III and Iago are also given depth and stature, but we don't feel sorry for them. If we regard *The Merchant* as a play of character rather haphazardly flung over a prefabricated plot, we cannot join, as unreservedly as we are meant to, in the joyful harmonies of the last Act; Shylock spooks in the background, an unappeased ghost.

The source of our unease is simple enough: Shylock gets more than his share of good lines. This is nowhere more evident than in the court-room scene, where he and Antonio, villain and hero, are pitted against each other in a rhetorical climax. Shylock is powerful in his vindictiveness:

> You'll ask me why I rather choose to have
> A weight of carrion flesh than to receive
> Three thousand ducats. I'll not answer that;
> But say it is my humour. Is it answer'd?
> What if my house be troubled with a rat
> And I be pleas'd to give ten thousand ducats
> To have it ban'd? What, are you answer'd yet?
> Some men there are love not a gaping pig;
> Some, that are mad if they behold a cat;
> And others, when the bagpipe sings i' th' nose,
> Cannot contain their urine: for affection,
> Master of passion, sways it to the mood
> Of what it likes or loathes. Now, for your answer:
> As there is no firm reason to be render'd
> Why he cannot abide a gaping pig;
> Why he, a harmless necessary cat;
> Why he, a swollen bagpipe, but of force
> Must yield to such inevitable shame
> As to offend, himself being offended;
> So can I give no reason, nor I will not,
> More than a lodg'd hate and a certain loathing
> I bear Antonio, that I follow thus
> A losing suit against him. Are you answer'd?

Antonio is grandiloquent:

> I pray you, think, you question with the Jew.
> You may as well go stand upon the beach
> And bid the main flood bate his usual height;
> You may as well use question with the wolf
> Why he hath made the ewe bleat for the lamb;
> You may as well forbid the mountain pines
> To wag their high tops and to make no noise

> When they are fretten with the gusts of heaven;
> You may as well do anything most hard,
> As seek to soften that – than which what's harder? –
> His Jewish heart.

Both men use the triple simile in parallel structure, but the similarity serves only to bring out the difference. The toughness of Shylock's argument is embodied in the toughness of his lines, his passion in their speed and directness; this is a man who *speaks*. We might simply say that Shakespeare here is writing close to his dramatic best; but if by this time he was able to give his devils their due, why does he leave his hero shamed? Antonio's lines are flaccidly oratorical; his similes move with a symmetry so slow and pedantic that our expectations continually outrun them. He strains so hard for the grand that when he has to bring his mountainous tropes around to the point of bearing, they bring forth only a pathetic anti-climax: 'You may as well do anything most hard.' True, the burden of his speech is resignation; but it is feeble rather than noble, a collapse from over-statement into helplessness.

The historical critic may protest at this point that such a judgment reflects a modern bias against rhetoric, a twentieth-century preference for the understated and purely dramatic. But the qualities which make us rank Shylock's lines over Antonio's have long been accepted among the criteria by which we seek to establish the sequence of Shakespeare's plays, on the assumption that where we find them we have evidence of greater maturity and mastery. Nor is this only an assumption. In *The Merchant* itself there is a crucial occasion where these qualities are preferred and where, had the choice been different, the consequence would have been disaster for Antonio. The occasion is Bassanio's choice of the right casket; he rejects the golden one, because it is 'mere ornament', and prefers lead:

> thou meagre lead,
> Which rather threat'nest than dost promise aught,
> Thy plainness moves me more than eloquence.*

* My interpretation here rests on an emendation; Folio and Quartos read 'paleness', not 'plainness'. But the emendation has the support of

At a decisive moment, Bassanio's critical judgment is the same as ours; so that, when we find ourselves more moved by Shylock's plainness than by Antonio's eloquence, we have the best possible reason for feeling sure that Shakespeare intended us to be.

For Bassanio's judgment is 'critical' in more senses than one: the play's happy outcome hangs on his taste. Had he judged wrongly, Portia could not have appeared in court to render her second and saving judgment. In the casket scene, the action turns on the *styles* of metals, conceived as modes of speech; the causalities of the play assume a significance which is, initially at least, only obscured by our being told that Shakespeare's plot is to be found in *Il Pecorone* and the *Gesta Romanorum*. Why does Portia come to Venice? Because Bassanio chooses plainness over eloquence. And how is Bassanio put into the position to make that choice? By Antonio's having bound himself to Shylock. That is how the causal chain of the story runs; it does not run from Fiorentino to Shakespeare.

And as in any good play, so here the causality reveals the meaning of the whole. It shows that the plot is *circular*: bound in such a way that the instrument of destruction, the bond, turns out to be the source of deliverance. Portia, won through the bond, wins Antonio's release from it; what is more, she wins it, not by breaking the bond, but by submitting to its rigour more rigorously than even the Jew had thought to do. So seen, one of Shakespeare's apparently most fanciful plots proved to be one of the most exactingly structured; it is what it should be: the play's controlling metaphor. As the subsidiary metaphors of the bond and the ring indicate, *The Merchant* is a play about circularity and circulation; it asks how the vicious circle of the bond's law

---

most editors since Warburton – and of sound sense. Bassanio means to contrast the three metals; and though both silver – 'thou pale and common drudge' – and lead are pale, it is contrary to his purpose, and to the logical structure of his speech, to fix on the one quality in which lead is *like* silver. The line as Folio has it would have to be read with a strong emphasis on 'Thy'; but even then there is no reason why the paleness of lead should move Bassanio, when that of silver left him unmoved. Moreover, and most decisively, the word is clearly antithetical to 'eloquence'; and while 'plainness' yields a natural antithesis, 'paleness' does not.

can be transformed into the ring of love. And it answers: through a literal and unreserved submission to the bond as absolutely binding. It is as though Shakespeare, finding himself bound to a story already drawn up for him in his source, had taken it as the test of his creative freedom and had discovered that this freedom lay, not in a feeble, Antonio-like resignation, which consoles itself with the consciousness of its inner superiority to the vulgar exigencies of reality, but in a Portia-like acceptance and penetration of these exigencies to the point where they must yield their liberating truth. The play's ultimate circularity may well be that it tells the story of its own composition, of its being created, wholly given and intractably positive though it seems, by the poet's discovery of what it is.

II

The world of *The Merchant* consists of two separate and mostly discontiguous realms: Venice and Belmont, the realm of law and the realm of love, the public sphere and the private. Venice is a community firmly established and concerned above all else with preserving its stability; it is a closed world, inherently conservative, because it knows that it stands and falls with the sacredness of contracts. Belmont, on the other hand, is open and potential; in it a union – that of lovers – is to be founded rather than defended. The happy ending arises from the interaction of the two realms: the bond makes possible the transfer of the action to Belmont, which then *re*-acts upon Venice. The public order is saved from the deadly logic of its own constitution by having been transposed, temporarily, to the private sphere.

But it is not a matter merely of transposition. Each realm has, as it were, its own language, so that the process is better described as a re-translation. Antonio's bonding is a necessary condition for Bassanio's winning Portia, but it is not a sufficient cause; the riddle of the caskets must be correctly *interpreted*. And in exactly the same way the winning of Portia is a necessary condition but not a sufficient cause for the redemption of the bond; it likewise cannot be bought but must be correctly interpreted. The language of love and liberality does not simply supersede that of 'use' (= usury) and law; it must first be translated from it and then back into it. Love must learn to speak the public language, grasp its peculiar grammar; Shylock, to be defeated, must be spoken to in his own terms. That he compels this retranslation is his triumph, Pyrrhic though it turns out to be.

The Jew draws his eloquence and dignity from raising to the level of principle something which by its very nature seems to deny principle: *use*. Antonio's most serious mistake – or rather failure of imagination – is that he cannot conceive of this possibility. He takes a fearful risk for Bassanio, but he cannot claim full credit for it, because he does not know what he is risking. Not only is he confident that his ships will come home a month before the day; he is taken in by Shylock's harmless interpretation of the 'merry jest', the pound-of-flesh clause:

> To buy his favour, I extend this friendship.

He is sure that the Jew wants to *buy* something, to make some kind of profit, and pleasantly surprised that the profit is to be of so 'gentle' (= gentile) a kind; he cannot conceive that a greedy usurer would risk three thousand ducats for a profitless piece of carrion flesh. His too fastidious generosity prevents him from reckoning with the generosity of hatred:

> . . . his flesh – what's that good for?
> To bait fish withal!

So he blindly challenges the usurer – the very man he is about to use – to do his worst:

> I am as like to call thee so again,
> To spit on thee again, to spurn thee too.
> If thou wilt lend this money, lend it not
> As to thy friends; for when did friendship take
> A breed of barren metal of his friend?
> But lend it rather to thine enemy,
> Who, if he break, thou mayest with better face
> Exact the penalty.

(Little wonder that his later words about Shylock's hardness come off so feebly.) The worst he expects is the exacting of 'barren metal'; that it will turn out to be a pound of his own flesh does not enter his haughtily gentle mind.

But the play, thanks largely to Shylock's imagination, insistently makes the point that metal is not barren; it does breed, is pregnant with consequences and capable of transformation into life and even love. Metal it is which brings Bassanio as a suitor to Belmont, metal which holds Portia's picture and with it herself. When Shylock runs through Venice crying, 'My ducats and my daughter', we are as shallow as Venetian dandies and street urchins if we simply echo him with ridicule. Jessica and Lorenzo turn fugitive thieves for the sake of these ducats; it is only at the very end, and by the grace of Portia, that they are given an honest competence:

> Fair ladies, you drop manna in the way
> Of starved people.

In this merchant's world money is a great good, is life itself. When Antonio, again through Portia, learns that three of his argosies are 'richly' come to harbour, he is not scornful of mere pelf but says:

> Sweet lady, you have given me life and living.

(Which makes him Shylock's faithful echo: 'You take my life, / If you do take the means whereby I live.') Bassanio, with Shylock's ducats, ventures to Belmont to win 'a lady richly left' and so to rid himself of his debts; it is a good deal worse than irrelevant to blame him (as some gentlemen critics, of independent income no doubt, have done) for being a fortune hunter. One, perhaps *the* lesson Antonio is made to learn is a lesson in metal-breeding.

Shylock is imaginative not only about money and flesh but about speech. We are, I am convinced, meant to understand that he draws his bloody inspiration directly from Antonio. In the lines just before the stating of the clause, we are shown how intimately and subtly the Jew responds to words, how they trigger his imagination, which thus proves more charged and sure than Antonio's. (That is why he has the better lines.) When Antonio proudly says, 'I do never *use* it', Shylock begins his

story of Jacob's *ewes*; shortly thereafter, when his calculations –
'Let me see, the *rate* . . .' – are brusquely interrupted by Antonio's
impatient: 'Well, Shylock, shall we be beholding to you?', he
picks up the thread again but with a new twist:

> Signior Antonio, many a time and oft
> In the Rialto you have *rated* me.

This is how he is brought to the idea of making his metal breed
flesh. Unlike Antonio, he does not speak in set pieces leading to
sententious commonplaces, 'as who should say: "I am Sir
Oracle, / And when I ope my lips, let no dog bark."' *His* speech
is for *use*, as it is of ewes; that is the secret of its effectiveness. Out
of context his lines are not as quotable as many of Antonio's; but
then we have reason to be suspicious of Shakespeare's quotable
lines; Polonius is probably the most quoted of his characters.
Shylock and Antonio provide the first major instance of Shakespeare's exploration of the conflict between noble-minded
orators and less scrupulous but more effective speakers: between
Brutus and Antony, Othello and Iago. The words of genuine
speakers are so fully part of the dramatic situation, so organically
flesh of the play's verbal body, that they resist excision. They
grow, as truly dramatic speech must, from their circumstances
and in turn change them; since the literal meaning of 'drama' is
'action', they are what they ought to be: language in action. It is
because Shylock speaks this language that he is able to transform
barren metal into living substance; the very mode of his speaking here becomes the mode of his doing.

III

In Belmont the Jew's money promises to breed in a more literal
sense: it helps to unite lovers. The equation money = offspring
is pointed up by Gratiano, in a line which echoes Shylock's 'My
ducats and my daughter':

> We'll play them the first boy for a thousand ducats.

More precisely, the money makes the union possible; the consummation turns out to be rather more complicated.

I have stressed the differences between Belmont and Venice;
but in one respect they are alike: both are governed by rigorously
positive laws, which threaten to frustrate the very purposes they
are meant to serve, but which must nevertheless be obeyed. In
fact, the rule which governs Belmont – the covenant of the
caskets – seems even more wilfully positive than that of Venice.
More rigidly even than the law of the bond, it puts obedience
above meaning, the letter above the spirit.

The harshly positive character of Venetian law is evident
enough. When Bassanio pleads a kind of natural law, man's in-
tuitive sense of justice, he is sternly corrected by Portia:

> *Bassanio.* If this will not suffice, it must appear
>   That malice bears down truth. And I beseech you,
>   Wrest once the law to your authority;
>   To do a great right, do a little wrong,
>   And curb this cruel devil of his will.
> *Portia.* It must not be; there is no power in Venice
>   Can alter a decree established.
>   'Twill be recorded for a precedent,
>   And many an error by the same example
>   Will rush into the state. It cannot be.

But Portia here can still appeal to reason, can show that the law
which is at the mercy of man's 'sense of justice' fails of its purpose, even though, taken as positively binding, it may also
frustrate that purpose. Nerissa, defending the wisdom of the
casket test against Portia's rebellious complaints, has no argument to fall back on except authority and faith:

> *Portia.* I may neither choose who I would nor refuse who I
>   dislike; so is the will of a living daughter curb'd by the
>   will of a dead father. Is it not hard, Nerissa, that I can-
>   not choose one nor refuse none?
> *Nerissa.* Your father was ever virtuous, and holy men at their
>   death have good inspirations.

The wisdom of the father's will can be proved only in the event.

The law of Belmont, then, demands submission quite as much
as that of Venice; it too disallows mere feeling. But it differs in
one decisive point: it permits, in fact (as the result shows)

requires interpretation by *substance* rather than by letter. Aragon and Morocco fail because they try to interpret the lines inscribed on the caskets rather than the substance; they calculate which of the inscriptions correctly states the relation between their own worth, Portia's worth and the risk of choosing wrongly. For them the caskets are mere clues; what they are really concerned with is themselves and the object of their suit. It is this intrusion of their selves and their purposes that misleads them; they are enmeshed in their reckonings. The noteworthy thing about Bassanio is that he disregards the inscriptions; he lets the metals themselves speak to him (quite literally: he apostrophizes them as speakers). Once before the caskets, he seems almost to forget Portia, himself and his purpose. He does not look for signs, pointers along the way to his goal; he stops – and listens to the things themselves. And so he wins.

When the predestined pair is happily united and everything seems to have dissolved into pure concord, we are promptly reminded that there is an accounting still due back in prosaic Venice. Belmont is bound to Venice as surely as Antonio is to Shylock. If the bond were not acknowledged, the bliss of the lovers would remain private, encapsuled in the barren half-fulfilment of fancy and sheer, useless poetry, while in the public world of prose and use time and the law would run their deadly course. The parthenogenesis of fancy has no lasting issue; the union of Portia and Bassanio must remain unconsummated until after the retranslation to Venice:

> First go with me to church and call me wife,
> And then away to Venice to your friend;
> For never shall you lie by Portia's side
> With an unquiet soul.

IV

In the Jessica plot Shakespeare breaks free of the bondage to his source and elopes into the untrammelled freedom of invention. Pure, spontaneous feeling governs the conduct of these lovers; they brush aside, without much compunction, the impediments to their union and celebrate careless honeymoons in Genoa,

Belmont or wherever their fancy and Shylock's ducats take them.

As lovers, Jessica and Lorenzo stand in the sharpest imaginable contrast to Portia and Bassanio. Their love is lawless, financed by theft and engineered through a gross breach of trust. It is subjected to no test: 'Here, catch this casket, it is worth the pains,' Jessica says to Lorenzo to underscore the difference. The ring which ought to seal their love is traded for a monkey. They are spendthrift rather than liberal, thoughtless squanderers of stolen substance; they are aimless, drifting by chance from Venice to Genoa to Belmont. They are attended by a low-grade clown, who fathers illegitimate children (Launcelot), while Bassanio and Portia are served by a true jester, who marries in due form (Gratiano). Wherever we look, the Jessica–Lorenzo affair appears as an inversion of true, bonded love.

More: the spontaneous love-match remains fruitless and useless; it redeems no one but is itself in urgent need of redemption.

What, then, does this subplot accomplish; why, it is now safe to ask, is it there at all? It is there to discover its own shame and uselessness and so, by contrast, to make clearer and firmer the outlines of bonded love.

If this judgment of Jessica and Lorenzo seems too narrowly puritanical – and at odds, moreover, with their gorgeous lines about night and music at the opening of the last Act – two things are to be remembered. *The Merchant* is a play of *use*; this word, among others, is rescued alike from Shylock's malice and Antonio's contempt. The people who ultimately count – Antonio, Bassanio, Portia and, in a negative way, Shylock – have all been useful, have freed and united not only each other but also the state. And they have done so – to repeat – by accepting the given, the letter of the law, as binding; something to be fulfilled, not evaded. The play's ethos, the standards by which we must judge, are defined by its causality: and the causality is wholly unambiguous. Here, as in the sphere of speech, it is action that counts, not sentiment, effect, not attitude; here too Shakespeare teaches us – and perhaps himself – the true meaning of 'drama'. Mere lyrical splendor is, in the world the play defines, a kind of sentimentality, a parasitical self-indulgence, possible only because, and insofar as, others bear the brunt of the law.

Which brings us to the concrete setting of the lyrical interlude. It opens with the oddly ambiguous hymn to night; what we are given is the genealogy of fly-by-night love: betrayal (Troilus and Cressida), disaster (Pyramus and Thisbe), desertion (Dido and Aeneas), sorcery (Medea) and theft (Jessica). Only with the arrival of good news from Venice does the tune change to the beautiful praise of music. And even then the music Lorenzo commands is not his but Portia's ('It is your music, madam, of the house'). She who pays the piper calls off the tune; to Lorenzo's borrowed authority ('Come, ho! and wake Diana with a hymn') there answers the real authority of the owner:

> Peace, ho! the Moon sleeps with Endymion
> And would not be awak'd.
>
> [*music ceases*]

Portia is known 'as the blind man knows the cuckoo, / By the bad voice'. Compared to the heavenly harmonies Lorenzo has summoned the voice *is* bad for it is the voice of daylight, of action. The scapegrace lovers have an unearned, nocturnal grace which transcends all that is earned and useful; if we are not moved by their concord of sweet sound, we are not to be trusted. But neither, clearly, were Jessica and Lorenzo to be trusted. Our surety lies in the sterner sound of redeemed prose which is won by the hazard of making the ethereal music of love answer to the letter of the law.

v

Belmont, left to itself, would end in sterile self-absorption; Venice, left to itself, would end in silence. There is an odd logic working in Shylock's bond: with its seal and letter it gradually deadens even the Jew's powerful speech. Increasingly his lines become monotonous and monomaniacal; where we heard him, earlier, responding acutely and flexibly to Antonio's hard scantness, he now grows deaf:

Antonio. I pray thee, hear me speak.
Shylock. I'll have my bond; I will not hear thee speak.

> I'll have my bond; and therefore speak no more . . .
> I'll have no speaking; I will have my bond.

The theme is continued in the trial scene:

> I'll never answer that . . .
> I am not bound to please thee with my answers . . .
> Till thou canst rail the seal from off my bond,
> Thou but offend'st thy lungs to speak so loud.

And finally:

> There is no power in the tongue of man
> To alter me. I stay here on my bond.

Thus 'bond', in Shylock's mouth, comes to mean the opposite of speech and hearing; and since the state must sustain him, we come to the point where the community, to preserve itself, must prohibit communion. He who stands on the bond is no longer answerable and need no longer listen; the instrument of exchange threatens to render the body politic tongue-tied. A gap opens between the private and utterly ineffectual speech of men as men and the deadening, unalterable letter of the law. Portia's oft-quoted lines about the quality of mercy are remarkable not so much for their eloquence as for their impotence; they are of no use, fall on deaf ears, *do* nothing and so remain, in the literal sense, un-dramatic.

But at this point there is a reversal. Very much as Shylock learned, from Antonio's hardness, how to transform metal into flesh, so Portia now learns from Shylock himself the art of winning life from the deadly letter. So far she has given no hint that she has come with the solution ready; her last plea, interrupting as it does her already begun judgment, has the desperate urgency of a final, hopeless effort. When she asks Shylock to provide a surgeon to staunch the blood, does she know yet that it is on this point she will presently hang him? Or is it not rather Shylock himself who leads her to the saving inspiration?

Shylock. Is it so nominated in the bond?
Portia. It is not so express'd; but what of that?
    'Twere good you do so much for charity.
Shylock. I cannot find it; 'tis not in the bond.

We cannot read Portia's mind and purposes, but this much is clear: here the crucial word is forced from her which then recurs in:

> This bond doth give thee here no jot of blood;
> The words *expressly* are 'a pound of flesh'.

The same process is at work as that which led to the framing of the bond; language, and with it Antonio and the state, have been revived and freed to act.

If we read Portia's judgment as a legal trick and Shylock's defeat as a foregone conclusion, the Jew's final humiliation must appear distressingly cruel. But there is good reason for reading the scene differently. Portia's ruling is one more hazard, and Shylock's moral collapse does not demolish the bond and all it stands for, but rather proves him unequal to the faith he has professed. Even after the judgment the issue is in doubt; it is still in Shylock's power to turn the play into a tragedy, to enforce the letter of the bond and to take the consequences. But at this point and before this choice he breaks, turns apostate to the faith he has so triumphantly forced upon his enemies. Having made the gentles bow before the letter of the law, he is now asked to become, literally, a blood witness. But he reneges and surrenders the bond's power, and like a renegade he is flogged into gentleness.

That it is the apostate rather than the bond that is brought into contempt is made clear in the last Act: the ring episode. We the spectators can view it as a mere frolic, because we know of Portia's double identity and so understand her threatening equivocations as being, in truth, binding pledges of fidelity. But Bassanio does not know and understand; to him the ring seems to continue the vicious circle of the bond. The cost of redeeming the public bond has been the forfeiture of the private one, the pledge of love; he now stands before Portia as Antonio stood before Shylock. His explanations, his appeals to circumstances and motives are in vain; she insists on the letter of the pledge and claims the forfeit. What redeems the bond of true love is not good intentions but the fact that Portia speaks with a double voice, functions both in Venice and in Belmont, is both man and woman ('the master-mistress of my passion', we may call her with Sonnet xx).

The ring is the bond transformed, the gentle bond. Since 'bond' has dinned its leaden echo into our ears for the better part of four Acts, 'ring' is now made to ring out with almost comic but still ominous iteration:

> *Bassanio.* If you did know to whom I gave the ring,
>   If you did know for whom I gave the ring,
>   And would conceive for what I gave the ring,
>   And how unwillingly I left the ring,
>   When nought would be accepted but the ring,
>   You would abate the strength of your displeasure.
> *Portia.* If you had known the virtue of the ring,
>   Or half her worthiness that gave the ring,
>   Or your own honour to contain the ring,
>   You would not then have parted with the ring.

Like the bond, the ring is of a piece with flesh, so that we can hardly tell whether it has made flesh into metal or has itself become flesh:

> A thing stuck on with oaths upon your finger,
> And riveted with faith unto your flesh.

Flesh, therefore, may have to be cut for it:

> Why, I were best to cut my left hand off,
> And swear I lost the ring defending it.

And in the end Antonio must once again bind himself:

> *Antonio.* I once did lend my body for his wealth,
>   Which, but for him that had your husband's ring,
>   Had quite miscarried. I dare be bound again,
>   My soul upon the forfeit, that your lord
>   Will never more break faith advisedly.
> *Portia.* Then you shall be his surety.

Only with this renewal of the bond is the secret discovered, the true meaning of the equivocations revealed. Shylock has been defeated and dismissed, but the words which he almost succeeded in making synonymous with himself are not. They enter

into the gentle contract of love, are requisite to the consummation; union, truth and faith are impossible without them.

So the action ends; or rather, the circle closes. The play comes
round with Shakespeare's happy discovery that poetry is an equi-
vocal language, public as well as private, common as well as
gentle, useful as well as beautiful. The poet draws upon the social
order's legal currency and so is bound and fully accountable. But
by binding himself with Antonio instead of stealing with
Lorenzo, he frees energies which will save the order from becoming deadlocked in a vicious circle of self-definition; by hazarding
all he has on the chance of making personal unions possible, he
frees himself from the twin futilities of uselessness and parasitical
exploitation of the public currency. For himself and for Venice
he gains Portia – the indefinable being who speaks most truly
when she sounds most faithless, who frees us through an absolute
literalness, who learns the grim prose of law in order to restore it
to its true function. The gain will serve him for the time of the
great romantic comedies; when, with *Julius Caesar* and *Hamlet*
he confronts the fact that the social order has neither the stability
nor the good will he supposed, a new and much grimmer search
will begin. The gentle bond will hold until Brutus speaks the
tragic epilogue to *The Merchant of Venice*: 'Portia is dead'.

SOURCE: Abridged from an essay in the *Journal of English
Literary History*, XXIX (Sept. 1962), 239.

W. H. Auden

BROTHERS AND OTHERS (1963)

The possible redemption from the predicament of irreversibility–
of being unable to undo what one has done–is the faculty of for-
giving. The remedy for unpredictability, for the chaotic un-
certainty of the future, is contained in the faculty to make and
keep promises. Both faculties depend upon plurality, on the
presence and acting of others, for no man can forgive himself and
no one can be bound by a promise made only to himself.

(HANNAH ARENDT)

THE England which Shakespeare presents in *Richard II* and
Henry IV is a society in which wealth, that is to say, social power,
is derived from ownership of land, not from accumulated capital.
The only person who is in need of money is the King who must
equip troops to defend the country against foreign foes. If, like
Richard II, he is an unjust king, he spends the money which
should have been spent on defense in maintaining a luxurious
and superfluous court. Economically, the country is self-sufficient
and production is for use, not profit. The community-forming
bond in this England is either the family tie of common blood
which is given by nature or the feudal tie of lord and vassal
created by personal oath. Both are commitments to individuals
and both are lifelong commitments. But this type of community
tie is presented as being ill suited to the needs of England as a
functioning society. If England is to function properly as a
society, the community based on personal loyalty must be converted into a community united by a common love of impersonal
justice, that is to say, of the King's Law which is no respecter of
persons. We are given to understand that in Edward III's day
this kind of community already existed, so that the family type
of community is seen as a regression. Centuries earlier, a war
between Wessex and Mercia, for example, would have been

regarded as legitimate as a war between England and France, but now a conflict between a Percy and a Bolingbroke is regarded as a civil war, illegitimate because between brothers. It is possible, therefore, to apply a medical analogy to England and speak of a sick body politic, because it is as obvious who are aliens and who ought to be brothers as it is obvious which cells belong to my body and which to the body of another. War, as such, is not condemned but is still considered, at least for the gentry, a normal and enjoyable occupation like farming. Indeed peace, as such, carries with it the pejorative associations of idleness and vice.

> Now all the youth of England are on fire
> And silken dalliance in the wardrobe lies.
> Now thrive the Armourers and Honour's thought
> Reigns solely in the breast of every man.
> They sell the pasture now to buy the horse.

The only merchants who appear in *Henry IV* are the 'Bacon-fed Knaves and Fat Chuffs' whom Falstaff robs, and they are presented as contemptible physical cowards.

In *The Merchant of Venice* and *Othello* Shakespeare depicts a very different kind of society. Venice does not produce anything itself, either raw materials or manufactured goods. Its existence depends upon the financial profits which can be made by international trade,

> . . . the trade and profit of the city
> Consisteth of all nations

that is to say, on buying cheaply here and selling dearly there, and its wealth lies in its accumulated money capital. Money has ceased to be simply a convenient medium of exchange and has become a form of social power which can be gained or lost. Such a mercantile society is international and cosmopolitan; it does not distinguish between the brother and the alien other than on a basis of blood or religion – from the point of view of society, customers are brothers, trade rivals others. But Venice is not simply a mercantile society; it is also a city inhabited by various communities with different loves – Gentiles and Jews, for example – who do not regard each other personally as brothers, but must tolerate each other's existence because both are indispensable to the proper functioning of their society, and this toleration is enforced by the laws of the Venetian state.

A change in the nature of wealth from landownership to money capital radically alters the social conception of time. The wealth produced by land may vary from year to year – there are good harvests and bad – but in the long run its average yield may be counted upon. Land, barring dispossession by an invader or confiscation by the State, is held by a family in perpetuity. In consequence, the social conception of time in a landowning society is cyclical – the future is expected to be a repetition of the past. But in a mercantile society time is conceived of as unilinear forward movement in which the future is always novel and unpredictable. (The unpredictable event in a landowning society is an Act of God, that is to say, it is not 'natural' for an event to be unpredictable.) The merchant is constantly taking risks – if he is lucky, he may make a fortune, if he is unlucky he may lose everything. Since, in a mercantile society, social power is derived from money, the distribution of power within it is constantly changing, which has the effect of weakening reverence for the past; who one's distant ancestors were soon ceases to be of much social importance. The oath of lifelong loyalty is replaced by the contract which binds its signatories to fulfill certain specific promises by a certain specific future date, after which their commitment to each other is over.

The action of *The Merchant of Venice* takes place in two locations, Venice and Belmont, which are so different in character that to produce the play in a manner which will not blur this contrast and yet preserve a unity is very difficult. If the spirit of Belmont is made too predominant, then Antonio and Shylock will seem irrelevant, and vice versa. In *Henry IV*, Shakespeare intrudes Falstaff, who by nature belongs to the world of *opera buffa*, into the historical world of political chronicle with which his existence is incompatible, and thereby, consciously or unconsciously, achieves the effect of calling in question the values of military glory and temporal justice as embodied in Henry of

Monmouth. In *The Merchant of Venice* he gives us a similar contrast — the romantic fairy-story world of Belmont is incompatible with the historical reality of money-making Venice – but this time what is called in question is the claim of Belmont to be the Great Good Place, the Earthly Paradise. Watching *Henry IV*, we become convinced that our aesthetic sympathy with Falstaff is a profounder vision than our ethical judgment which must side with Hal. Watching *The Merchant of Venice*, on the other hand, we are compelled to acknowledge that the attraction which we naturally feel towards Belmont is highly questionable. On that account, I think *The Merchant of Venice* must be classed among Shakespeare's 'Unpleasant Plays'.

Omit Antonio and Shylock, and the play becomes a romantic fairy tale like *A Midsummer Night's Dream*. The world of the fairy tale is an unambiguous, unproblematic world in which there is no contradiction between outward appearance and inner reality, a world of being, not becoming. A character may be temporarily disguised – the unlovely animal is really the Prince Charming under a spell, the hideous old witch transforms herself into a lovely young girl to tempt the hero – but this is a mask, not a contradiction: the Prince is *really* handsome, the witch *really* hideous. A fairy story character may sometimes change, but, if so, the change is like a mutation; at one moment he or she is this kind of person, at the next he is transformed into that kind. It is a world in which people are either good or bad by nature; occasionally a bad character repents, but a good character never becomes bad. It is meaningless therefore to ask why a character in a fairy tale acts as he does because his nature will only allow him to act in one way. It is a world in which, ultimately, good fortune is the sign of moral goodness, ill fortune of moral badness. The good are beautiful, rich and speak with felicity, the bad are ugly, poor and speak crudely.

In real life we can distinguish between two kinds of choice, the strategic and the personal. A strategic choice is conditioned by a future goal which is already known to the chooser. I wish to catch a certain train which will be leaving in ten minutes. I can either go by subway or take a taxi. It is the rush hour, so I have to decide which I believe will get me sooner to the station. My choice may turn out to be mistaken, but neither I nor an observer will have any difficulty in understanding the choice I make. But now and again, I take a decision which is based, not on any calculation of its future consequences, for I cannot tell what they will be, but upon my immediate conviction that, whatever the consequences, I must do this now. However well I know myself, I can never understand completely why I take such a decision, and to others it will always seem mysterious. The traditional symbol in Western Literature for this kind of personal choice is the phenomenon of falling-in-love. But in the fairy-tale world, what appear to be the personal choices of the characters are really the strategic choices of the storyteller, for within the tale the future is predestined. We watch Portia's suitors choosing their casket, but we know in advance that Morocco and Arragon cannot choose the right one and that Bassanio cannot choose the wrong one, and we know this, not only from what we know of their characters but also from their ordinal position in a series, for the fairy-tale world is ruled by magical numbers. Lovers are common enough in fairy tales, but love appears as a pattern-forming principle rather than sexual passion as we experience it in the historical world. The fairy tale cannot tolerate intense emotions of any kind, because any intense emotion has tragic possibilities, and even the possibility of tragedy is excluded from the fairy tale. It is possible to imagine the serious passion of Romeo and Juliet having a happy ending instead of a tragic one, but it is impossible to imagine either of them in Oberon's Wood or the Forest of Arden.

The fairy tale is hospitable to black magicians as well as to white; ogres, witches, bogeys are constantly encountered who have their temporary victories but in the end are always vanquished by the good and banished, leaving Arcadia to its unsullied innocent joy where the good live happily ever after. But the malevolence of a wicked character in a fairy tale is a given premise; their victims, that is to say, never bear any responsibility for the malice, have never done the malevolent one an injury. The Devil, by definition malevolent without a cause, is presented in the medieval miracle plays as a fairy-story bogey, never victorious but predestined to be cheated of his prey.

Recent history has made it utterly impossible for the most unsophisticated and ignorant audience to ignore the historical reality of the Jews and think of them as fairy-story bogeys with huge noses and red wigs. An Elizabethan audience undoubtedly still could – very few of them had seen a Jew – and, if Shakespeare had so wished, he could have made Shylock grotesquely wicked like the *Jew of Malta*. The star actors who, from the eighteenth century onwards have chosen to play the role, have not done so out of a sense of moral duty in order to combat anti-Semitism, but because their theatrical instinct told them that the part, played seriously, not comically, offered them great possibilities.

The Merchant of Venice is, among other things, as much a 'problem' play as one by Ibsen or Shaw. The question of the immorality or morality of usury was a sixteenth-century issue on which both the theologians and the secular authorities were divided. Though the majority of medieval theologians had condemned usury, there had been, from the beginning, divergence of opinion as to the correct interpretation of Deuteronomy, XXIII 19–20:

Thou shalt not lend upon usury to thy brother; usury of money, usury of victuals, usury of any thing that is lent upon usury: Unto a stranger thou mayest lend upon usury

and Leviticus XXV 35–7 which proscribe the taking of usury, not only from a fellow Jew, but also from the stranger living in their midst and under their protection.

Some Christian theologians had interpreted this to mean that, since the Christians had replaced the Jews as God's Chosen, they were entitled to exact usury from non-Christians. [1]

Who is your brother? He is your sharer in nature, co-heir in grace, every people, which, first, is in the faith, then under the Roman Law. Who, then, is the stranger? the foes of God's people. From him, demand usury whom you rightly desire to harm, against whom weapons are lawfully carried. Upon him usury is legally imposed. Where there is the right of war, there also is the right of usury. (St Ambrose)

Several centuries later, St Bernard of Siena, in a statement of which the sanctity seems as doubtful as the logic, takes St Ambrose's argument even further.

Temporal goods are given to men for the worship of the true God and the Lord of the Universe. When, therefore, the worship of God does not exist, as in the case of God's enemies, usury is lawfully exacted, because this is not done for the sake of gain, but for the sake of the Faith; and the motive is brotherly love, namely, that God's enemies may be weakened and so return to Him; and further because the goods they have do not belong to them, since they are rebels against the true faith; they shall therefore devolve upon the Christians.

The majority, however, starting from the Gospel command that we are to treat all men, even our enemies, as brothers, held that the Deuteronomic permission was no longer valid, so that under no circumstances was usury permissible. Thus, St Thomas Aquinas, who was also, no doubt, influenced by Aristotle's condemnation of usury, says:

The Jews were forbidden to take usury from their brethren' i.e., from other Jews. By this we are given to understand that to take usury from any man is simply evil, because we ought to treat every man as our neighbour and brother, especially in the state of the Gospel whereto we are called. They were permitted, however, to take usury from foreigners, not as though it were lawful, but in order to avoid a greater evil, lest to wit, through avarice to which they were prone, according to Deuteronomy, XXIII 19–20, they should take usury from Jews, who were worshippers of God.

On the Jewish side, talmudic scholars had some interesting interpretations. Rashi held that the Jewish debtor is forbidden to pay interest to a fellow Jew, but he may pay interest to a Gentile. Maimonides, who was anxious to prevent Jews from being tempted into idolatry by associating with Gentiles, held that a Jew might borrow at usury from a Gentile, but should not make loans to one, on the ground that debtors are generally anxious to avoid their creditors, but creditors are obliged to seek the company of debtors.

Had Shakespeare wished to show Shylock the usurer in the most unfavorable light possible, he could have placed him in a medieval agricultural society, where men become debtors through misfortunes, like a bad harvest or sickness for which they are not responsible, but he places him in a mercantile society, where the role played by money is a very different one.

When Antonio says:

> I neither lend nor borrow
> By taking nor by giving of excess

he does not mean that, if he goes into partnership with another merchant contributing, say, a thousand ducats to their venture, and their venture makes a profit, he only asks for a thousand ducats back. He is a merchant and the Aristotelian argument that money is barren and cannot breed money, which he advances to Shylock, is invalid in his own case.

This change in the role of money had already been recognized by both Catholic and Protestant theologians. Calvin, for example had come to the conclusion that the Deuteronomic injunction had been designed to meet a particular political situation which no longer existed.

The law of Moses is political and does not obligate us beyond what equity and the reason of humanity suggest. There is a difference in the political union, for the situation in which God placed the Jews and many circumstances permitted them to trade conveniently among themselves without usuries. Our union is entirely different. Therefore I do not feel that usuries are forbidden to us simply, except in so far as they are opposed to equity and charity.

The condemnation of usury by Western Christendom cannot be understood except in relation to the severity of its legal attitude, inherited from Roman Law, towards the defaulting debtor. The pound of flesh story has a basis in historical fact for, according to the Law of the Twelve Tables, a defaulting debtor could be torn to pieces alive. In many medieval contracts the borrower agreed, in the case of default, to pay double the amount of the loan as a forfeit, and imprisonment for debt continued into the nineteenth century. It was possible to consider interest on a loan immoral because the defaulting debtor was regarded as a criminal, that is to say, an exception to the human norm, so that lending was thought of as normally entailing no risk. One motive which led the theologians of the sixteenth century to modify the traditional theories about usury and to regard it as a necessary social evil rather than as a mortal sin was their fear of social revolution and the teachings of the Anabaptists and other radical utopians. These, starting from the same premise of Universal Brotherhood which had been the traditional ground for condemning usury, drew the conclusion that private property was unchristian, that Christians should share all their goods in common, so that the relation of creditor to debtor would be abolished. Thus, Luther, who at first had accused Catholic theologians of being lax towards the sin of usury, by 1524, was giving this advice to Prince Frederick of Saxony:

It is highly necessary that the taking of interest should be regulated everywhere, but to abolish it entirely would not be right either, for it can be made just. I do not advise your Grace, however, to support people in their refusal to pay interest or to prevent them from paying it, for it is not a burden laid upon people by a Prince in his law, but it is a common plague that all have taken upon themselves. We must put up with it, therefore, and hold debtors to it and not let them spare themselves and seek a remedy of their own, but put them on a level with everybody else, as love requires.

Shylock is a Jew living in a predominantly Christian society, just as Othello is a Negro living in a predominantly white society. But, unlike Othello, Shylock rejects the Christian community as firmly as it rejects him. Shylock and Antonio are at one in refusing to acknowledge a common brotherhood.

> *Shylock.* I will buy with you, sell with you, talk with you, walk with you, and so following, but I will not eat with you, drink with you, nor pray with you.

Antonio. I am as like. . . .
>   To spit on thee again, to spurn thee, too.
>   If thou wilt lend this money, lend it not
>   As to thy friends . . .
>   But lend it rather to thine enemy,
>   Who if he break, thou mayst with better face
>   Exact the penalty.

In addition, unlike Othello, whose profession of arms is socially honourable, Shylock is a professional usurer who, like a prostitute, has a social function but is an outcast from the community. But, in the play, he acts unprofessionally; he refuses to charge Antonio interest and insists upon making their legal relation that of debtor and creditor, a relation acknowledged as legal by all societies. Several critics have pointed to analogies between the trial scene and the medieval *Processus Belial* in which Our Lady defends man against the prosecuting Devil who claims the legal right to man's soul. The Roman doctrine of the Atonement presupposes that the debtor deserves no mercy – Christ may substitute Himself for man, but the debt has to be paid by death on the cross. The Devil is defeated, not because he has no right to demand a penalty, but because he does not know that the penalty has been already suffered. But the differences between Shylock and Belial are as important as their similarities. The comic Devil of the mystery play can appeal to logic, to the letter of the law, but he cannot appeal to the heart or to the imagination, and Shakespeare allows Shylock to do both. In his 'Hath not a Jew eyes . . .' speech in Act iii, scene i, he is permitted to appeal to the sense of human brotherhood, and in the trial scene, he is allowed to argue, with a sly appeal to the fear a merchant class has of radical social revolution:

>   You have among you many a purchased slave
>   Which, like your asses and your dogs and mules,
>   You use in abject and in slavish parts,

which points out that those who preach mercy and brotherhood as universal obligations limit them in practice and are prepared to treat certain classes of human beings as things.

Furthermore, while Belial is malevolent without any cause except love of malevolence for its own sake, Shylock is presented as a particular individual living in a particular kind of society at a particular time in history. Usury, like prostitution, may corrupt the character, but those who borrow upon usury, like those who visit brothels, have their share of responsibility for this corruption and aggravate their guilt by showing contempt for those whose services they make use of.

It is, surely, in order to emphasize this point that, in the trial scene, Shakespeare introduces an element which is not found in *Pecorone* or other versions of the pound-of-flesh story. After Portia has trapped Shylock through his own insistence upon the letter of the law of Contract, she produces another law by which any alien who conspires against the life of a Venetian citizen forfeits his goods and places his life at the Doge's mercy. Even in the rush of a stage performance, the audience cannot help reflecting that a man as interested in legal subtleties as Shylock, would, surely, have been aware of the existence of this law and that, if by any chance he had overlooked it, the Doge surely would very soon have drawn his attention to it. Shakespeare, it seems to me, was willing to introduce what is an absurd implausibility for the sake of an effect which he could not secure without it: at the last moment when, through his conduct, Shylock has destroyed any sympathy we may have felt for him earlier, we are reminded that, irrespective of his personal character, his status is one of inferiority. A Jew is not regarded, even in law, as a brother.

If the wicked Shylock cannot enter the fairy story world of Belmont, neither can the noble Antonio, though his friend, Bassanio, can. In the fairy story world, the symbol of final peace and concord is marriage, so that, if the story is concerned with the adventures of two friends of the same sex, male or female, it must end with a double wedding. Had he wished, Shakespeare could have followed the *Pecorone* story in which it is Ansaldo, not Gratiano, who marries the equivalent of Nerissa. Instead, he portrays Antonio as a melancholic who is incapable of loving a woman. He deliberately avoids the classical formula of the

Perfect Friends by making the relationship unequal. When Solanio says of Antonio's feelings for Bassanio

> I think he only loves the world for him

we believe it, but no one would say that Bassanio's affections are equally exclusive. Bassanio, high-spirited, elegant, pleasure-loving, belongs to the same world as Gratiano and Lorenzo; Antonio does not. When he says:

> I hold the world but as the world, Gratiano,
> A stage, where every man must play a part,
> And mine a sad one

Gratiano may accuse him of putting on an act, but we believe him, just as it does not seem merely the expression of a noble spirit of self-sacrifice when he tells Bassanio:

> I am a tainted wether of the flock,
> Meetest for death; the weakest kind of fruit
> Drops earliest to the ground, and so let me.

It is well known that love and understanding breed love and understanding.

> The more people on high who comprehend each other,
> the more there are to love well, and the more
> love is there, and like a mirror, one giveth
> back to the other.
>
> *(Purgatorio,* xv)

So, with the rise of a mercantile economy in which money breeds money, it became an amusing paradox for poets to use the ignoble activity of usury as a metaphor for love, the most noble of human activities. Thus, in his Sonnets, Shakespeare uses usury as an image for the married love which begets children.

> Profitless usurer, why dost thou use
> So great a sum of sums, yet canst not live?
> For having traffic with thyself alone
> Thou of thyself thy sweet self dost deceive.
>
> (Sonnet iv)

That use is not forbidden usury
Which happies those that pay the willing loan,
That's for thyself, to breed another thee,
Or ten times happier, be it ten for one.
                                        (Sonnet VI)

And, even more relevant, perhaps, to Antonio are the lines

But since she pricked thee out for women's pleasure
Mine be thy love, and thy love's use their treasure.
                                        (Sonnet XX)

There is no reason to suppose that Shakespeare had read Dante, but he must have been familiar with the association of usury with sodomy of which Dante speaks in the Eleventh Canto of the Inferno.

It behoves man to gain his bread and to prosper. And because the usurer takes another way, he contemns Nature in herself and her followers, placing elsewhere his hope. . . . And hence the smallest round seals with its mark Sodom and the Cahors. . . .

It can, therefore, hardly be an accident that Shylock the usurer has as his antagonist a man whose emotional life, though his conduct may be chaste, is concentrated upon a member of his own sex.

In any case, the fact that Bassanio's feelings are so much less intense makes Antonio's seem an example of that inordinate affection which theologians have always condemned as a form of idolatry, a putting of the creature before the creator. In the sixteenth century, suretyship, like usury, was a controversial issue. The worldly-wise condemned the standing surety for another on worldly grounds.

Beware of standing suretyship for thy best friends; he that payeth another man's debts seeketh his own decay: neither borrow money of a neighbour or a friend, but of a stranger.
                                        (Lord Burghley)

Suffer not thyself to be wounded for other men's faults, or scourged for other men's offences, which is the surety for another: for thereby, millions of men have been beggared and destroyed. . . . from suretyship as from a manslayer or enchanter, bless thyself.

(Sir Walter Raleigh)

And clerics like Luther condemned it on theological grounds

Of his life and property a man is not certain for a single moment, any more than he is certain of the man for whom he becomes surety. Therefore the man who becomes surety acts unchristian like and deserves what he gets, because he pledges and promises what is not his and not in his power, but in the hands of God alone. . . . These sureties act as though their life and property were their own and were in their power as long as they wished to have it; and this is nothing but the fruit of unbelief. . . . If there were no more of this becoming surety, many a man would have to keep down and be satisfied with a moderate living, who now aspires night and day after high places, relying on borrowing and standing surety.

The last sentence of this passage applies very well to Bassanio. In *Pecorone*, the Lady of Belmonte is a kind of witch and Gianetto gets into financial difficulties because he is the victim of magic, a fate which is never regarded as the victim's fault. But Bassanio had often borrowed money from Antonio before he ever considered wooing Portia and was in debt, not through magic or unforeseeable misfortune, but through his own extravagances,

> 'Tis not unknown to you, Antonio,
> How much I have disabled mine estate
> By something showing a more swelling port
> Than my faint means would grant continuance

and we feel that Antonio's continual generosity has encouraged Bassanio in his spendthrift habits. Bassanio seems to be one of those people whose attitude towards money is that of a child; it will somehow always appear by magic when really needed. Though Bassanio is aware of Shylock's malevolence, he makes no serious effort to dissuade Antonio from signing the bond because, thanks to the ever-open purse of his friend, he cannot believe that bankruptcy is a real possibility in life.

Shylock is a miser and Antonio is openhanded with his

money; nevertheless, as a merchant, Antonio is equally a member of an acquisitive society. He is trading with Tripoli, the Indies, Mexico, England, and when Solanio imagines himself in Antonio's place, he describes a possible shipwreck thus:

> . . . the rocks
> Would scatter all her spices on the stream,
> Enrobe the roaring waters with my silks.

The commodities, that is to say, in which the Venetian merchant deals are not necessities but luxury goods, the consumption of which is governed not by physical need but by psychological values like social prestige, so that there can be no question of a Just Price. Then, as regards his own expenditure, Antonio is, like Shylock, a sober merchant who practises economic abstinence. Both of them avoid the carnal music of this world. Shylock's attitude towards the Masquers

> Lock up my doors and when you hear the drum
> And the vile squealing of the wry-necked fife
> Clamber not you up to the casements then, . . .
> Let not the sound of shallow foppery enter
> My sober house

finds an echo in Antonio's words a scene later:

> Fie, fie, Gratiano. Where are all the rest?
> Tis nine o'clock: our friends all stay for you.
> No masque to-night – the wind is come about.

Neither of them is capable of enjoying the carefree happiness for which Belmont stands. In a production of the play, a stage director is faced with the awkward problem of what to do with Antonio in the last Act. Shylock, the villain, has been vanquished and will trouble Arcadia no more, but, now that Bassanio is getting married, Antonio, the real hero of the play, has no further dramatic function. According to the Arden edition, when Alan McKinnon produced the play at the Garrick theatre in 1905, he had Antonio and Bassanio hold the stage at the final curtain, but I cannot picture Portia, who is certainly no Victorian doormat of a wife, allowing her bridegroom to let her enter the house by herself. If Antonio is not to fade away into a nonentity, then the married couples must enter the lighted house and leave Antonio standing alone on the darkened stage, outside the Eden from which, not by the choice of others, but by his own nature, he is excluded.

Without the Venice scenes, Belmont would be an Arcadia without any relation to actual times and places, and where, therefore, money and sexual love have no reality of their own, but are symbolic signs for a community in a state of grace. But Belmont is related to Venice though their existences are not really compatible with each other. This incompatibility is brought out in a fascinating way by the difference between Belmont time and Venice time. Though we are not told exactly how long the period is before Shylock's loan must be repaid, we know that it is more than a month. Yet Bassanio goes off to Belmont immediately, submits immediately on arrival to the test of the caskets, and has just triumphantly passed it when Antonio's letter arrives to inform him that Shylock is about to take him to court and claim his pound of flesh. Belmont, in fact, is like one of those enchanted palaces where time stands still. But because we are made aware of Venice, the real city, where time is real, Belmont becomes a real society to be judged by the same standards we apply to any other kind of society. Because of Shylock and Antonio, Portia's inherited fortune becomes real money which must have been made in this world, as all fortunes are made, by toil, anxiety, the enduring and inflicting of suffering. Portia we can admire because, having seen her leave her Earthly Paradise to do a good deed in this world (one notices, incidentally, that in this world she appears in disguise), we know that she is aware of her wealth as a moral responsibility, but the other inhabitants of Belmont, Bassanio, Gratiano, Lorenzo and Jessica, for all their beauty and charm, appear as frivolous members of a leisure class, whose carefree life is parasitic upon the labours of others, including usurers. When we learn that Jessica has spent fourscore ducats of her father's money in an evening and bought a monkey with her mother's ring, we cannot take this as a comic punishment for Shylock's sin of avarice; her behaviour seems rather an example of the opposite sin of conspicuous waste. Then, with the example in our minds of self-sacrificing love as displayed by

Antonio, while we can enjoy the verbal felicity of the love duet between Lorenzo and Jessica, we cannot help noticing that the pairs of lovers they recall, Troilus and Cressida, Aeneas and Dido, Jason and Medea, are none of them examples of self-sacrifice or fidelity. Recalling that the inscription on the leaden casket ran, 'Who chooseth me, must give and hazard all he hath', it occurs to us that we have seen two characters do this. Shylock, however unintentionally, did, in fact, hazard all for the sake of destroying the enemy he hated, and Antonio, however un-thinkingly he signed the bond, hazarded all to secure the happi-ness of the friend he loved. Yet it is precisely these two who cannot enter Belmont. Belmont would like to believe that men and women are either good or bad by nature, but Shylock and Antonio remind us that this is an illusion: in the real world, no hatred is totally without justification, no love totally innocent.

SOURCE: *The Dyer's Hand* (1963).

NOTE

1. N.B. For the quotations which follow, I am indebted to Ben-jamin Nelson's fascinating book *The Idea of Usury* (Princeton, 1949).

SELECT BIBLIOGRAPHY

Geoffrey Bullough, *Narrative and Dramatic Sources of Shakespeare*, vol. 1 (Routledge and Columbia U.P., 1957). Reprints the complete texts of Shakespeare's sources and discusses them in detail.

H. B. Charlton, *Shakespearian Comedy* (Methuen and The Macmillan Company of New York, 1938). In his chapter on 'Shakespeare's Jew' Charlton presents the fullest and most sympathetic defence of Shylock.

Nevill Coghill, 'The Basis of Shakespearean Comedy', in *Essays and Studies*, N.S., vol. III (1950). An allegorical interpretation of the play as a contrast between Justice and Mercy.

Stratford-upon-Avon Studies 3: Early Shakespeare, ed. J. R. Brown and Bernard Harris (Edward Arnold and St Martin's Press, 1962). Includes essays by John Russell Brown on theatrical interpretations of Shylock, and Frank Kermode on 'The Mature Comedies'. Kermode sees the play as an examination of 'judgement, redemption and mercy'. 'It begins with usury and corrupt love; it ends with harmony and perfect love.'

G. Wilson Knight, *Principles of Shakespearean Production* (Faber and The Macmillan Company of New York, 1936). Suggests how the meaning of the play can be realised visually in the theatre.

Toby Lelyveld, *Shylock on the Stage* (Western Reserve U.P., 1960; Routledge, 1961). The most detailed survey of the stage-history of the play.

A. D. Moody, *Shakespeare: The Merchant of Venice* (Edward Arnold, 1964). According to Moody, much of the play is written ironically. It 'does not celebrate the Christian virtues so much as expose their absence'.

Richard G. Moulton, *Shakespeare as a Dramatic Artist* (Oxford, 1885); reissued with an introduction by Eric Bentley (Dover Publications, 1966). Only a sample of Moulton's analysis is included in the present selection. His examination of the Jessica sub-plot and the episode of the rings is equally valuable.

J. Middleton Murry, *Shakespeare* (Jonathan Cape and Harcourt Brace, 1936). The play is 'a true folk story made drama . . . Shylock is both the embodiment of an irrational hatred and a credible human being.'

H. P. Pettigrew, 'Bassanio, the Elizabethan Lover', in *Philological Quarterly*, vol. XVI (1937). Relates Bassanio's prodigality to the conventional behaviour of the Elizabethan nobility.

William Shakespeare, *The Merchant of Venice,* ed. John Russell Brown (New Arden Shakespeare: Methuen and Harvard U.P., 1955). The best modern edition with an extensive commentary and textual and critical introduction.

Herman Sinsheimer, *Shylock: the History of a Character; or the Myth of the Jew* (Gollancz, 1947).

NOTES ON CONTRIBUTORS

W. H. AUDEN. Poet and critic. With *Poems* (1930) and *The Orators* (1932) he established himself as the leading poet of the 1930s. He moved to America in 1939 and became an American citizen in 1946. He has since written poetry, libretti and literary criticism, including *The Dyer's Hand* (1963) – a collection of essays, some of them on Shakespeare.

C. L. BARBER, Professor of English, University of Indiana, is the author of *Shakespeare's Festive Comedy* (1959).

M. C. BRADBROOK, Professor of English, University of Cambridge and Fellow of Girton College, is the author of *Themes and Conventions of Elizabethan Tragedy* (1935), *Shakespeare and Elizabethan Poetry* (1951), *The Growth and Structure of Elizabethan Comedy* (1955), and *The Rise of the Common Player* (1962).

JOHN RUSSELL BROWN, Professor and Head of the Department of Drama and Theatre Arts, University of Birmingham, is the author of *Shakespeare and his Comedies* (1957) and *Shakespeare's Plays in Performance* (1966). He is the editor of the New Arden edition of *The Merchant of Venice* and of Webster's *The White Devil* and *The Duchess of Malfi* for the Revels Plays.

SIGURD BURCKHARDT (1916–66). Professor of German Literature at the University of California at San Diego and author of essays on Goethe, Kleist and Shakespeare.

MARK VAN DOREN, poet and critic, is Professor of English at Columbia University. He was literary editor of the *Nation* 1924–8 and the author of *The Poetry of John Dryden* (1920), *Shakespeare* (1939), *Nathaniel Hawthorne* (1950) and *Selected Poems* (1954).

FRANCIS GENTLEMAN (1728–84). Actor, dramatist and critic, he adapted Shakespeare's *Richard II* and plays by Ben Jonson for the eighteenth-century stage. His most successful play was *The Modish Wife* (1774). He edited Bell's acting edition of Shakespeare.

G. G. GERVINUS (1805–71). German historian and literary scholar, Professor at the University of Heidelberg. His *Shakespeare* (1849–52), translated by F. E. Bunnett as *Shakespeare Commentaries*, includes a thorough analysis of individual plays with particular emphasis on the unity of plot.

HAROLD C. GODDARD (1878–1950). Scholar and critic, Professor of English, Swarthmore College, he was the author of *Studies in New England Transcendentalism* (1908) and *The Meaning of Shakespeare* published posthumously in 1951.

HARLEY GRANVILLE-BARKER (1877–1946). Actor, playwright, director and critic. He played leading roles in the first productions of many of Shaw's plays and revolutionised Shakespearean production at the Court theatre where he simplified settings and emphasised the rapid, continuous flow of action. On retiring from the theatre he wrote five volumes of *Prefaces to Shakespeare* (1927–47), largely derived from his experience as a theatrical director.

G. WILSON KNIGHT. Critic, actor and playwright, Professor Emeritus of English, University of Leeds. He is the foremost expositor of the symbolic interpretation of Shakespeare. His chief works of criticism include *The Wheel of Fire* (1930), *The Imperial Theme* (1932), *The Shakespearean Tempest* (1932; new edition 1953), *The Crown of Life* (1947) and *The Sovereign Flower* (1958).

GRAHAM MIDGLEY, Fellow and Tutor in English Literature at St Edmund Hall, Oxford.

RICHARD G. MOULTON (1849–1924). Professor of Literary Theory and Interpretation, University of Chicago, 1892–1919, he wrote and edited several texts on the Bible as literature. In his

Shakespeare as a Dramatic Artist (1885) he attempted to develop 'an inductive science of literary criticism' by close analysis of five plays. He was also the author of *Shakespeare as Dramatic Thinker* (1907).

JOHN PALMER (1885–1944). Literary and dramatic critic. He was the author of *Studies in the Contemporary Theatre* (1927), *Molière* (1930), *The Political Characters of Shakespeare* (1945), and *The Comic Characters of Shakespeare* (1946).

E. C. PETTET, Head of Department of English, Goldsmiths' College, University of London, is the author of *Shakespeare and the Romance Tradition* (1949), *On the Poetry of Keats* (1957) and *Of Paradise and Light: A Study of Vaughan's Silex Scintillans* (1960). He is co-editor of the new Warwick Shakespeare.

MAX PLOWMAN (1883–1941). Poet, critic and journalist. He was the editor of *The Adelphi* 1938–41, and the author of four books of verse, numerous writings in support of pacificism and *An Introduction to the Study of Blake* (1927).

NICHOLAS ROWE (1674–1718). Dramatist, poet, first editor and first authoritative biographer of Shakespeare. His best-known plays are *The Tragedy of Jane Shore* 'written in imitation of Shakespeare's style' (1714) and *The Fair Penitent* (1703). He became Poet Laureate in 1715.

E. E. STOLL (1874–1959). American scholar and critic, Professor of English, University of Minnesota. He was notable for his insistence that Shakespeare should be studied in the light of the conventions of Elizabethan drama. He was the author of *Shakespeare Studies* (1927), *Poets and Playwrights* (1930) and *Art and Artifice in Shakespeare* (1933).

HERMANN ULRICI (1806–84). German scholar, Professor of Philosophy at the University of Halle, he published several philosophical treatises, studies of Greek poetry and *Uber Shakespeares Dramatische Kunst* (1839), an early attempt to trace the development of Shakespeare's dramatic art.

INDEX